T0053859

SOPHOCLES II

THE COMPLETE GREEK TRAGEDIES

Edited by David Grene & Richmond Lattimore

THIRD EDITION *Edited by Mark Griffith & Glenn W. Most*

AJAX *Translated by John Moore*

THE WOMEN OF TRACHIS *Translated by Michael Jameson*

ELECTRA *Translated by David Grene*

PHILOCTETES *Translated by David Grene*

THE TRACKERS *Translated by Mark Griffith*

The University of Chicago Press CHICAGO & LONDON

MARK GRIFFITH is professor of classics and of theater, dance, and performance studies at the University of California, Berkeley.

GLENN W. MOST is professor of ancient Greek at the Scuola Normale Superiore at Pisa and a visiting member of the Committee on Social Thought at the University of Chicago.

DAVID GRENE (1913-2002) taught classics for many years at the University of Chicago.

RICHMOND LATTIMORE (1906-1984), professor of Greek at Bryn Mawr College, was a poet and translator best known for his translations of the Greek classics, especially his versions of the *Iliad* and the *Odyssey*.

The University of Chicago Press, Chicago 60637
The University of Chicago Press, Ltd., London
© 2013 by The University of Chicago

Ajax, The Women of Trachis, Electra, Philoctetes
© 1957, 2013 by the University of Chicago
The Trackers © 2013 by the University of Chicago

22 21 20 19 18 17 16 15 14 13   1 2 3 4 5

ISBN-13: 978-0-226-31154-8 (cloth)
ISBN-13: 978-0-226-31155-5 (paper)
ISBN-13: 978-0-226-31156-2 (e-book)
ISBN-10: 0-226-31154-6 (cloth)
ISBN-10: 0-226-31155-4 (paper)
ISBN-10: 0-226-31156-2 (e-book)

Library of Congress Cataloging-in-Publication Data

Sophocles.
[Works. Selections. English]
Sophocles. — Third edition / edited by Mark Griffith and Glenn W. Most.
volumes. cm. — (The complete Greek tragedies)
ISBN 978-0-226-31150-0 (v. 1 : cloth : alk. paper) — ISBN 978-0-226-31151-7 (v. 1 : pbk. : alk. paper) — ISBN 978-0-226-31153-1 (v. 1 : e-book) — ISBN 978-0-226-31154-8 (v. 2 : cloth : alk. paper) — ISBN 978-0-226-31155-5 (v. 2 : pbk. : alk. paper) — ISBN 978-0-226-31156-2 (v. 2 : e-book) 1. Sophocles—Translations into English. 2. Greek drama (Tragedy)—Translations into English. 3. Mythology, Greek—Drama. I. Wyckoff, Elizabeth, 1915- II. Grene, David. III. Fitzgerald, Robert, 1910-1985. IV. Griffith, Mark (Classicist) V. Most, Glenn W. VI. Title. VII. Series: Complete Greek tragedies (Unnumbered)
PA4414.A1G7 2013
882'.01—dc23

2012043847

CONTENTS

EDITORS' PREFACE TO THE THIRD EDITION

The first edition of the *Complete Greek Tragedies*, edited by David Grene and Richmond Lattimore, was published by the University of Chicago Press starting in 1953. But the origins of the series go back even further. David Grene had already published his translation of three of the tragedies with the same press in 1942, and some of the other translations that eventually formed part of the Chicago series had appeared even earlier. A second edition of the series, with new translations of several plays and other changes, was published in 1991. For well over six decades, these translations have proved to be extraordinarily popular and resilient, thanks to their combination of accuracy, poetic immediacy, and clarity of presentation. They have guided hundreds of thousands of teachers, students, and other readers toward a reliable understanding of the surviving masterpieces of the three great Athenian tragedians: Aeschylus, Sophocles, and Euripides.

But the world changes, perhaps never more rapidly than in the past half century, and whatever outlasts the day of its appearance must eventually come to terms with circumstances very different from those that prevailed at its inception. During this same period, scholarly understanding of Greek tragedy has undergone significant development, and there have been marked changes not only in the readers to whom this series is addressed, but also in the ways in which these texts are taught and studied in universities. These changes have prompted the University of Chicago Press to perform another, more systematic revision of the translations, and we are honored to have been entrusted with this delicate and important task.

Our aim in this third edition has been to preserve and strengthen as far as possible all those features that have made the Chicago translations successful for such a long time, while at the same time revising the texts carefully and tactfully to bring them up to date and equipping them with various kinds of subsidiary help, so they may continue to serve new generations of readers.

Our revisions have addressed the following issues:

- Wherever possible, we have kept the existing translations. But we have revised them where we found this to be necessary in order to bring them closer to the ancient Greek of the original texts or to replace an English idiom that has by now become antiquated or obscure. At the same time we have done our utmost to respect the original translator's individual style and meter.
- In a few cases, we have decided to substitute entirely new translations for the ones that were published in earlier editions of the series. Euripides' *Medea* has been newly translated by Oliver Taplin, *The Children of Heracles* by Mark Griffith, *Andromache* by Deborah Roberts, and *Iphigenia among the Taurians* by Anne Carson. We have also, in the case of Aeschylus, added translations and brief discussions of the fragments of lost plays that originally belonged to connected tetralogies along with the surviving tragedies, since awareness of these other lost plays is often crucial to the interpretation of the surviving ones. And in the case of Sophocles, we have included a translation of the substantial fragmentary remains of one of his satyr-dramas, *The Trackers* (*Ichneutai*). (See "How the Plays Were Originally Staged" below for explanation of "tetralogy," "satyr-drama," and other terms.)
- We have altered the distribution of the plays among the various volumes in order to reflect the chronological order in which they were written, when this is known or can be estimated with some probability. Thus the *Oresteia* appears now as volume 2 of Aeschylus' tragedies, and the sequence of Euripides' plays has been rearranged.
- We have rewritten the stage directions to make them more consistent throughout, keeping in mind current scholarly under-

standing of how Greek tragedies were staged in the fifth century BCE. In general, we have refrained from extensive stage directions of an interpretive kind, since these are necessarily speculative and modern scholars often disagree greatly about them. The Greek manuscripts themselves contain no stage directions at all.

· We have indicated certain fundamental differences in the meters and modes of delivery of all the verse of these plays. Spoken language (a kind of heightened ordinary speech, usually in the iambic trimeter rhythm) in which the characters of tragedy regularly engage in dialogue and monologue is printed in ordinary Roman font; the sung verse of choral and individual lyric odes (using a large variety of different meters), and the chanted verse recited by the chorus or individual characters (always using the anapestic meter), are rendered in *italics*, with parentheses added where necessary to indicate whether the passage is sung or chanted. In this way, readers will be able to tell at a glance how the playwright intended a given passage to be delivered in the theater, and how these shifting dynamics of poetic register contribute to the overall dramatic effect.

· All the Greek tragedies that survive alternate scenes of action or dialogue, in which individual actors speak all the lines, with formal songs performed by the chorus. Occasionally individual characters sing formal songs too, or they and the chorus may alternate lyrics and spoken verse within the same scene. Most of the formal songs are structured as a series of pairs of stanzas of which the metrical form of the first one ("strophe") is repeated exactly by a second one ("antistrophe"). Thus the metrical structure will be, e.g., strophe A, antistrophe A, strophe B, antistrophe B, with each pair of stanzas consisting of a different sequence of rhythms. Occasionally a short stanza in a different metrical form ("mesode") is inserted in the middle between one strophe and the corresponding antistrophe, and sometimes the end of the whole series is marked with a single stanza in a different metrical form ("epode")—thus, e.g., strophe A, mesode, antistrophe A; or strophe A, antistrophe A, strophe B, antistrophe B, epode. We have indicated these metrical structures by inserting the terms

STROPHE, ANTISTROPHE, MESODE, and EPODE above the first line of the relevant stanzas so that readers can easily recognize the compositional structure of these songs.

- In each play we have indicated by the symbol ° those lines or words for which there are significant uncertainties regarding the transmitted text, and we have explained as simply as possible in textual notes at the end of the volume just what the nature and degree of those uncertainties are. These notes are not at all intended to provide anything like a full scholarly apparatus of textual variants, but instead to make readers aware of places where the text transmitted by the manuscripts may not exactly reflect the poet's own words, or where the interpretation of those words is seriously in doubt.

- For each play we have provided a brief introduction that gives essential information about the first production of the tragedy, the mythical or historical background of its plot, and its reception in antiquity and thereafter.

- For each of the three great tragedians we have provided an introduction to his life and work. It is reproduced at the beginning of each volume containing his tragedies.

- We have also provided at the end of each volume a glossary explaining the names of all persons and geographical features that are mentioned in any of the plays in that volume.

It is our hope that our work will help ensure that these translations continue to delight, to move, to astonish, to disturb, and to instruct many new readers in coming generations.

MARK GRIFFITH, *Berkeley*
GLENN W. MOST, *Florence*

INTRODUCTION TO SOPHOCLES

Sophocles was born in about 495 BCE, into a wealthy family from the deme of Colonus, close to the city center of Athens. He was thus about thirty years younger than Aeschylus (who died in 455), and about ten or fifteen years older than Euripides (who died just a few months before Sophocles, in 405).

In addition to being the most successful tragedian of his time, Sophocles was active in Athenian public life: he was appointed a treasurer (*hellenotamias*) in 443-42, elected a general (*strategos*) in 441-40 along with Pericles, and perhaps again in the 420s with Nicias; and he was selected to be a special magistrate (*proboulos*) during the emergency administration of 412-11, all of this in marked contrast to the apolitical life of Euripides. There was also an ancient tradition (perhaps apocryphal) that when the cult of the healing god Asclepius was first brought to Athens, it was for a while located in Sophocles' house.

Although we know for certain few details of Sophocles' personal life, he apparently had at least one son, Iophon, by his wife Nicostrate, and another, Ariston, by his mistress Theoris. Ariston's son was in turn named Sophocles, and both Iophon and Sophocles Jr. became successful tragedians. Among his friends were such luminaries as Herodotus, Pericles, and Ion of Chios, and he was said to be sociable and a "good-natured" man. He had a reputation for being something of a flirt and bisexual playboy. Stories that were later told of the octogenarian Sophocles' legal feuds with his sons may have been triggered by his depiction of fierce, lonely, embittered men in his plays (Ajax, Philoctetes,

Teiresias, and especially Oedipus cursing his son in *Oedipus at Colonus*).

Sophocles' career as a dramatist was long, prolific, and immensely successful. His first production in the annual tragedy competition at Athens was in 468 BCE. The plays he entered are not known, but they resulted in a victory over Aeschylus. Sophocles was still composing plays right up to his death in 405 (*Philoctetes*, produced in 409; *Oedipus at Colonus*, produced posthumously in 401).

Ancient sources knew the titles of 120 plays by Sophocles, which should mean thirty groups of four for the annual competition, each comprising three tragedies and a satyr-play. It is recorded that he won eighteen victories (thus even outdoing Aeschylus' thirteen, and far more than Euripides' five), and that he was never ranked lower than second in the competition. Unlike Aeschylus, Sophocles never composed a connected trilogy, that is, a sequence of plays performed together that focused on the same characters or family (like, for example, the *Oresteia*). Unfortunately we do not know what principles he may have used in designing each set of four plays in any given year. All of the seven plays we possess seem to have been performed in different years, and we do not even know the titles of any of the lost plays that accompanied them. As far as we can tell, however, each play was intended to be treated as a separate masterpiece—fully intelligible and self-contained on its own terms.

Any attempt to trace a development in Sophocles' style or worldview during his long career is hampered not only by the loss of all but seven of his plays, but also by the uncertain dating of several of the ones we do have. Sophocles' tragedies rarely contain references to actual current events or issues, and they rarely elicited parodies from Aristophanes (as several of Euripides' did). For only two Sophoclean plays do we possess definite information about their date of production, based on the original fifth-century festival competition records: *Philoctetes* (409) and *Oedipus at Colonus* (405/401). There is good external evidence for dating *Antigone* to 442 or 441, but for the other four plays we have to rely on stylistic—hence subjective—criteria. Most scholars nowadays are inclined to date *Ajax* and *The Women of Trachis* quite early (to the 460s–440s). *Electra* is probably late (perhaps 415–10). The date of *Oedipus the King* is uncertain, though many would like to place it in the early 420s because of its vivid depiction of plague—not a compelling argument.

Sophocles inherited from Aeschylus and the other early tragedians a well-established set of dramatic conventions and formal structures, and he does not appear to have made radical innovations of his own, except perhaps in the musical aspects, since he is credited with being the first Athenian playwright to introduce "Phrygian" and "Lydian" scales into the melodies of his lyrics. (None of this music survives.) Ancient critics disagreed as to whether it was Aeschylus or Sophocles who first employed a third speaking actor—earlier the rule had been that only two were allowed. Aristotle says that Sophocles was first, and that he also introduced scene-painting. In general, however, it was Euripides, along with his younger contemporary Agathon, who were generally regarded as the chief iconoclasts and experimenters in artistic forms and subject matter. Sophocles' gifts lay rather in refining and elaborating the possibilities of the tragic form: tightly constructed plots, more complex dialogue scenes, exploration of extreme emotional states and character contrasts, the subtle interweaving of spoken and musical elements, and an extraordinary richness and fluidity of verbal expression that is often very difficult to capture in English translation. To Aristotle in the fourth century, as to many lovers of drama since, Sophocles' plays appear to represent the pinnacle of what Greek tragedy was capable of achieving, the fulfilment of its very "nature."

After Sophocles died, his plays continued for centuries to be widely read and (presumably) performed all over the Greek-speaking world. A more or less complete collection of his plays was made in Alexandria during the third century BCE, though this no longer exists. Hundreds of fragments from his lost plays are found in quotations by other authors and in anthologies, and while he was never as widely read or imitated as Euripides or Menander (let alone Homer), Sophocles remained a classic both in the ancient schools and among later practitioners of the dramatic arts (including Ennius, Accius, and Pacuvius; Seneca; Corneille and Racine). The seven plays we possess today were probably selected in the second century CE, and from that point gradually the other plays ceased to be copied, and thus eventually were lost to posterity. At Byzantium (Constantinople, now Istanbul), three plays in particular were most widely copied: the "triad" of *Ajax*, *Electra*, and *Oedipus the King*. But the rest were never as close to extinction as the tragedies of Aeschylus, whose difficult style and more old-fashioned dramaturgy made his works less appealing to later readers.

A large papyrus unearthed at Oxyrhynchus (first published in 1912) contains a substantial chunk of the previously lost satyr-play titled *The Trackers* (*Ichneutai*), which is included in translation in this new edition of the Chicago Greek tragedies. Further papyrus finds have continued to add important scraps to our knowledge both of Sophocles' tragedies and of his satyr-dramas. But for the most part, even though we know that, for example, his *Phaedra* was influential and popular throughout antiquity, as were *Polyxena*, *Thyestes*, *Tereus* (about Procne and Philomela), *Inachus* (a satyr-play about Zeus and Io), and numerous other lost plays, Sophocles' reputation in the modern era has rested almost entirely on the seven plays that survive in medieval manuscripts. Of these, *Oedipus the King*, *Antigone*, and *Electra* have always been the most widely read and often staged, but all seven have been central to the discussions of theater historians, philosophers, and theorists of tragedy, and all of them have provoked adaptations, paintings, and translations in abundance, all over the world. Indeed, since the late eighteenth century, for many critics and philosophers it has been Sophocles' plays—along with Shakespeare's—that have been taken to represent the culmination of the genre of tragedy and its capacity to represent human experience and heroic suffering.

HOW THE PLAYS WERE ORIGINALLY STAGED

Nearly all the plays composed by Aeschylus, Sophocles, and Euripides were first performed in the Theater of Dionysus at Athens, as part of the annual festival and competition in drama. This was not only a literary and musical event, but also an important religious and political ceremony for the Athenian community. Each year three tragedians were selected to compete, with each of them presenting four plays per day, a "tetralogy" of three tragedies and one satyr-play. The satyr-play was a type of drama similar to tragedy in being based on heroic myth and employing many of the same stylistic features, but distinguished by having a chorus of half-human, half-horse followers of Dionysus—sileni or satyrs—and by always ending happily. Extant examples of this genre are Euripides' *The Cyclops* (in *Euripides*, vol. 5) and Sophocles' *The Trackers* (partially preserved: in *Sophocles*, vol. 2).

The three competing tragedians were ranked by a panel of citizens functioning as amateur judges, and the winner received an honorific prize. Records of these competitions were maintained, allowing Aristotle and others later to compile lists of the dates when each of Aeschylus', Sophocles', and Euripides' plays were first performed and whether they placed first, second, or third in the competition (unfortunately we no longer possess the complete lists).

The tragedians competed on equal terms: each had at his disposal three actors (only two in Aeschylus' and in Euripides' earliest plays) who would often have to switch between roles as each play progressed, plus other nonspeaking actors to play attendants and other subsidiary characters; a chorus of twelve (in Aeschylus' time) or fifteen (for most of the careers of Sophocles and Euripides), who would sing and dance formal songs and whose Chorus Leader would engage in dialogue with the characters or offer comment on the action; and a pipe-player, to accompany the sung portions of the play.

All the performers were men, and the actors and chorus members all wore masks. The association of masks with other Dionysian rituals may have affected their use in the theater; but masks had certain practical advantages as well—for example, making it easy to play female characters and to change quickly between roles. In general, the use of masks also meant that ancient acting techniques must have been rather different from what we are used to seeing in the modern theater. Acting in a mask requires a more frontal and presentational style of performance toward the audience than is usual with unmasked, "realistic" acting; a masked actor must communicate far more by voice and stylized bodily gesture than by facial expression, and the gradual development of a character in the course of a play could hardly be indicated by changes in his or her mask. Unfortunately, however, we know almost nothing about the acting techniques of the Athenian theater. But we do know that the chorus members were all Athenian amateurs, and so were the actors up until the later part of the fifth century, by which point a prize for the best actor had been instituted in the tragic competition, and the art of acting (which of course included solo singing and dancing) was becoming increasingly professionalized.

The tragedian himself not only wrote the words for his play but also composed the music and choreography and directed the productions. It was said that Aeschylus also acted in his plays but that Sophocles chose not to, except early in his career, because his voice was too weak. Euripides is reported to have had a collaborator who specialized in musical composition. The costs for each playwright's production were shared between an individual wealthy citizen, as a kind of "super-tax" requirement, and the city.

The Theater of Dionysus itself during most of the fifth century BCE probably consisted of a large rectangular or trapezoidal dance floor, backed by a one-story wooden building (the *skênê*), with a large central door that opened onto the dance floor. (Some scholars have argued that two doors were used, but the evidence is thin.) Between the *skênê* and the dance floor there may have been a narrow stage on which the characters acted and which communicated easily with the dance floor. For any particular play, the *skênê* might represent a palace, a house, a temple, or a cave, for example; the interior of this "building" was generally invisible to the audience, with all the action staged in front of it. Sophocles is said to have been the first to use painted scenery; this must have been fairly simple and easy to remove, as every play had a different setting. Playwrights did not include stage directions in their texts. Instead, a play's setting was indicated explicitly by the speaking characters.

All the plays were performed in the open air and in daylight. Spectators sat on wooden seats in rows, probably arranged in rectangular blocks along the curving slope of the Acropolis. (The stone semicircular remains of the Theater of Dionysus that are visible today in Athens belong to a later era.) Seating capacity seems to have been four to six thousand—thus a mass audience, but not quite on the scale of the theaters that came to be built during the fourth century BCE and later at Epidaurus, Ephesus, and many other locations all over the Mediterranean.

Alongside the *skênê*, on each side, there were passages through which actors could enter and exit. The acting area included the dance floor, the doorway, and the area immediately in front of the *skênê*. Occasionally an actor appeared on the roof or above it, as if flying. He was actually hanging from a crane (*mêchanê*: hence *deus ex machina*, "a god from the machine"). The *skênê* was also occasionally opened up—the mechanical details are uncertain—in order to show the audience what was concealed within (usually dead bodies). Announcements of entrances and exits, like the setting, were made by the characters. Although the medieval manuscripts of the surviving plays do not provide explicit stage directions, it is usually possible to infer from the words or from the context whether a particular entrance or exit is being made through a door (into the *skênê*) or by one of the side entrances. In later antiquity, there may have been a rule that one side entrance always led to the city center, the other to the countryside or harbor. Whether such a rule was ever observed in the fifth century is uncertain.

AJAX

Translated by JOHN MOORE

AJAX: INTRODUCTION

The Play: Date and Composition

We do not know when *Ajax* was first produced. Presumably Sophocles presented it along with three other plays for the annual competition in Athens; but we have no idea which plays they were, out of the 120 or so tragedies and satyr-dramas by Sophocles that we know about. In the absence of any reliable historical evidence, modern scholars' opinions about the date of the play are based mostly on formal and stylistic criteria. The technique of the dialogue scenes in particular, in which we do not find three characters all engaged in conversation together as we do in Sophocles' late plays, and also the relative paucity of actors' solo songs, seem more characteristic of early than late fifth-century tragedies. Overall, the majority of scholars believe the play was probably written early in Sophocles' career, perhaps in the 440s BCE; but it could be even earlier, or considerably later. The issue remains open.

The Myth

Ajax was one of the most famous heroes of the Trojan War. Son of the mighty hero Telamon (who had himself fought successfully at Troy in a previous campaign), Ajax plays a prominent role in the *Iliad* and is regarded by everyone there as the greatest Greek warrior after Achilles. Among several memorable scenes involving Ajax is one in which he engages in single man-to-man combat with the Trojan champion Hector, ending in a stalemate and exchange of gifts (book 7: an episode directly recalled in our play). Ajax is also found from time to time fighting in collaboration with his half brother Teucer, an archer. In several other poems of the epic Trojan Cycle, of which only brief fragments and summaries survive, it was narrated that, after Achilles had been killed by the Trojans, Ajax carried his body off the battlefield and it was then proposed that the armor should be awarded to "the best of the Greeks." Somehow Odysseus, not Ajax, ended up receiving it. In rage and humiliation Ajax committed suicide with his sword; and in the *Odyssey* (book 11) we find his ghost, still enraged, refusing to speak to Odysseus when he visits the underworld.

Depictions of particular moments from this story are common in the visual art of the sixth and fifth centuries BCE, especially on Athenian vases. As with all Greek myths, the details varied considerably from one version to another, and in the early fifth century, before Sophocles came to write his play, additional accounts were composed, including some lyric poems by Pindar (extant) and a tragic trilogy by Aeschylus of which the titles, but little else, are preserved: *The Judgment of the Arms*, *The Thracian Women*, and *The Women of Salamis*. The process whereby the armor of Achilles came to be awarded—surprisingly—to Odysseus was explained in various ways, often involving some foul play. Sophocles leaves this issue tantalizingly open. Then in some versions of the story, including this one, Ajax becomes so angry, even to the point of temporary insanity, that he attempts to kill Odysseus and Agamemnon in revenge. In our play Athena directly intervenes to cloud Ajax's mind so that his violence is directed against animals instead of the Greek leaders: this may have been Sophocles' own invention. (Of course Athena was always known to be a devoted protector and helper of Odysseus.) Sophocles has also added a characteristic new twist to his plot by including an unexpected prophecy about Athena's desire to punish Ajax, which we are told may be averted if he survives this one day. After Ajax's suicide, Agamemnon and the other Greek leaders are sometimes, as in our play, described as denying a proper burial to his body, but the idea of having Odysseus intervene to bring about his archrival's due burial, out of enlightened fellow-feeling, seems to be another innovation by Sophocles.

This play is not only about Ajax, of course. The rest of his family is intimately involved. Neither Ajax's father (the mighty, intimidating Telamon) nor his mother (Eriboea) actually appears in the play, though they are frequently mentioned. More crucial to the action and pathos of the tragedy are Tecmessa, Ajax's war-captive concubine, and their baby son, Eurysaces. Sophocles depicts the affectionate relationship between Tecmessa and Ajax and their concerns about their son's future in terms vividly reminiscent of the relationship of Hector, Andromache, and Astyanax in the *Iliad* (and again, in Euripides' *Trojan Women*), though Ajax's harshness of character contrasts sharply with the more considerate Hector. Another prominent character in the play is Ajax's half brother, Teucer (son of Telamon's own slave-captive, herself of Trojan ancestry); he seems to have been a major character also in Aeschylus' trilogy (see above). In our play Teucer's loyal defense of his half brother provides much of the dramatic energy of the later scenes, and the bond of respect and gratitude forged between Teucer and Odysseus at the end helps bring about some degree of comfort and resolution.

According to tradition, Ajax and his family were based on Salamis, which in Homer's time had been an independent island but by the sixth century was an integral part of Attica and hence (by Sophocles' time) of the Athenian democratic city-state. One of the ancestral Athenian tribes was named after Ajax (Aiantis), and he and his son were worshipped in several hero cults. Of all the major Homeric heroes Ajax was thus by far the most closely associated with Athens, and the issue of his burial and the honor to be shown to his corpse, and to his son, was therefore of particular importance to Sophocles' audience. This play is also unusual in having as its chorus a group of young men: these Salaminian sailors, played by young Athenian citizens, seem likewise to stand in a particularly close relationship to the spectators themselves.

Problems of Staging and the Suicide

In its first production, *Ajax* seems to have involved some unusual experiments in staging, not all of which are possible for modern scholars to sort out. In the opening scenes, the action takes place in front of Ajax's hut or tent in the Greek camp at Troy. But in the middle of the play, not only does the chorus rush out in different directions to search for Ajax, leaving the orchestra empty—which very rarely happens in Greek tragedy—but when Ajax reappears with his sword and prepares to commit suicide, the scene seems to be the beach at some distance from the Greek camp. The details of the staging of the suicide are also unclear to us (see Textual Notes on lines 815-65). Ajax apparently places his sword hilt-down in the earth within the audience's line of vision, and then falls on it—a highly unusual example of a violent death in tragedy actually represented on stage. Scholars have debated how this was managed, and how Ajax's body could have remained visible for the rest of the play, as it clearly did, even while the actor somehow departed in order to return shortly in the role of Teucer. The visual spectacle of Ajax placing his sword in the earth, or doubled-up and impaled on it, was a favorite topic for Athenian vase painters: how Sophocles represented this unforgettable moment in the Theater of Dionysus remains a fascinating puzzle.

Transmission and Reception

While the story of Ajax continued to be well known throughout antiquity and was often depicted in literature and art, it is impossible to know exactly how widely Sophocles' play was performed and read after its first production. Other successful plays on this topic were composed, both Greek and Roman, including tragedies (now lost) by the Roman Republican playwrights Livius Andronicus (*Ajax the Whipbearer*), Ennius, and Pacuvius. Some of these doubtless drew directly upon Sophocles, and Ovid includes the episode in his *Metamorphoses*. Thus Ajax endured into late antiquity and the Middle Ages as a (good) example of stalwart courage and heroic commitment to the maintenance of honor, and as a (bad) example of excessive passion for vengeance—and also of the vulnerability of great men to divine displeasure or human lies and envy. *Ajax* does not seem to have been among the most widely read of Sophocles' plays in antiquity (few papyrus fragments have been found, and the play is not often quoted), though it is cited quite often by ancient grammarians and lexicographers. It was one of the seven Sophoclean tragedies selected for school use during the Roman period, and a few copies thus survived until the Byzantine revival of classical learning in the tenth century and beyond. Along with *Oedipus the King* and *Electra*, *Ajax* was included among the "triad" of Sophoclean plays most often copied between the eleventh and fifteenth centuries, and so it exists in more than a hundred manuscript copies.

In the Early Modern period, the story was frequently adapted in dramas, operas, ballets, and paintings. Few of them stayed close to Sophocles' original. Productions of the Sophoclean play itself have been relatively frequent ever since the sixteenth century, mostly in schools and colleges, doubtless because of the predominantly male cast of characters and the focus on masculine virtue. The twentieth century has witnessed a few more ambitious professional productions, including one by the National Theatre of Greece, directed by Takis Mouzenidis (1961) with music by Mikis Theodorakis, and one by the London Small Theatre, directed by Peter Meineck (1991; available on video). An inventive production directed by Peter Sellars (1986, etc.) of Robert Auletta's adaptation of the play, which adheres closely to Sophocles' original, was performed widely in the United States and Europe. (It was filmed by Dutch TV and is available on video.) Several freer adaptations have emphasized Ajax's uncompromising ethical principles in contrast to the political corruption and tyrannical impulses of Agamemnon and Odysseus: for example, Ugo Foscolo's *Ajace* (1811; with reference to Napoleon); H. J. Rehfisch's *Die goldenen Waffen* (1913); and Heiner Müller's *Germania 3: Ghosts at the Dead Man* (1995).

Sophocles' *Ajax* has always been appreciated by readers and audiences for its classic depiction of the proud, even obsessive, commitment of a "great man" to his own honor and aristocratic principles, as he collides with the principles of loyalty and obedience demanded by smaller-minded political authorities. The dramatic impact of Sophocles' exploration of the ferocious and intransigent passion of this old-style Homeric hero, and of the patient devotion and vulnerability of his family, have not faded.

AJAX

Characters   ATHENA
                 ODYSSEUS
                 AJAX
                 CHORUS of Salaminian sailors
                 TECMESSA, war captive and concubine of Ajax
                 EURYSACES (silent character), the baby son of
                 Ajax and Tecmessa
                 MESSENGER
                 TEUCER, half brother of Ajax
                 MENELAUS
                 AGAMEMNON

Scene: The tent of Ajax in the Greek encampment at Troy.

*(Enter Athena, on high,° and Odysseus from the side, moving
eagerly across the orchestra as though tracing footprints.)*

ATHENA
Odysseus, I have always seen and marked you
stalking to pounce upon your enemies;
and now by the tent of Ajax, where he keeps
last station upon the shore, I find you busy
tracing and scanning these fresh tracks of his,   5
new-printed on the sand, to see if he's inside.
You've tracked him down like a keen-nosed Spartan hound.
In fact, he has just come in. His head is dripping
with sweat and his murderous hands drip too . . . But now   10

you need not go on peering in—no, tell me,
what was the reason for your eager search?
For I have knowledge and can set you right.

ODYSSEUS

Voice of Athena, dearest utterance
of all the gods' to me—I cannot see you,   15
and yet how clearly I can catch your words
that speak as from a trumpet's throat of bronze!
You guess my purpose; I have been circling
steadily on the trail of a man I hate,
shield-bearing Ajax.   20
He has done a thing—sometime this last night—
an act of staggering horror . . . aimed at us,
if indeed he's done it; for nothing about these things
is surely known—we are floundering in conjecture,
and I have volunteered to search it out.
This much is sure: we found not long ago   25
our flocks and herds of captured beasts all devastated
and struck with havoc by some butchering hand.
Their guards were slaughtered with them. Everyone
puts the blame of it on Ajax. A scout saw him
alone, bounding over the plain and carrying   30
a sword still wet with blood—this man informed me
and set me on the track. I leapt to the scent
at once; and partly I can trace it still,
though partly, too, I'm baffled. How can these prints be his?
You come just as I need you. Now and always:
as heretofore, your hand shall steer me straight.   35

ATHENA

I know, Odysseus;
some time ago I felt your need and came
on the path to guard and help you in your chase.

ODYSSEUS

Tell me, dear Mistress: am I working to some purpose?

ATHENA

Yes, this is the man that did the things you speak of.

ODYSSEUS

What motive, though, prompted that senseless hand?   40

ATHENA

He was aggrieved, because of Achilles' armor.

ODYSSEUS

But why this wild assault upon the flocks?

ATHENA

He thought it was *you, your* blood, that was staining his hands.

ODYSSEUS

It was a stroke, then, aimed at the Greek army?

ATHENA

A successful one, if I had not been watchful.   45

ODYSSEUS

What desperate daring nerved him to this attempt?

ATHENA

In the night he was moving upon you, stealthily and alone.

ODYSSEUS

And did he come close? Was he reaching near his goal?

ATHENA

To the very doors of the two supreme commanders.

ODYSSEUS

And how did he check that hand that yearned for murder?   50

ATHENA

I checked him; I threw before his eyes
obsessive notions, thoughts of insane joy,
to fall on the mingled droves of captured livestock,
the undistributed loot which the herdsmen had in charge.
He fell upon them,

hewed out a weltering shambles of horned beasts,   55
chopping them down in a circle all around him.
Sometimes he thought he held the sons of Atreus
in his grip to kill them, and then again
his fancy would seize some other of the chiefs.
The man was wandering in diseased delusions;
and I urged him, drove him into the fatal net.
At last, when he was weary of the slaughter,   60
he hobbled the cattle that were still alive,
and the sheep, and brought them to his tent, thinking
it was men he had captured and not poor horned beasts.
And now he has them bound inside the lodge
and is tormenting them. But I shall show you   65
his madness in plain view. Take note of it;
then you can proclaim it to all the Greeks.
Get a grip on your nerves and wait. You're in no danger
to see the man. I'll turn his glance away.   70
He'll never see you or know your face.

                                                        (To Ajax.)

Hey!
You there, who are binding fast your captives' arms
with fetters, come outside! Ajax! Come out!

ODYSSEUS
Athena, what can you be thinking of?
Don't call him out!

ATHENA
Quiet, now! Don't be a coward!   75

ODYSSEUS
No, no, for heaven's sake!
It'd be much better if he stayed inside.

ATHENA
What are you afraid of? He was only a man before.

ODYSSEUS

Yes, but he was my enemy and still is.

ATHENA

But to laugh at your enemies—
what sweeter laughter can there be than that?

ODYSSEUS

It's enough for me if he stays just where he is.   80

ATHENA

You're afraid, then, to see a madman face to face?

ODYSSEUS

Certainly if he were sane, I should never shrink from him.

ATHENA

No need to do so now. He will stand near you,
and yet not see you.

ODYSSEUS

How is that possible, if he sees with the same eyes still?

ATHENA

I can darken even the most acute vision.   85

ODYSSEUS

I know that a god's contriving may do anything.

ATHENA

Be still, then, and remain right where you are.

ODYSSEUS

If I must, I must. But I wish I were anywhere but here!

ATHENA

Hello there, Ajax, I call you once again!
Why so little care for your old ally?   90

(Enter Ajax from inside, carrying a whip.)

AJAX

Hail, Athena! Daughter of Zeus,
hail and welcome! How well you have stood by me!
I shall garland you with trophies all of gold
from the spoils of this hunting, in thanksgiving.

ATHENA

Excellent. But tell me, did you dye
your blade well in the Greeks' blood?   95

AJAX

Indeed, I can boast as much. I don't deny it.

ATHENA

Did you even turn your weapon against Atreus' sons?

AJAX

I don't think they will slight Ajax again.

ATHENA

Those men are dead, if I understand you correctly.

AJAX

Dead they are. Let them rob my armor now!   100

ATHENA

Tell me, please, what happened to Laertes' son?
He didn't escape you?

AJAX

Oho, that villainous fox! You want to know where *he* is?

ATHENA

Yes. Your adversary, you know. Odysseus.

AJAX

He's sitting there inside, my sweetest prisoner.   105
I don't intend for him to die just yet.

ATHENA

What are you going to do first?

AJAX

First bind him to the pole that props my tent . . .

ATHENA

Poor miserable man! What treatment will you give him?

AJAX

Crimson his back with this whip first, then kill him.   110

ATHENA

Poor wretch! In pity don't mistreat him so!

AJAX

Have your way, goddess, in all else, and welcome;
but that man's punishment shall not be changed.

ATHENA

Well, then, if your good pleasure wills it so,
put your hand to work, spare nothing of what you plan.   115

AJAX

I must be at my work. Goddess, I bid you:
stand always my ally as you have today.

                                        (*Exit Ajax inside.*)

ATHENA

Do you see, Odysseus, how great the gods' power is?
Who was more full of foresight than this man,
or abler, do you think, to act as needed?   120

ODYSSEUS

None that I know of. And I pity
his wretchedness, though he is my enemy,
for the terrible yoke of blindness that is on him.
I think of him, yet also of myself;
for I see the true state of all us that live—   125
phantoms we are, no more, and weightless shadow.

ATHENA

Look well at this, and speak no towering word

yourself against the gods, nor walk too grandly
because your hand is weightier than another's,
or your great wealth deeper founded. One short day   130
inclines the balance of all human things
to sink or rise again. Know that the gods
love men of steady sense and hate the wicked.

> *(Exit Athena; exit Odysseus to one side. Enter the Chorus*
> *of Salaminian sailors, from the other side.)*

CHORUS [*chanting*]
Son of Telamon, lord of the firm foundation
of Salamis, where the sea circles and swirls,   135
Ajax, my lord,
when you are fortunate, I too feel gladness;
but when the fury of Zeus or the virulent
slur of the Greeks' slander
strikes you, I shrink in fear, and my eye
like a bird's, like a dove's, shows terror.   140
Now out of this fading night
come huge oppressive rumors of dismay,
wretched and shameful;
for you, they say, in the dark went striding out
over the horse-delighting grassland,
swinging your bright sword, slaughtering and wasting   145
all that remained of our plunder,
flocks and herds belonging to the Greeks.
Such tales as these, whisperings and fabrications,
Odysseus is supplying to every ear.
And many believe him. For as he speaks of you,   150
his words win credit, and each new hearer
even more than the teller relishes his chance
to gloat over your distress.
> *Strike at a great man, and you will not miss;*
but if one should bend such slander at me,   155
none would believe him. Envy stalks
after magnates of wealth and power;

yet small men without the great
are a frail support for a fortress. They
should best depend upon the great,   160
and the great ones too be upheld by the lesser.
But the foolish cannot be taught these things.
Such are the men who are raising this clamor;
and against it we have no defense, my lord,   165
but you. When once they are out of your sight,
they screech like a gaggle of angry birds;
but fear of the mighty eagle,°
all of a sudden, I think,
if you should only appear,   170
would make them cower and be silent.

[singing]

STROPHE A

    Can it have been wild, bull-consorting Artemis
that stirred you, evil Rumor,
mother of my disgrace, to move against the flocks?   175
    Was she angered perhaps over victory dues unpaid,
    cheated of some rich spoils of war,
    or the recompense for a hunted stag?
Or was it Enyalios, the bronze-cased lord of war
    that begrudged your co-operant spear,
and spitefully paid you out in the night's error?   180

ANTISTROPHE A

    For never, son of Telamon, of your own heart's prompting,
would you so far have strayed,
as to fall upon the flocks. A god-sent sickness   185
must have come on you. May Apollo and Zeus ward off
    the evil tales of the Greeks!
    Yet if the high kings or Odysseus,
    he of the accursed family of Sisyphus,
are artfully weaving some lying tale,   190
        then no longer hide your face like this, my lord,
in your tent beside the sea, as they destroy your good name!

Rise, up from the place
where you have sat too long, refusing to fight your cause,
while ruin flares up toward heaven.   195
Your enemies' gross outrage
sweeps fearlessly, breezing through all the glades
in a blast of ringing laughter and hard spite.
But I am fixed in my distress.   200

(Enter Tecmessa from the tent.)

TECMESSA [chanting]
Mariners who serve with Ajax,
our prince of the old and kingly line
sprung from Athenian earth, we
who care for him and his father's far-off home
have cause indeed for grief;
for he, our great grim man of power, lies low,   205
sickened with a storm of troubles.

CHORUS [chanting]
But what, following on yesterday's
load of wretchedness, has this night brought?
Tell us, daughter of Phrygian Teleutas;   210
for the valiant Ajax loves
and honors you, his spear-won bride—
perhaps you can speak with knowledge.

TECMESSA
But how shall I speak a thing that appalls
my speech? You shall hear all too clearly
of a suffering awful as death.   215
Madness has seized our noble Ajax;
he has come to ignominy in the night.
What a sight is to be seen within the tent!
Victims, slain by his hand, deep-dyed
in blood, this man's sacred offerings.   220

CHORUS [*singing while Tecmessa chants in response*]

STROPHE B

You have vouched it true, then, that report
about our hot-tempered chief,
that tale we cannot bear, yet may not escape:
huge it grows, and the words of powerful Greeks   225
give it further reinforcement. Oh, I fear
for that which is moving upon us. He will be done to death,
our glorious prince, because
with frenzied hands and a dark sword he killed   230
herds and their mounted guardians.

TECMESSA

Alas, then, it can only have been from there
that he brought those bound beasts home!
And some he slew on the tent's floor   235
cleanly with a neck-cut; others he hacked to pieces
with slashes at their ribs. But two special
white-footed rams he caught up; the head of one
he cut off, and the tip of its tongue, and threw them away;
the other he bound upright against a pillar,   240
seized a stout length of harness, using it
as a singing whip, two-thonged, to lash him with.
And, amid the blows, poured forth such awful curses
as no man, but some demon, must have taught him.

CHORUS

ANTISTROPHE B

Now is the time for a man to muffle his head   245
and over the land to make his escape in stealth,
or else, sitting the thwarts to row,
to trust his life to a ship's swift course on the deep—   250
such are the threats that the sons of Atreus, two in power,
stir toward us. I am in dread to share
with him the blows and hurt of the killing stones;   255
for awful is the doom that holds him.

TECMESSA

No longer so. After the lightning
flash and leap of the storm-wind,
he is calm. But now, being clear in mind,
he is freshly miserable. It is a painful thing
to look at your own trouble and know   260
that you yourself and no one else has made it.

CHORUS LEADER [*now speaking*]

But still, if it is past, I should think he is lucky;°
once the trouble has gone, there is less talk about it.

TECMESSA [*speaking*]

If someone posed the question, which would you choose: 265
to grieve your friends while feeling joy yourself,
or to be wretched with them, shares alike?

CHORUS LEADER

The last, lady, is twice as bad a thing.

TECMESSA

Since he is ill no longer, only we feel ruined.°

CHORUS LEADER

What do you mean? I cannot understand you.   270

TECMESSA

Ajax, so long as the mad fit was on him,
himself felt joy at all his wretchedness,
though we, his sane companions, grieved indeed.
But now that he's recovered and breathes clear,
his own anguish totally masters him,   275
while we are no less wretched than before.
Is not this a redoubling of our grief?

CHORUS LEADER

You are quite right. Lady, I wonder
if a fearful blow of god's anger may have hit him.
It is strange that he feels no happier sane than sick.   280

TECMESSA

   Strange, perhaps. But the facts are as they are.

CHORUS LEADER

   How at the start did this catastrophe
   swoop down? Tell us: we share the pain of it.

TECMESSA

   Indeed, you are partners and shall hear it all.
   In the depth of night, after the evening flares   285
   had all gone out, Ajax, with sword in hand,
   began to move toward the door, intent
   upon some pointless errand. I objected,
   and said, "Ajax, what are you doing? Why
   do you stir? No messenger has summoned you: 290
   you have heard no trumpet. Why, the whole army now's
      asleep!"
   He answered briefly in a well-worn phrase,
  "Woman, a woman's decency is silence."
   I heard, and said no more; he headed out alone.
   I don't know what horrors occurred outside,   295
   but when he came back in, he brought with him
   a mass of hobbled bulls and shepherd dogs
   and woolly captives. He struck the heads off some;
   others' throats he slit with an upward cut;
   and some, held fast in bonds, he kept abusing
   with words and blows, as though they were human beings—
   and all the while he was abusing poor dumb beasts.   300
   At length he darted out the door and spoke
   wild, rending words, directed toward some phantom,
   exulting with a harsh laugh how he'd paid them,
   Odysseus and the sons of Atreus. Then
   he sprang back in again, and somehow, slowly,   305
   by painful stages came to his right mind.
   And when he saw his dwelling full of ruin,
   he beat his head and bellowed. There he sat,

wreckage himself among the wreck of corpses,
the sheep slaughtered; and in an anguished grip
of fist and fingernail he clutched his hair.   310
He sat so, without speaking, for some time;
then finally spoke those fearful, threatening words—
what he would do to me if I failed to say
all that had happened: he asked me where he stood.
Friends, I was terrified by all he'd done,   315
and told him, simply, everything I knew.
Then he cried out—long wails of shattering pain,
like none I ever heard from him before;
he always used to say such cries were cowardly,
marks of an abject spirit. His own way   320
was not to wail aloud in his distress,
but keep his moans low, like a roaring bull.
Now, though, quite overcome by his misfortune,
refusing food and drink, he sits there motionless,
relapsed among the beasts his sword brought down.   325
      There are clear signs, too,
that he's aiming to do some dreadful thing; his words
and his lamentations both somehow suggest it.
Friends—this was the thing I came to ask of you—
won't you come in and help us, if you can?
Men like him will listen to their friends.   330

CHORUS LEADER
Tecmessa, Teleutas' daughter, what a frenzy,
by your account, his griefs have moved him to!

AJAX   (From inside the tent.)
Ah, ah!

TECMESSA
Worse may be coming. Didn't you hear his voice,
Ajax's, distorted in that ghastly cry?   335

AJAX   (From inside.)
Ah, ah!

CHORUS LEADER

Either he still is mad, or else can't bear
to face the results of his former madness.

AJAX   (From inside.)

Boy! Where is my son?

TECMESSA

Oh no! Eurysaces, it's you he's calling.   340
What can he want? Where are you? What shall I do?

AJAX   (From inside.)

Teucer! Where are you? Where is my brother Teucer?
Is he out there raiding, forever? And I here ruined!

CHORUS LEADER

No, he seems to be sane. Open the door.
Perhaps seeing someone, though it's only us,
may help him to compose himself.   345

                    (Tecmessa opens the door, revealing Ajax sitting in
                    the middle of slaughtered bulls and sheep.)

TECMESSA

There, now you see.
You can judge for yourself the state of his affairs,
and how the man is too.

AJAX [singing, perhaps from inside the tent or from the doorway, while
the Chorus Leader and Tecmessa speak in response]

                        STROPHE A

Ah!
Dear fellow sailors, my only friends,
still faithful in the old proved way,   350
look at this swirling tide of grief
and the storm of blood behind it,
coursing around and round me.

CHORUS LEADER

Horrible!

Tecmessa, what you told us was too true—
insanity stands here revealed indeed!   355

AJAX

Ah!
Stout hearts and skillful navigators,
strong hands to move the oar,
I see no friend but you,
no, none, to watch out for me.   360
So now, please, help by killing me!

CHORUS LEADER

Hush! Check those awful words!
Don't seek a worse cure for a bad disease,
and make your pain still heavier than it is.

AJAX

Here I am, the bold, the valiant,
unflinching in the shock of war—   365
a terrible threat to unsuspecting beasts.
Oh! What a mockery I have come to! What indignity!

TECMESSA

Ajax, my lord and master,
I beg you not to say such things.

AJAX

Go away! Take yourself out of my sight!   370
Ah, ah!

CHORUS LEADER

In god's name, be more gentle and more temperate.

AJAX

How could I be so unfortunate?
To let those accursed ones out of my hand,

and fall instead on goats and cattle,
curving horns and splendid flocks,   375
shedding their dark blood!

CHORUS LEADER
The thing is done. Why grieve about it now?
You cannot make it undone.

AJAX

ANTISTROPHE B

Ah, yes, son of Laertes
spying everywhere, always   380
the tool of every mischief,
filthiest scoundrel of all the army:
what a huge laugh you're laughing now, what gloating!

CHORUS LEADER
It is the god's giving if we laugh or weep.

AJAX
Ah, if I could just once catch sight of him!
Crushed as I am, I'd . . .
Ah, ah!   385

CHORUS LEADER
My lord, no blustering words.
Your situation's desperate; can't you see?

AJAX
Zeus, father of my forefathers,
how might I strike them down,
that devious, hateful rogue and the two joint kings,   390
and finally find death myself?

TECMESSA
When you utter that prayer, why, pray for my death too;
why should I go on living after you are dead?

AJAX

O
darkness that is my light,
murk of the underworld, my only brightness,
oh, take me to yourself to reside with you,   395
receive and keep me. I cannot look
to any of the race of gods for help,
being no longer worthy,
nor yet to humankind.   400
But the mighty goddess, daughter of Zeus, cruelly works my ruin.
Where shall a man flee?
Where shall I turn for refuge?
All that I was has perished°   405
with these poor creatures here,
and I abused by a fool's dream
of stalk and capture. Friends, friends,
the massed army will take my life
with bloody swords in hand.

TECMESSA

What wretchedness, to hear a brave man speak   410
such words as formerly he'd never deign to use!

AJAX

O
sounding straits of the sea,
caves by the sea's edge, meadows on the shore,
long and long have you kept me here at Troy;   415
but now I shall not revive again, never again—
a man of sense may know it.
Scamander, neighboring river, gentle to Greeks,   420
you shall no longer see this man,
such a man (let me now speak my boast)
as Troy never saw the like of, not in all
the army that came from the land of Greece.   425

But now in dishonor
I lie abject.

CHORUS LEADER
I cannot restrain you, and yet I can't allow you
to keep talking, surrounded by such miseries.

AJAX [*now speaking*]
Agony. Who would have thought my name and fortune   430
could square so well together! My name is Ajax;
agony is its meaning.° And my fortunes
are cause indeed for an agony of wailing,
cause and enough twice over. How my father,
fighting here under Ida long ago,
won with his sword the loveliest prize of all   435
for valor, and sweet praise at his return;
but I, his son,
coming in my turn with a force no less
to this same land of Troy, no less than he a champion,
nor less deserving, yet am left an outcast,
shamed by the Greeks, to perish as I do!   440
And yet I seem to know this simple truth:
if the bestowing of the famous armor
had rested with Achilles while he lived,
to give them as a war prize to the bravest,
no rival then would have filched them from my hands.
But now the sons of Atreus have contrived   445
that a man of most dishonest mind should have them,
pushing my brave deeds aside. And I say this,
that if my eyes and mind had not leapt whirling
wide from my aim, those two would never again
cheat anyone with their awards and ballots!
But, instead, the fierce-eyed, overpowering   450
daughter of Zeus, just then as I was readying
my hand and plot against them, set me sprawling,
distraught and frenzied, and I dipped my hands
in the blood of beasts like these. And now they are laughing

and triumph in their clear escape, which I
never intended for them. But when a god   455
strikes harm, a worse man often foils his better.
     And now, Ajax—what is to be done now?
I am hated by the gods, that's plain; the Greek camp hates me:
Troy and the ground I stand upon detest me.
Shall I go, then, from this place where the ships ride,   460
desert the Atridae, and cross the Aegean to my home?
But when I get there,
what face can I show to my father Telamon?
How will he ever stand the sight of me
if I stand there empty-handed, armed with no glory,
when he himself won the crown of men's top praise?   465
That won't bear thinking of. Well, then,
shall I make a rush against the walls of Troy,
fight with them all in single combat, do
some notable exploit, and find my death in it?
But that might give some comfort to the sons of Atreus.
No. I must find some better way entirely—   470
an enterprise which will prove to my old father
that the son of his loins is not by nature a weakling.
It's a contemptible thing for a man to want long life
when his whole existence brings no relief from trouble.
What joy is there in a long file of days,   475
edging you forward toward the goal of death,°
then back again a little? I wouldn't give much for a man
who warms himself with the comfort of vain hopes.
Let a man nobly live or nobly die
if he *is* a nobleman: I have said what I had to say.   480

CHORUS LEADER
    Ajax, no one could ever call those words
    spurious or alien to you. They are your own heart's speech.
    Pause, though, a moment; put aside these thoughts,
    and give your friends a chance to win you over.

TECMESSA

Ajax, my lord, life knows no harder thing   485
than to be at the mercy of compelling fortune.
I, for example, was born of a free father;
if any man in Phrygia was lordly and prosperous, he was.
Now I'm a slave. Such, it seems, was the gods' will,
and the will of your strong hand. But since I've come   490
to share your bed with you, my thoughts are loyal
to you and yours. And I beg you
in the holy name of Zeus who guards your hearth fire,
and by your bed, in which you were united with me,
don't give me up to hear the harsh speech
of your enemies and to be owned by one of them.   495
For this is certain: the day you die
and by your death desert me, that same day
will see me outraged too, forcibly dragged
by the Greeks, together with your boy, to lead a slave's life.
And then some one of my masters, lashing out   500
with a cruel word, will make his hateful comment:
"There she is, Ajax's woman;
he was the greatest man in the whole army.
How enviable her life was then, and now how slavish!"
Some speech in that style. And my ill fate
will be driving me before it, but these words
will be a reproach to you and all your family.   505
Ajax, revere your father; do not leave him
in the misery of his old age—and your mother,
shareholder in many years, revere her too!
She prays the gods for your safe return, how often!
And last, dear lord, show pity to your child,   510
if robbed of his infant nurture and deprived of you,
he's to live his life out under the rule of guardians
not kind nor kindred—what a wretchedness
you by your death will deal to him and me!
For I no longer have anywhere to look for help,

if not to you. My country was destroyed   515
utterly by your spear, and another fate
brought down my mother and my father too,
to dwell in death with Hades. Then what fatherland
shall I ever have but you? Or what prosperity?
You are my only safety. O my lord,
remember even me. A man ought to remember   520
if he has perhaps experienced some pleasure.
Kindness it is that brings forth kindness always;
but when a man ignores good done to him
and lets the recollection of it slip away,
how shall I any longer call him noble?

CHORUS LEADER
Ajax, I wish you could have pity in your heart   525
as I do. For then you might approve her words.

AJAX
Well, she can certainly count on my approval
if only she sets her mind to do as I bid her.

TECMESSA
Dearest Ajax, I will be all obedience.

AJAX
Then bring me my son and let me see him.   530

TECMESSA
It was only because of my fears that I removed him.

AJAX
In all this terrible business? Or do I understand you?

TECMESSA
Yes, in case the poor boy might come in your way and be
  killed.

AJAX
Yes, that would have been in accord with my misfortune.

TECMESSA

At all events I took care that it shouldn't happen.   535

AJAX

You did well and deserve credit for your foresight.

TECMESSA

Is there anything, then, you want me to do for you?

AJAX

Yes. Let me speak to my boy and see his face.

TECMESSA

He's not far off. The servants are looking after him.

AJAX

Why doesn't he come at once, then?   540

TECMESSA

Eurysaces! Your father is calling for you

(To one of the servants inside.)

You there, whose hands have care of him—bring him here!

AJAX

Is he coming? Doesn't he hear your words?

(Enter Eurysaces, led by a servant.)

TECMESSA

Here he is. See, the servant's bringing him.

AJAX

Lift him up, lift him to me. He won't be frightened,   545
even by seeing this fresh-butchered gore,
not if he really is my son. Break in
the colt straight off to his father's savage ways;
train him to have a nature like his sire.

My boy, may you have better luck than your father,   550
but be like him in all else; and you will not be bad.
You know, even now I somewhat envy you:

you have no sense of all this misery.
Not knowing anything's the sweetest life—
ignorance is bliss°—
till the time comes when you learn of joy and grief.   555
But when you come to that,
then you must show your father's enemies
what sort of a man you are, and what man's son.
Till then feed on light breezes, basking
in the tenderness of young life, your mother's joy.
For rest assured, the Greeks will not offer you outrage   560
or hatefully insult you, even when you're without me.
I leave you a strong guardian as doorkeeper,
Teucer. He will protect and rear you up
and stint you nothing, even though now he's far away,
gone on a distant raid in enemy country.   565
    You, men at arms and seafarers, my followers,
I enjoin this act of kindness on you all:
pass on my command to Teucer; bid him take
my boy here to my home, present him
to Telamon and my mother, Eriboea,
and let him tend and nourish their old age   570
with constancy, till at the last they find
their dark apartments with the god below.°
As for my arms—
I say no arbiter of the Greeks shall set them
as a prize of competition for the army;
certainly my destroyer shall not. Rather
you, my boy, take from me this great weapon
from which you have your name, Eurysaces;°   575
hold and direct it by its stalwart strap,
this sevenfold-oxhide-thick unbreachable shield.
The rest of my armor shall be buried with me.
But there's enough. Come, take the child quickly;
close up the house. And let there be no wailing
here out of doors. Lord, what a plaintive creature   580
womankind is!

Make fast, and hurry!
No good physician moans incantations
when the malady he's treating needs the knife.

CHORUS LEADER

I'm terrified by your eager urgency,
and take no comfort in your sharpened tongue.

TECMESSA

Ajax, my lord, what is your mind bent upon?   585

AJAX

Don't probe and question me! Restraint is best.

TECMESSA

How my heart falters! Ajax, by your child
and by the gods I beg you, don't be our betrayer!

AJAX

You're growing tedious. Don't you know by now
that I owe the gods no service any more?   590

TECMESSA

What impious words!

AJAX

                              Reprove those who hear you.

TECMESSA

And will you not relent?

AJAX

                              You've said too much already.

TECMESSA

My lord, it is my fear that speaks!

AJAX   *(To the servants.)*

                              Shut the doors at once!

TECMESSA

In the gods' name, soften!

AJAX

You have a foolish thought
if you think at this late date to school my nature.   595

(Ajax, Tecmessa, and Eurysaces go inside.)

CHORUS [*singing*]

STROPHE A

O glorious Salamis, my heart recalls,
blessed island, where you lie
at peace in the surf's pounding,
radiant in all men's sight and prized forever.
But Time has grown old since I   600
have kept this wretched campsite under Ida,°
losing count of the months' passing,
feeling the slow wear and abrasion;   605
and dark is my thought's forecast:
shall I yet come, shall my coming be
to the somber and detested house of Death?

ANTISTROPHE A

And now I face a further struggle,
for Ajax, incurable, sits by, ah,   610
with god-sent madness as his consort.
You sent him forth, fair island, in a time long past,
a warrior mighty among warriors. Now
he feeds his thoughts in loneliness   615
and brings grief to his friends.
And the works of war that once his strong hands did
now are fallen, fallen away,
unappreciated, unloved by those unloving kings.   620

STROPHE B

I think, too,
of his mother, with the white of age upon her:
surely when the news of his mind's devouring sickness   625
is brought to her, lamenting, lamenting,

like the pitiful nightingale
she will not hold back the cry of her heart's anguish,
but high, rending strains will break from her,   630
her hands will thud, beating her breast,
and her gray hair will be torn.

Better if he
were hidden in Hades, now his mind is gone;   635
for though his proud lineage
excelled the other warlike Greeks,
he keeps no more the steady heart we knew,
but ranges in extravagant madness. Wretched father!   640
What an unendurable word you must hear! Calamity
fallen upon your son, such as no other
of all Aeacus' family has borne, but only he.   645

(Enter Ajax from the tent with a sword in
his hand, followed by Tecmessa.)

AJAX
Strangely the long and countless drift of time
brings all things forth from darkness into light,
then covers them once more. Nothing so unexpected
that anyone can say it surely will not be—
strong oath and iron intent come crashing down.
My mood, which just before was strong and rigid,   650
like hardened steel, now has lost its edge—
my speech is womanish for this woman's sake;
and pity touches me for wife and child,
widowed and lost among my enemies.
But now I'm going to the bathing place
and meadows by the sea, to cleanse my stains,   655
in hope the goddess' wrath may pass from me.
And when I've found a place that's quite deserted,
I'll dig in the ground, and hide this sword of mine,

hatefullest of weapons, out of sight. May Darkness
and Hades, god of death, hold it in their safe keeping.   660
For never, since I took it as a gift
which Hector, my great enemy, gave to me,
have I known any kindness from the Greeks.
I think the ancient proverb speaks the truth:
an enemy's gift is ruinous and no gift.   665
Well, then,
from now on this will be my rule: Give way
to the gods, and bow before the sons of Atreus.
They are our rulers, they must be obeyed.
I must give way, as all dread strengths give way,
in turn and deference. Winter's hard-packed snow
cedes to the fruitful summer; stubborn night   670
at last withdraws, so white-horsed day can shine.
The dread blast of the gale slackens and gives
peace to the sounding sea; and Sleep, strong jailer,
in time yields up his captive. Shall not I   675
learn place and wisdom? Have I not learned this,
only so much to hate my enemy
as though he might again become my friend,
and so much good to wish to do my friend,   680
as knowing he may yet become my enemy?
Most men have found friendship a treacherous harbor.
Enough: this will be well.
        You, my wife, go in
and fervently and continually pray the gods   685
to grant fulfillment of my soul's desire.
And you, my friends, heed my instructions too,
and when he comes, deliver this to Teucer:
let him take care for me and thought for you.
Now I am going where my way must go;   690
do as I bid you, and you yet may hear
that I, though wretched now, have found my safety.

(Exit Ajax to the side; exit Tecmessa into the tent.)

CHORUS [singing]

I shudder and thrill with joy,
I leap and take wings—lord Pan!
Come to me over the sea   695
from your snow-buffeted mountain,
from the long, rocky ridge of Cyllene.
Teach me (since you, self-taught, are the gods' dance leader),
teach me the excited Mysian and Cnosian steps—°   700
I am eager to dance!
And over the open sea . . .
may Apollo come to me, clear to see,
the lord of Delos—
to be with me in kindness always.   705

Ares the war god has cleared
the grim grief from our eyes.
Ah, I exult with joy!
Once again, Zeus,
king of the bright air, your perfect daylight
can bathe our skimming seacraft in its whiteness.
Ajax forgets his pain,   710
and now, with holy rite and due observance,
once more recognizes divine law.
Great Time makes all things dim and ignites them again;°
and nothing seems beyond the verge of the speakable,   715
since Ajax has been converted
(amazing!) from his heart's fierceness and his stern
strife with the sons of Atreus.

(Enter Messenger, from the side.)

MESSENGER

Friends, I would deliver this news first to you:
Teucer has just come back from rugged Mysia.   720
No sooner did he reach headquarters than

the whole Greek army gathered to abuse him.
They'd seen him coming quite a long way off
and, when he arrived, stood around him in a circle,
jabbing at him with jeers from every side: 725
called him the brother of a lunatic
and traitor to the army, threatened him
with stoning to a torn and bloody death.
So far they went that eager fingers then
had plucked forth swords from scabbards, but the strife,   730
just as it hurried toward its uttermost,
grew quiet at the elders' peaceful words.
But where is Ajax? I must speak my news,
the whole story, to my lord himself.

CHORUS LEADER
He is not here. He went away just now;   735
his heart is changed, and bends to bear the yoke
of a changed purpose.

MESSENGER
Oh no!
Perhaps the man that sent me was too slow
in sending, or I lingered on the way.

CHORUS LEADER
What is so urgent? Why do you think you're late?   740

MESSENGER
Teucer declared the man should not go out,
but stay indoors, till he himself arrives.

CHORUS LEADER
He *has* gone out, though—seeking his truest good.
He wants to be relieved of the gods' anger.

MESSENGER
A very foolish and misguided thought,   745
if Calchas can foresee events at all!

CHORUS LEADER
  What are you saying? What can you know of it?

MESSENGER
  This much I know—I happened to be near:
  for Calchas rose and left the kingly circle   750
  and came to speak with Teucer separately
  without the Atridae; gently he placed his hand
  in Teucer's own, and urged and pled with him
  to use all means to keep his brother safe
  under his tent roof, and confine him there
  throughout the length of this now present day,   755
  if ever he wished to see him alive again.
  Only for this one day, the prophet said,
  will the goddess Athena drive him with her anger.
  "Wherever men forget their human nature,
  thinking thoughts too high, they are not helped
  by bodily bulk and stupid° boldness; no,   760
  they fall, through heavy disasters sent by Heaven.
  Ajax, even when he first set out from home,
  proved himself foolish, when his father gave him
  his good advice at parting. 'Child,' he said,
  'Resolve to win, but always with god's help.'   765
  But Ajax answered with a senseless boast:
  'Father, with god's help even a worthless man
  could triumph. I propose without that help
  to win my prize of fame.' In such a spirit
  he boasted. And when once Athena stood   770
  beside him in the fight, urging him on
  to strike the enemy with his deadly hand,
  he answered then, that second time, with words
  to shudder at, not speak: 'Goddess,' he said,
  'go stand beside the other Greeks; help them.
  For where I'm stationed, no enemy will break through.'   775
  With such words as these that kept no human measure

he won from the goddess hatred and fierce anger.
But if he lives this day out, then perhaps,
with god's help, we may be his saviors still."
This was the seer's message. Teucer rose   780
at once and sent me off, bearing you these
instructions, with strict charge to keep them. But
if things already have deprived us of our hopes,
then Ajax's life is done—or Calchas knows nothing.

CHORUS LEADER

Tecmessa, I think you were born for every misery.
Come and attend to this man's fearful story.   785
The razor grazes near, and we feel no comfort.

(*Enter Tecmessa from the tent, carrying Eurysaces.*)

TECMESSA

I have only just found respite from that other
siege of calamities. What new alarm is this?

CHORUS LEADER

Listen to the message this man has brought.
It concerns Ajax, and it sounds grim.   790

TECMESSA

Alas, what is your message? Not that we're ruined?

MESSENGER

As to your own case, I can't say. But if Ajax
has left his tent, there is no hope for him.

TECMESSA

But he *has* gone out. I tremble in suspense
to know your meaning.

MESSENGER

Teucer sends strict directions that Ajax   795
must be kept under the cover of his tent
and not permitted to go out alone.

TECMESSA

    But where is Teucer? And why does he say this?

MESSENGER

    He has just returned. And he apprehends
    that Ajax's going out will be his ruin.

TECMESSA

    Heaven help us! Who was the man that told him this?   800

MESSENGER

    Calchas the prophet. He warned us to be on our guard
    all day, for it brings him either life or death.°

TECMESSA

    Alas, friends, stand between me and my doom!
    Hurry, some of you, and bring Teucer quickly;
    the rest divide—let one group search the eastward
    and one the westward bendings of the shore,   805
    to trace his evil journey. I can see now
    that I have been deceived of his intent
    and exiled from his kindness which I knew.
        But oh! my child, what shall I do? Not stay,
    but join the search as far as my strength supports me.   810
    Come, let's be at the work! No time to linger,
    if we aim to save a man that's bent on death.

CHORUS LEADER

    I am ready. More than my words shall show it:
    you'll find me swift of foot and prompt in action.

          (Exit Tecmessa to the side bearing Eurysaces, along with
          the Messenger. The Chorus divides into two semichoruses
          and exits to both sides. The stage is empty.)

Scene: An empty place by the seashore. Enter Ajax, carrying a sword.

AJAX   *(He fixes the sword in the ground.)*°
    My slayer's set there, firm in the ground, so the cut   815

(if I have time even for this reflection)
should now be deadliest. This very sword
was Hector's gift, a token of guest-friendship,
and he of all guest-friends my bitterest foe;
here now it stands, lodged in this hostile ground
of Troy, its edge renewed with the gnawing whetstone.   820
And also I've fixed it firmly, with every care,
to help me quickly and kindly to my death.

    This preparation I have made. And now,
making my invocation, as is right,
I call first, Zeus, on you. Grant me one small thing: 825
send some messenger, please, to bring
the evil news about me first to Teucer,
so that he may be first to lift me up
when I have fallen on this fresh-stained sword.
I would not have some enemy spy me out
and cast me forth, a prize for birds and dogs.   830
Grant me, O Zeus, this one thing. And I call
on Hermes, conductor to the world below,
to put me to sleep quickly, in one leap
without convulsions on this piercing blade.
And I ask those dread Furies, who are ever maidens   835
and watch all the fates and sufferings of men,
to come with long strides, my helpers; mark my end,
how Atreus' sons have brought me to my ruin,
and sweep upon them for their ruin too.°
They see me falling now by my own hand;   840
so may they fall too by loved and kindred hand!
Go, swift and punishing Erinyes,
taste the whole army's blood, and spare them nothing.

    And you that drive your chariot up steep heaven,   845
lord Helios—when you next shall see my own
dear country, hold in check your golden reins,
and bring the tale of my death and downfall
to my old father and to her that nursed me.
Poor mother! When she hears this wretched word,   850

how her laments will echo through the town!
　　But it does no good to bemoan things pointlessly.
I must set about my business with all speed.
Strong god of death, attend me now and come.
And yet I shall converse with you hereafter° 855
and be with you in the world below. But you,
sweet gleam of daylight now before my eyes,
and sun god, splendid charioteer, I greet you
for this last time and never any more.
　　O radiance, O my home and hallowed ground
of Salamis, and my father's hearth, farewell! 860
And glorious Athens, and my peers and kin
nurtured with me—and also here the springs
and streams and plains of Troy, my nurses all—
farewell! This last word Ajax speaks to you;
the rest he'll utter in Hades to those below. 865

(He falls on the sword.° Enter, from the sides,
the two divisions of the Chorus.)

FIRST SEMICHORUS [alternating between singing and speaking, as
does the Second Semichorus]
　Toil breeds toil upon toil;
　where, where have I not searched?
　No place allows me to share its secret.°
　Listen! What noise was that? 870

SECOND SEMICHORUS
　Only us, your shipmates.

FIRST SEMICHORUS
　What news?

SECOND SEMICHORUS
　From the ships to westward we've scanned all the ground.

FIRST SEMICHORUS
　And discovered? 875

SECOND SEMICHORUS
  Labor enough; but nothing to see.

FIRST SEMICHORUS
  Nor yet on the path to eastward, facing the sunrise:
  no sign of him at all.

(The two halves of the Chorus unite.)

CHORUS [*alternating between singing and speaking, as does Tecmessa*]
                STROPHE
  What struggling fisherman
  of those that seek their haul
  with labor in the hours of sleep;   880
  what nymph of mountainside
  or seaward-rolling river
  has seen the fierce man   885
  wandering somewhere and might cry out to me?
  I wish one would! For surely
  it's a hard thing that I must range and toil
  with never a fair course
  to bring me near my goal;
  but I cannot see the afflicted man's faint trace.   890

TECMESSA   *(From the side.)*
  Oh! No! No!

CHORUS
  Whose is that harsh cry bursting from the grove?

(Enter Tecmessa.)

TECMESSA
  Oh! Oh!

CHORUS LEADER
  It is she, I see her now, the poor captive wife,
  Tecmessa. She is lost in lamentation.   895

TECMESSA
  Friends, I am ruined, overwhelmed, undone.

CHORUS

What is the matter?

TECMESSA

Here at my feet lies Ajax, newly slaughtered.
His fallen body enfolds and hides the sword.

CHORUS

Oh, now I shall not win home!   900
You have dealt me death, my lord,
your poor unhappy shipmate.
—And I feel for her, poor wretched one, poor wife!

TECMESSA

He is dead, dead. We can only weep for him.

CHORUS LEADER

Whose hand helped him to his fate?   905

TECMESSA

His own hand and act. It's plain to see.
This blade, packed in the ground, on which he fell,
declares it.

CHORUS

How blind I was! And you bled alone, unprotected by friends!   910
I was all deaf and stupid, totally heedless.
Let me see him,
rugged and ill-starred Ajax, where he lies.

TECMESSA

He is not to be looked at! I will cover him   915
with this enfolding garment from all sight.

(She places a cloak over Ajax's body.)

Surely no one who loved him could endure
to see the foam at his nostrils and the spout
of darkening blood from the wound his own hand made.
Alas, what shall I do? Which of your friends   920

will bear you up? Where's Teucer? Oh, may he come in time
to give fit tendance to his fallen brother!
Ajax! To be so great, and suffer this!
Even your enemies, I think, might weep for you.

CHORUS

ANTISTROPHE

You were bound, hard spirit,   925
bound in the end (it is clear now)
to work the term of your luckless
life's share of affliction, that vast journey.
What could they mean but that,
those groans your fierce heart uttered
by night and in the sunlight,   930
fraught with hate
for the sons of Atreus,
fraught with a mind for harm?
That was indeed a great
inaugural time of sorrows,
when the contest for greatest warrior   935
was held over the priceless armor . . .°

TECMESSA [*singing*]
   Oh! The pain of it!

CHORUS LEADER [*speaking*]
   A noble grief, I know, goes to the heart.

TECMESSA
   Oh! Oh!

CHORUS LEADER
   I don't wonder, lady, that you cry out,
   and again cry out, your grief, deprived just now   940
   of such a loved one.

TECMESSA [*now speaking*]
   You may conjecture that;
   I know and feel it all too certainly.

CHORUS [*singing*]
> *That is true.*

TECMESSA
> Poor little child! What a yoke of servitude
> we go to! What harsh masters stand over us!   945

CHORUS
> *They are ruthless indeed, the two sons of Atreus,*
> *if they do the unspeakable thing*
> *you have spoken in your distress:*
> *may the god prevent it!*

TECMESSA
> Even in what we suffer I see the gods' hand.   950

CHORUS LEADER
> Yes, they have given an overload of grief.

TECMESSA
> I think it's Pallas, Zeus' dreadful daughter,
> who breeds this trouble, to benefit Odysseus.

CHORUS
> *Indeed, that much-enduring man,*   955
> *how he insults us in his black heart!*
> *He mocks our frenzied griefs*
> *with loud laughter, bitter to bear,*
> *and the pair of kings hear and join him.*   960

TECMESSA
> Well, let them laugh their laughter and exult
> in Ajax's downfall. They didn't want him living;
> perhaps, now he is dead, they will yearn for him
> when the fighting presses. Ignorant men
> don't know what good they hold in their hands until   965
> they've flung it away. His death was as bitter to me
> as it's sweet to them; but for himself a happiness.
> For he won his great desire, the death he looked for.

Why should those others mock him any more?
His death concerns the gods, not them at all.   970
Let Odysseus think of this and make his empty insult.
For them there is no Ajax; but for me,
he's gone, and left great anguish, pain, and grief.

TEUCER   *(Entering from the side.)*
  Oh! Oh!

CHORUS LEADER
  Be silent! I think it's Teucer's voice I hear;   975
  and his cry goes straight to the mark of this disaster.

TEUCER [*speaking*]
  O my dear brother Ajax, have you come
  to grief, as this strong rumor says you have?

CHORUS LEADER
  He is dead, Teucer. Know the simple truth.

TEUCER
  Then my ill luck is bearing heavily down!   980

CHORUS LEADER
  It is true.

TEUCER
                Ah, I am miserable!

CHORUS LEADER
  You may well groan.

TEUCER
                So rash and calamitous!

CHORUS LEADER
  Yes, Teucer.

TEUCER
                The grief comes sharp. But what
  of his child? Where in Troy's land can he be found?

CHORUS LEADER

He is alone by the tents.   985

TEUCER   *(To Tecmessa.)*
                                Go quickly, then,
quickly, and bring him here. Some enemy else
may snatch him, as one would a lion cub
torn from its lonely mother. Hurry and lose
no time! When a man lies dead and helpless,
all the world delights to mock and injure him.

                                        (Exit Tecmessa.)°

CHORUS LEADER

Teucer, that was his last command to you,   990
to take care for his child, as you are doing.

TEUCER

This sight of all sights that my eyes have seen
to me is harshest, and no other road,
of all my feet have taken, so has grieved
my heart as this, dear Ajax, which I took   995
as I sought the truth and tried to track it down
after I heard the news about your fate.
It was sharp news, and sped through all the army
as if some god had sent it: you were dead.
And when I heard it, still a long way off,   1000
I groaned with inward misery; now I see;
it is true, and it destroys me.
Ah!
Come, uncover him; let me see the worst.
              Hard face to gaze on, face of fierce resolve,
how can I look at you? Oh, what a crop
of anguish you have sown for me in death!   1005
Where can I go? Who ever will receive me,
now I have failed to help you in your need?
Old Telamon is your father, and mine too:
no doubt he'll welcome me and beam on me
when I come home without you. Very likely!   1010

He's not much given to smiling, even when things go well.
What will he not say? What reproach will he spare me?
"Bastard, born from the war spear, wretched coward,
deserter and abandoner"—of you,
dear Ajax! Or perhaps he will suggest   1015
I did it out of treachery, so that I
might get your house and power by your death.
These will be that harsh old man's reproaches:
age makes him morose and stirs him up
to causeless anger. In the end I'll be
cast into exile and denied my country,
a slave in his account, no more a free man.   1020
At home those are my expectations; here in Troy
my enemies are numerous, my assets small,
and even these have vanished with your death.°

     What shall I do? How shall I pull you free,
brother, from off this bitter, gleaming spike,   1025
your murderer, by whose cut you gasped your life out?
Do you see how in time Hector, though dead,
was to destroy you? Only consider this
amazing thing, the fortunes of two men:
the sword-belt Hector had as Ajax's gift
was that which dragged him from the chariot rails,   1030
clamping his flesh and grating him until
he breathed out his life; this sword Hector gave Ajax,
who perished on it with a deadly fall.
Did not a Fury make this blade of bronze?
And was it not Hades, that grim craftsman,   1035
who made that belt? In my opinion,
this was the gods' contrivance, like all other
fortunes of men, for the gods design them all;
and if anyone should find my thought at fault,
let him keep his opinion, and I mine.

CHORUS LEADER
    Cut short your speech, and quickly consider   1040

how best to hide him in some sort of grave,
and what you must say next. I see a man
coming, our enemy, to laugh no doubt,
like any troublemaker, at our misfortunes.

TEUCER

Which chief of the army is it that you see?

CHORUS LEADER

Menelaus, the one for whom we made this voyage.   1045

TEUCER

I see him now.
At closer range he's not hard to distinguish.

(Enter Menelaus from the side, with attendants.)

MENELAUS

You, there! I tell you not to lift that corpse
nor bury it, but leave it where it is.

TEUCER

Why take such trouble to make this grand announcement?

MENELAUS

It's my decision, and the high command's decree.   1050

TEUCER

Perhaps you'd care to give some justification for it.

MENELAUS

Listen, then.
When we brought Ajax here from Greece,
we thought he would be our ally and our friend:
but instead we've found him worse than any Trojan—
plotting a murderous strike at the whole army,   1055
a night attack, to kill us with his spear.
And unless some god had smothered that attempt,
we should have met the end that he has met,
done to a helpless, miserable death,

and he be living still. But a god diverted   1060
his criminal rage to fall on sheep and cattle.
Therefore I say, no man exists on earth
who shall have the power to give him burial;
but he shall be tossed forth
somewhere on the pale sand, to feed the seagulls.   1065
There it is, and don't attempt resistance.
Maybe we couldn't rule him while he lived;
but now he is dead, we most assuredly will,
with a firm directing hand, whether you like it or not.
So long as he lived, he never would heed our words,   1070
never. Yet only a rotten common soldier
would feel no duty to obey his betters.
Laws will never be rightly kept in a city
that knows no fear or reverence, and no army
without its shield of fear can be well governed.   1075
And a man, even if he develops a mighty body,
had better know how small a lapse can down him.
When a man is moved by wholesome fear and shame,
you may know that combination makes for safety;   1080
but insubordination and the rule
of do-as-you-like invariably, mark my words,
sooner or later drive a city on
before the winds to sink beneath the depths.
There should be, I say, some salutary fear:
and let's not think we can do just what we please,   1085
and then not pay a price—and one that hurts.
There's turnabout in these things. A while ago
he was the hot aggressor; now it's I
who entertain large ideas. And I give you notice,
don't bury him. For you may find, if you do,
that you may fall right into your own grave.   1090

CHORUS LEADER
    Menelaus, these are fine principles you've outlined;
    don't shame them now by outrage to the dead.

TEUCER

Friends, I never shall be amazed again
to see a man of humble birth go wrong,
when those who claim the noblest birth of all   1095
utter words as wrong as the ones that you've just heard.
Come, tell me again: you say you brought this man
here for the Greeks as an ally *you* enlisted?
Didn't he make the voyage here on his own,
as his own master? How, then, are you his general?   1100
What gives you title to command his people,
who followed him from home? King of Sparta
you came, no general over us. You've no more claim
to discipline him than he had to give you orders.
Why, you sailed here in a subordinate place,°   1105
not lord of all, that you should ever claim
the right to captain Ajax! Rule your own;
chastise their arrogant speech. But Ajax,
in spite of your prohibitions and your brother's,
I shall lay in his tomb, reverently and justly,
regardless of your tongue. It wasn't at all   1110
for your wife's sake he made the expedition,
like some poor, toiling subject; but for the oaths
which he had sworn—no service due to you.
He took no stock of nobodies. Think this over,
and come then with more heralds at your back,   1115
and maybe the general too. As for your empty noise,
I'll ignore it, so long as you are what you are.

CHORUS LEADER

I can't approve such bold speech in misfortune;
harsh words, however just they are, still bite.

MENELAUS

This archer seems to think quite well of himself.   1120

TEUCER

My archery is no contemptible science.

MENELAUS

Think how he'd boast if he bore a true warrior's shield!

TEUCER

I'm a match light-armed for you in heavy armor.

MENELAUS

That tongue of yours! What a fierce heart it fosters!

TEUCER

A man who's in the right may have some boldness.   1125

MENELAUS

So! It was right he should kill me and then prosper!

TEUCER

Kill? Truly this *is* a miracle,
if you've been killed and still are living!

MENELAUS

A god saved me; I was dead in *his* intention.

TEUCER

Then don't affront the gods, if the gods have saved you.

MENELAUS

Could it be that I'd find fault with the gods' laws?   1130

TEUCER

Yes, if you stand there and forbid the dead to be buried.

MENELAUS

My own enemies! It's right that they not be buried.

TEUCER

Ajax, then, was your enemy on the field of battle?

MENELAUS

He hated me, as I did him. You knew that well.

TEUCER

There was some reason for it:
you were found out procuring fraudulent votes.   1135

MENELAUS

Charge his defeat to the judges, not to me.

TEUCER

You have a gift for suave and stealthy villainy.

MENELAUS

Someone is going to get hurt for saying that.

TEUCER

No worse, I judge, than the hurt I shall inflict.

MENELAUS

I tell you one thing. This man must not be buried.   1140

TEUCER

And this shall be your answer. He shall be
buried at once.

MENELAUS

I once saw a man of fast and saucy speech
who had pressed sailors to make a voyage in a storm;
when the weather got really rough, you couldn't hear
him chirping anywhere: he'd hid himself in his cloak,   1145
and anybody aboard could step on him at will.
And very possibly you and your reckless speech—
if a big whistling storm should suddenly come
out of a little cloud—your clamorous uproar
might be quenched in a very similar fashion.

TEUCER

And I once saw a man inflated with foolishness,   1150
who insulted the misfortunes of his neighbors.
And another man, closely resembling me,
quite like me in temperament, gave him a straight look
and said to him, "Man, don't outrage the dead.
You certainly shall regret it if you do."   1155
That was the advice he gave that worthless man.
I see him now, and he is, it seems to me,
you, and nobody else. Am I speaking in riddles?

MENELAUS

I'm leaving. I shall only look absurd
to stay and chide you, when I might use force.   1160

(*Exit to the side.*)

TEUCER

Go, then. It does me little credit, either,
to listen to an empty man's loud talk.

CHORUS [*chanting*]

A great and wrathful contest is shaping.
Teucer, hurry and find for him,
as quickly as you can, some hollow   1165
cavity in the earth, which shall
become his dank tomb, a signal
reminder of him to men in aftertime.

TEUCER

Here, just in time for that, his wife and child
are coming, to perform with kindred touch
the burial due his pitiable body.   1170

(*Enter Tecmessa with Eurysaces.*)

Come, little one, stand close by as a suppliant,
grasp your father, the creator of your life.
Hold in your hands this lock of hair of mine

(*Cuts it, and puts it in the boy's hand.*)

and one from her, and this, a third, your own
—a suppliant's treasure.
Keep your station, and make your supplication;   1175
and if anyone in the army tries to drag you
forcibly from this corpse, may his corpse be
thrown out unburied from his land and home,
wretchedly, as he is a wretch, cut off
at the root with all his family, even as I
have cut this lock of hair.

Take hold of him, child, and guard him; let no one   1180
remove you, but throw yourself on the body and cling fast.

(To the Chorus.)

And you, don't huddle near like a crowd of women,
instead of the men you are, but rally round
and help, till I come back, having provided
a tomb for him, though all the world oppose me.

(Exit Teucer to the side.)

CHORUS [*singing*]

STROPHE A

Which year, I wonder, shall be our long toil's last,   1185
and when shall the battered count of them all be full?
They bring upon me a ceaseless curse of spear-sped
trouble over the length and breadth of Troy,   1190
a grief and a shame to all Greeks.

ANTISTROPHE A

Whoever it was that first revealed to Hellas
their common scourge, detested arms and war,   1195
I curse him. Would the large sky first had taken him up
or else the impartial house of Death. Generation
after generation of toil. Ah,
there indeed was a destroyer of men!

STROPHE B

It was he that denied me my share
in the sweet companionship   1200
of garlands and deep wine cups;
and miserly he grudged me
the pipe's soft lovely clamor
and a pleasant bed in the night;
and love, the joys of love he also stopped.   1205
Ah! I lie here, and no one cares
that my hair is soaked in the thick continual dew,
reminders of foul Troy.   1210

And he, valorous Ajax,
who was once my shield
from every flying missile
and terror in the hours of night,
now is handed over to his harsh destiny.
What joy, then, is left to me?   1215
Oh, if somehow I might find myself
rounding the wood-topped promontory,
Sunium's flat top where the surf crashes,
and make my salutation   1220
to holy Athens!

(Enter Teucer from the side.)

TEUCER

I hurried back when I saw the commander in chief,
Agamemnon, approaching. And here he is,
looking ready to let loose his clumsy tongue.   1225

(Enter Agamemnon with retinue, from the side.)

AGAMEMNON

You, there! Are you the one they tell me of,
who has made bold to open his big mouth
and utter nasty speeches against me?
And you're unpunished, so far? You,
the son of a captive slave woman! What if your mother
had been a princess? Then I think you'd strut,   1230
then you'd talk big! Why, as it is, being
nothing yourself you have risen up to protect
that man who now is nothing, and have sworn
that I am not the general nor the admiral
either of the Achaeans or of you,
since Ajax, as you say, came under his own command!
These are quite some taunts to hear from a slave.   1235
And what was the man on whose behalf you've shouted
these arrogant claims? Where did he go,

or stand in battle, where I did not too?
Was he the one real man in the whole Greek army?   1240
Ah! That contest for Achilles' armor!
We shall regret the day we published it
if every moment we must be defamed
and slandered by this Teucer, since he won't
accept defeat or yield to the majority,
the verdict of the judges.
No! But you losers pelt us still with slanders,
and seek to wound us with your crafty plots.   1245
Yet if such tactics and behavior rule,
no law can stand unshaken, not when we
are to shove the lawful victors from their place,
and give precedence to those ranked behind.
This must be curbed. It's not a man's great muscles   1250
or breadth of shoulders makes his value sure:
it's men of sense that always come out on top.
Just a small whip can suffice to guide
a hulking ox straight forward on his road;
and I fancy something of that medicine   1255
is coming for you, unless you get some sense!
That man is dead, now—just a shadow;
and yet you seem to count on him to protect
your loose speech! I say, learn common sense!
Think of your slave's birth; bring someone else,   1260
a free man, here to plead your case before me.
I'm disinclined to hear more words from you,
being not much versed in your barbarian tongue.

CHORUS LEADER

I wish you both might learn to have some sense!
That is the best I have to say to you.   1265

TEUCER

Ah! How fleeting is the gratitude
men owe the dead, how soon shown to deceive,
if this man now hasn't even the smallest memory,

of you, Ajax, though oftentimes for him
you risked your life and bore the stress of war.   1270
All that is gone now, easily tossed away.
You, who just now spoke that long, foolish speech,
can't you remember any more at all
how once you were penned close behind your defenses,
and all but reduced to nothing in the fighting,   1275
with flames licking the ships' quarterdecks
already, and Hector high in the air, leaping
over the ditch to board, but Ajax came,
alone, to save you? Who fended off that ruin?
Wasn't it he, the very man you now   1280
declare fought nowhere but where you fought too?
What do you say? Did he do his duty then?
And when that other time he faced Hector
alone in single combat, not conscripted,
but chosen when each champion put his lot
into the crested helmet—Ajax then   1285
put in no coward's lot among the rest,
no clod of moist earth, no! but one to leap
lightly, first and victorious, from the helmet.
It was he that did those things, and I stood by him:
the slave, yes! The barbarian mother's son!
Wretched man, why do you light upon *that* taunt?   1290
Aren't you aware that your own grandfather,
old Pelops, was a barbarous Phrygian? Or
that Atreus, yes, your very own father, set
before his brother a most unholy dish
of his own sons' flesh? And you yourself
had a Cretan for your mother, in whose bed   1295
an interloping foreigner was discovered,
and she consigned, and by your father's order,
to be eaten by the fishes of the deep.
These are your origins. Can you censure mine?
Telamon was my father, and he won
my mother as his valorous prize of war.   1300

She was a princess by her birth, the child
of King Laomedon, and Heracles
distinguished her to be my father's gift.   ⟍⟋⟍
Two royal races gave me to the world.
How shall I shame my kin if I defend them   1305
in their adversity, when you with shameless words
would fling them out unburied? Listen to this:
if you should venture to cast Ajax out,
you must cast out the three of us as well,
together in one heap with him. I make my choice
to stand in public and to die for him,   1310
rather than for your wife—or was it your brother's wife?
So! Think of your own case, and not merely mine;
for if you hurt me, you may wish one day
you had been a coward, rather than bold, with me.   1315

(Enter Odysseus from the side.)

CHORUS LEADER

You arrive, my lord Odysseus, just in time,
if you have come to reconcile and not provoke.

ODYSSEUS

What is this, gentlemen? From quite some distance
I could hear the sons of Atreus raising their voices
over this valiant corpse.

AGAMEMNON

                    Indeed we were.
Hadn't we just been hearing shameful language,   1320
my lord Odysseus, from this fellow here?

ODYSSEUS

What language do you complain of? If he gave
insult for insult, I could pardon him.

AGAMEMNON

I gave him ugly words:
it was an ugly wrong he offered me.

ODYSSEUS

What did he do to injure you?   1325

AGAMEMNON

He says
he will not leave that corpse unburied, but
declares he'll bury it in spite of me.

ODYSSEUS

Agamemnon, may a friend speak truth to you,
and still enjoy your friendship as before?

AGAMEMNON

Speak. I would be foolish to resent your words;   1330
you are my truest friend in the whole army.

ODYSSEUS

Then listen. Don't cast out this brave man's body
unburied; don't in the gods' name be so hard.
Vindictiveness should not so govern you
as to make you trample on the right. I too   1335
found this man hateful once, beyond the rest
of all my fellow soldiers, since the time
I won Achilles' armor. Nevertheless,
in spite of his enmity, I cannot wish
to pay him back with dishonor, or refuse
to recognize in him the best of all   1340
the men that came to Troy, except Achilles.
It would be wrong to do him injury;
in acting so, you'd not be injuring him—
rather the gods' laws. It is not right to harm
a valiant man in death, even if you hate him.   1345

AGAMEMNON

Do you, Odysseus, take his side against me?

ODYSSEUS

I do.
But I hated him while it was fair to hate.

AGAMEMNON
  But now he is dead,
  shouldn't you also trample on his corpse?

ODYSSEUS
  Do not seek pleasure, my lord, in unworthy triumphs.

AGAMEMNON
  Reverence doesn't come easily to a ruler.   1350

ODYSSEUS
  But regard for a friend's advice is not so hard.

AGAMEMNON
  A good man should defer to his superiors.

ODYSSEUS
  No more, now.
  You win the victory when you yield to friends.

AGAMEMNON
  Think what a man you're showing favor to!

ODYSSEUS
  My enemy, it's true. But he was noble.   1355

AGAMEMNON
  What will you do? Respect a corpse you hate?

ODYSSEUS
  His greatness weighs more than my hate with me.

AGAMEMNON
  Men who act so are changeable and unsteady.

ODYSSEUS
  Men's minds are given to change in hate and friendship.

AGAMEMNON
  Do you, then, recommend such changeable friends?   1360

ODYSSEUS
  I cannot recommend a rigid spirit.

AGAMEMNON

You'll make us look like cowards in this transaction.

ODYSSEUS

Honorable, though, as all the Greeks will say.

AGAMEMNON

You want me, then, to let this corpse be buried?

ODYSSEUS

Yes. For I too shall come to that necessity.   1365

AGAMEMNON

In everything, I see, men labor for themselves.

ODYSSEUS

For whom should I rather labor than myself?

AGAMEMNON

Let this be called your doing, and not mine.

ODYSSEUS

However you do it, you will deserve praise.

AGAMEMNON

Understand my position. I would do   1370
this and much more at your request. But as for him,
whether on earth or in the underworld,
I hate him. You may do whatever you wish.

(Exit Agamemnon with his retinue to the side.)

CHORUS LEADER

Whoever fails to recognize your wisdom
and value it, Odysseus, is a fool.   1375

ODYSSEUS

And now I have a promise,
Teucer, to make to you. From now on, I
shall be as much a friend as I was once
an enemy; and I should like to join

in the burial of your dead—doing with you
that labor, and omitting none of it,
which men should give the noblest of their fellows. 1380

TEUCER

Noble Odysseus, I can only praise you.
How greatly you deceived my expectations!
For though you hated him worst of the Argives,
you alone came to help, and did not wish,
because you lived, to outrage him in death. 1385
That half-brained general did otherwise—
he and his brother—and wanted Ajax's corpse
to be thrown out and left to rot unburied.
Therefore, may Zeus who rules on high Olympus,
remembering Fury, and avenging Justice, 1390
destroy them miserably, just as they
sought to work outrage and abomination
on my dear brother's body.
                    Son of Laertes,
I feel some hesitation at your offer
and fear I cannot let you touch the corpse:
that might offend the dead. But bear your part 1395
in all the rest, and if you wish to bring
any others of the army, they shall be welcome.
I'll see to all the rest. And you, Odysseus,
are written in our hearts as truly noble.

ODYSSEUS

I could have wished to help. 1400
But if your preference is otherwise,
I shall respect your wish and take my leave.

                                        (*Exit Odysseus.*)

TEUCER [*chanting*]
Enough then. Delay
has grown too long already.
Some of you hurry and dig

the hollow trench; others
set the tall cauldron   1405
amid the surrounding flames
to ready the holy bath;
and one troop bring from within the tent
his glorious suit of armor.

Now you, my boy,
take hold with your little strength
upon your father's body,   1410
and help in tenderness to lift him up;
for still the warm conduits
spout forth his life's dark force.
Come now, come, everyone
that claims to be his friend,
begin, proceed, and bear him up,
this man of perfect excellence—   1415
no nobler one has ever been than he:
I speak of Ajax, while he lived.°

                                                    (*The funeral cortege forms.*)

CHORUS [*chanting*]   .
    What men have seen they know;
    but what shall come hereafter
    no man before the event can see,
    nor what end waits for him.   1420

                                                    (*Exit all, following the body.*)

THE WOMEN OF TRACHIS

Translated by MICHAEL JAMESON

THE WOMEN OF TRACHIS: INTRODUCTION

The Play: Date and Composition

Sometimes ancient tragedies were named after their chorus, rather than a main character or event (for example, *The Libation Bearers* of Aeschylus and *The Phoenician Women* of Euripides). *The Women of Trachis* could just as well have been entitled *Deianira* or *The Death of Heracles*, and we do not know who actually assigned the play its title. As with the majority of Sophocles' plays, we have no evidence as to when this one was first produced. Presumably it was performed for the annual competition in Athens; but we have no idea which other plays accompanied it nor whether Sophocles won the prize that year. On stylistic grounds, most scholars are inclined to believe that the play was written in the middle of Sophocles' career, perhaps in the 440s or 430s BCE, but this is no more than a conjecture.

The Myth

Heracles was the greatest of all Greek heroes, and an extraordinary number of stories grew up around him. In our play, as in many ancient sources, he is described as being "best" of mortals: this does not mean that he was morally the finest, but that through his strength, courage, and determination he was physically and mentally capable of achieving feats that other men could not. Greek literature and art are replete with narratives and images of Heracles' exploits: killing animals and monsters, punishing human wrongdoers, surviving visits to the underworld, but also losing his temper and attacking innocent victims, fighting against divinities, and sexually violating young women. His short temper, sexual appetite, and tendencies to violence were as renowned as his courage and strength.

Heracles was the son of Zeus and the human Alcmene. The fact that Alcmene was married to Amphitryon of Thebes meant that Zeus' paternity was occasionally called into question (as it is by Heracles himself in this play), and this ambiguous status was part of Heracles' mythological identity throughout antiquity. There were also rival traditions about his death or apotheosis. The ending of our play alludes tantalizingly to this ambiguity, as preparations are made to place his dying body on a funeral pyre on Mount Oeta. Sophocles does not specify whether the immolation will put Heracles finally out of his misery in death or transform him into an immortal.

Plots focused primarily on Heracles were not all that common in Greek tragedy: Euripides' *Heracles* is the only other surviving play in which he is the main character, though he also plays a significant role in Sophocles' *Philoctetes* and in Euripides' *Alcestis*. He was more prominent in satyr-plays and comedies, which often focused on his extreme eating and drinking habits or his success in slaying monsters. The so-called twelve labors of Heracles (there are almost twenty of them, in fact) were favorite topics for artists and poets, and several of them are mentioned in our play. One is of particular importance: Heracles killed the Hydra by cutting off all of its many heads, and then he collected the monster's poisonous blood, which he used to tip his arrows and thus guarantee the deadliness of his archery. It is the Hydra's blood that ends up killing Heracles—thereby fulfilling the prophecy referred to in the play (probably Sophocles' invention) that he would be killed "by someone dead."

Sophocles' *Women of Trachis* focuses on the events that lead up to Heracles' death, and places his wife Deianira at the center of the action. She is the most engaging and pathetic character in the play. The sequence of events that unfolds around her comprises elements that were for the most part traditional and well known; we find these episodes mentioned by earlier poets such as Hesiod and Bacchylides, and also depicted in vase paintings and sculptures. But, as usual, Sophocles has added particular new twists and ironies in weaving them together into a taut and heart-rending plot.

Deianira, whose name in Greek means literally "manslayer" or "husband killer," was the daughter of Oeneus and Althaea and the sister of Meleager. She was betrothed and married to Heracles after he defeated the monstrous river god Acheloüs, who was courting her for himself (an episode vividly described twice in the play). She and Heracles have been married for many years by the time the play begins, for they have an almost grown son, Hyllus. (Heracles' previous marriage to Megara had ended in catastrophe and the death of all his children, an episode presented in Euripides' *Heracles*; there is no mention of this previous wife and family in our play.) At one point early in their marriage, Heracles had shot to death the Centaur Nessus, who, while ferrying Deianira across a river, was attempting to violate her. As he died, Nessus advised the naive young bride that she should collect some of his blood to use as a love charm in the event that her husband might one day lose his affection for her. Deianira did so and kept it in reserve. (Of course, this blood was poisoned by the venom of the Hydra from Heracles' arrowhead. But Deianira did not realize this.) Heracles continued to travel and perform labors and adventures all over the world. While visiting King Eurytus of the town of Oechalia, he committed a series of terrible crimes: first, he killed the king's son, Iphitus, by pushing him off a cliff—an offense for which Heracles was sentenced to spend a year as a slave to the Lydian queen Omphale in Anatolia. Then he fell in love with Eurytus' daughter, Iole, and when the king refused him permission to sleep with her, he destroyed the whole town, killed Eurytus, and took Iole to be his slave concubine. This is where our play begins.

Deianira is waiting anxiously at home in Trachis, Thessaly (where she and Heracles are living in exile from both their homelands), hoping for her husband's final return after completing all his labors. When the news arrives that Heracles is indeed on his way home, she is at first overjoyed, but then she quickly learns about Iole—and that Heracles expects his wife to welcome her into their home as his concubine. Even while she is strongly sympathetic to Iole's plight and struggles not to be angry at her husband's behavior, she finds herself unable to endure the prospect of sharing his affections with a younger woman. Hesitatingly, she resorts to what she thinks is a magical charm, the ointment from Nessus. The robe she anoints with this and sends off to her husband causes his slow and agonizing death. Deianira commits suicide; Hyllus first blames her, then realizes her innocence and laments his loss. In the closing scenes of the play, the tormented Heracles makes his son agree to burn him, barely alive, on a funeral pyre and then marry Iole. The audience recognizes that these two will form the origin of the clan of Heraclids (children of Heracles), who are destined to rule over the Peloponnesus and become the ancestral heroes of all Dorian Greek people (a story portrayed in part in Euripides' *Children of Heracles*).

Transmission and Reception

We do not know what kind of impact *The Women of Trachis* had in its first performance, nor what its subsequent performance history in antiquity may have been. Episodes from the life (and death) of Heracles continued to be widely depicted in literature and art; but there are few direct signs that Sophocles' play was particularly well known. In the Augustan period, the Roman poet Ovid, in the ninth of his *Letters from Heroines* (*Heroides*), has Deianira write to Heracles to express her concern about Iole; and in book 9 of his *Metamorphoses* Ovid narrates the death of Heracles very much along the lines of Sophocles' play. In the next generation (late first century CE) a tragedy dubiously attributed to Seneca titled *Hercules on Mount Oeta* likewise covers much of the same material. These Latin versions—especially Ovid—were far more widely known than Sophocles' play during the Middle Ages and early modern era.

The Greek text of *The Women of Trachis* was included among the seven plays to be read in schools during the later classical period, and so it survived to be copied once pagan Greek literature began to be studied again, from the tenth century onward. But up until the twentieth century it remained the least read of Sophocles' seven surviving plays, in part perhaps because of the rival Latin versions, but also because of the centrality of sexual and erotic themes, the unpleasant portrayal of the hero Heracles, and the play's intense focus on female victimization, as embodied in Deianira and Iole. Such themes were felt to be quite suitable for musical adaptation, however, and during the seventeenth and eighteenth centuries ballets and operas about Deianira and the death of Heracles were composed and performed all over Europe, including G. F. Handel's *Hercules* (1745, with libretto by T. Broughton). None of them show much direct awareness of Sophocles' play. It was only in the twentieth century that it finally began to attract more attention from both readers and college performers. Ezra Pound achieved a leap forward in his highly engaging modern adaptation (1957), even though it was at first much derided by scholars. Pound's version was used in the Living Theatre's staged readings, directed by Julian Beck (1960-61). The National Theatre of Greece presented Sophocles' play in a full-scale production in Modern Greek directed by Alexis Solomos (1970); and Timberlake Wertenbaker more recently presented a reading for BBC radio in 1999 and a staged reading at the Royal National Theatre in 2001. Nowadays the play is one of the most widely read Greek tragedies, especially because of its sensitive representation of issues of love, marital abuse, and feminine affect and subjectivity. Overall, however, it still has received far fewer performances than any of Sophocles' other plays.

THE WOMEN OF TRACHIS

Scene: Trachis, before the house of Heracles and Deianira.

(Deianira and the Nurse enter from the house.)

DEIANIRA
It was long ago that someone first said:
you can't know a person's life before that person
has died, then only can you call it good or bad.
But I know mine before I've come to Death's house,
and I can tell that mine is heavy and sorrowful.   5
While I still lived in Pleuron, with Oeneus my father,
I conceived an agonizing fear of marriage.
No other Aetolian woman ever felt such fear,
for my suitor was the river Acheloüs,
who used to come to ask my father for my hand,   10
taking three forms—first, clearly a bull, and then

a serpent with shimmering coils, then a man's body
but a bull's face, and from his clump of beard
whole torrents of water splashed like a fountain.
I had to think this suitor would be my husband,   15
and in my unhappiness I constantly prayed for death
before I should ever come to his marriage bed.

But, after a time, to my joy there came
the famous Heracles, son of Alcmene and Zeus.
In close combat with Acheloüs, he won the contest   20
and set me free. I do not speak of the manner
of their struggles, for I do not know. Someone
who watched the spectacle unafraid could tell.
I sank down, overwhelmed with terror lest
my beauty should end up bringing me pain. But Zeus   25
of the contests made the end good—if it has been good.
Chosen partner for the bed of Heracles,
I nurse fear after fear, always worrying
over him. I have a constant relay of troubles;
some each night dispels—each night brings others on.   30
We have had children now, whom he sees at times,
like a farmer working an outlying field,
who sees it only when he sows and when he reaps.
This has been his life, that only brings him home
to send him out again, to serve some man or other.   35

But now he's won through to the end of all his labors,
and now I find I am more than ever afraid.
Ever since he killed the mighty Iphitus,
we, his family, live here in Trachis, a stranger's guests,
forced to leave our home. But no one seems to know   40
where Heracles himself can be. I only know
he's gone and left with me a sharp pain for him.
I am almost sure that he is in some trouble.
It has not been a short time—it's fifteen months,
by now, and still there has been no word of him.   45
Yes, this tablet he left behind makes me think

it must surely be some terrible trouble. Often
I pray the gods I do not have it for my sorrow.

NURSE

Deianira, my mistress, many times before
I have watched as you wept and sobbed, bewailing   50
your absent Heracles, and I said nothing. But now
I wonder—if it is proper that the free should learn
from the thoughts of slaves and I give you advice—
how is it that your family abounds with sons, and yet
you send none of them to inquire for your husband?   55
Hyllus, especially, it would be natural to send
if he is at all concerned for his father's safety.
See, here he is, running to the house,
so if what I have said seems of any value,
you can use the boy and follow my advice.   60

                    (Hyllus enters from the side.)

DEIANIRA

O my child, my son, even the lowborn throw
a lucky cast when they speak well. This woman is
a slave, but what she says is worthy of the free.

HYLLUS

What is it she said? Tell me, Mother, if you may.

DEIANIRA

That with your father abroad so long, it does not   65
look well that you have made no inquiry for him.

HYLLUS

But I know where he is, if I can believe what I hear.

DEIANIRA

My child, have you heard in what country he stays?

HYLLUS

All this past year, in all its length of time
they say he worked as servant to a Lydian woman.   70

DEIANIRA

If he could really endure that, then anything might be said
of him.

HYLLUS

But he is free now, I hear.

DEIANIRA

Then where is he now? Is he reported alive or dead?

HYLLUS

They say he is in Euboea, where he campaigns against
the city of Eurytus, unless he is still preparing.   75

DEIANIRA

Did you know, my child, that it was about
this very place he left me a trusty prophecy?°

HYLLUS

What prophecy, Mother? I knew nothing about this.

DEIANIRA

It said that either he would come to his life's end
or have by now, and for the rest of his time,   80
a happy life, once he had carried out this task.
Child, his future lies in the balance. Surely, then,
you will go to help him, since we are only safe
if he can save himself. His ruin is ours.°   85

HYLLUS

I shall go, Mother, and had I known the contents
of this oracle before, I would have been there
long ago. As it was, my father's usual
good luck kept me from worrying and being too fearful.
Now that I know of it, I shall not stop until   90
I have learned the whole truth about his fate.

DEIANIRA

Go now, my son. There is always some advantage
in learning good news, even if one learns it late.

(Exit Hyllus to the side; the Nurse goes inside.
The Chorus enters from the other side.)

CHORUS [*singing*]

STROPHE A

Shimmering night as she lies despoiled brings you
to birth at dawn, lays you to bed ablaze—   95
O Sun, Sun! I beg you,
tell me of Alcmene's child.
Where, where is Heracles?
All afire with the flashing brilliance of light, tell me!
—is he in the narrows of the Black Sea,   100
or does he rest against the twin
continents? Your vision is the strongest.

ANTISTROPHE A

With longing in her heart for him, I learn
that Deianira, over whom men fought,
like some unhappy bird,   105
never lays to bed her longing,
her eyes never dry from tears, but
she nurses fear that well remembers her husband's
journey, worn out upon her troubled
husbandless bed, miserable,   110
with expectation of misfortune.

STROPHE B

As many waves under
the untiring south wind or north
may be seen on the wide
ocean coming on   115
and going by, so he, the descendant
of Cadmus, is twisted, but on life's
next toilsome surge, as on the Cretan
deep, he will be raised up.
Some god always pulls him   120
safely back from the house of Death.

(The Chorus turns toward Deianira.)

ANTISTROPHE B

Therefore, I reprove you,
respectfully, but still
dissenting. You should not let
all expectation of good   125
be worn away. Nothing painless
has the all-accomplishing king, Cronus' son,
dispensed for mortal men. But
grief and joy come circling
to all, like the turning paths   130
of the Bear among the stars.

EPODE

The shimmering night does not last
for mortals, nor does calamity,
nor wealth, but swiftly they are gone,
and to anyone there comes
both joy and its loss.   135
Therefore, I bid even you, O Queen, always
hold fast to this knowledge in your expectations.
For who has seen Zeus be so careless of his children?   140

DEIANIRA

You are here, I suppose, because you have heard
of my suffering. May you never learn
by your own suffering how my heart is torn.
You do not know now. So the young thing
grows in her own places; the heat of the sun god   145
does not disturb her, nor does the rain, nor any wind.
Pleasurably she enjoys an untroubled life
until the time she is no longer called a maiden
but woman, and takes her share of worry in the night,
fearful for her husband or for her children. Then,   150
by looking at their own experience, people may come
to understand the troubles with which I am weighed down.

Many sufferings have made me weep before.
But I shall tell you of one unlike all the rest.   155
When lord Heracles set off from home on his
last journey, he left an old tablet in the house,
on which some signs had been inscribed. Never before
could he bring himself to speak to me of this,
though he went out to many contests; he used to go   160
as if for some great achievement, not to die.
This once, as though he were no longer living, he told me
what property from our marriage I should take and how
he wished the portions of ancestral land divided
among the children, first fixing the time at three months
after he had been away from here one year: 165
then he would either die exactly at this time,
or, by getting past this time limit, he would
in the future live a life without grief.
He said that this was fated by the gods to be
the final limit of the labors of Heracles,   170
as once at Dodona he heard the ancient oak
declare on the lips of the twin Doves, the priestesses.
The period of their prediction exactly coincides
with the present time, when all must come true;
so that I leap up from pleasant sleep in fright,   175
my friends, terrified to think that I may have to live
deprived of the one man who is the finest of all.

CHORUS LEADER
Peace—speak words of good omen. I see a man
with laurel on his head who comes to tell good news.

(The Messenger enters from the side.)

MESSENGER
O Deianira, my mistress, I am the first messenger   180
to free you from your uncertainty. You should know
that Alcmene's son lives and is victorious
and brings from battle first fruits for the gods of the land.

DEIANIRA

What did you say, old man? What are you telling me?

MESSENGER

Soon there shall come to your halls that most enviable man,   185
your husband, appearing in his victorious might.

DEIANIRA

Who told you this? Some townsman or a stranger?

MESSENGER

This is what Lichas, the herald, proclaims to many
in the meadow where the cattle pasture. I heard him
and rushed off, that, as the first to bring the news, I might   190
profit from your gratitude and gain your favor.

DEIANIRA

Why is he not here himself if all is well?

MESSENGER

He is not free to move as he would like, lady.
Around him in a circle stand all the people of Malis
and question him. He is not able to take a step.   195
Everyone is curious; they want to know all
and will not let him go until they've heard him
to their heart's content. So though he does not want to, he
    stays
with those who want him. You will see him soon in person.

(The Messenger goes to the side but remains on stage.)

DEIANIRA

O Zeus, master of the unharvested meadow of Oeta,   200
though it has been long, you have given us joy.
Cry out, O you women who are inside the house
and you who are outside—now that the unhoped-for
    sunshine
of this news has risen high, we pluck its gladness.

CHORUS [*singing*]

 Let there be joyous shouting for this house and jubilation   205
 around the hearth by girls whose wedding is to come; and let the
  clamor
 of men among them go in chorus to honor Apollo,
 who wears the fine quiver, our defender. Together
 raise on high the paean, paean, O maidens,   210
 and shout aloud the name of his sister,
 Artemis Ortygia, deer hunter, who holds the twin torches,
 and of the nymphs her neighbors.   215
 I rise up; I shall not
 push aside the reed pipe, you master of my heart.
 See how it excites me—
 Euoi!—
 the ivy that just now sets me whirling in Bacchant rivalry.   220
 Oh, oh, Paean! See, see, dear lady,
 you are face to face with it now,
 it is clear to look upon.

       (*Enter Lichas from the side, followed by a group*
         of captive women, among them Iole.)

DEIANIRA

 I do see the group that comes to us, ladies.   225
 The sight did not slip past my sentinel eyes.
 I proclaim our welcome to the herald, here after
 a long time—if the news he brings is welcome.

LICHAS

 Our coming is good, lady, and good, too, your greeting,
 which fits accomplished fact. When a man prospers,   230
 his profit must be to earn an excellent report.

DEIANIRA

 O kindest of men, tell me first what I want first
 to hear: Shall I have Heracles alive?

LICHAS

    I can tell you that I left him not only alive
    but strong and flourishing and unburdened by disease.   235

DEIANIRA

    Where? In a Greek or in a foreign land? Tell me.

LICHAS

    On a shore of Euboea, where he marks out altars
    and tributes of the land's harvest for Cenaean Zeus.

DEIANIRA

    Is he fulfilling a vow or obeying an oracle?

LICHAS

    A vow he took while he sought with his spear to overthrow   240
    the country of these women whom you see before you.

DEIANIRA

    And by the gods, who are they, and who is their master?
    They are pitiable, if their misfortune does not deceive me.

LICHAS

    He selected them when he sacked the city of Eurytus
    as possessions for himself and a choice gift for the gods.   245

DEIANIRA

    Was it against this city, then, that he was gone
    an unforeseeable time, days beyond number?

LICHAS

    No, most of this time he was kept in Lydia,
    and, as he himself declares, he was not free
    but a bought slave. (One should not hesitate, lady,   250
    to tell a tale where it is seen Zeus did the work.)
    He was sold to Omphale, the foreign queen,
    and served her a full year, as he says himself,
    and was so stung by this disgrace he had to bear
    that he set himself an oath and swore that he   255
    would live to see the author of his suffering,
    along with wife and child, all in slavery.

These were not empty words, but when he was pure again,
he raised a mercenary army and came against the city
of Eurytus, who alone of mortals was   260
responsible, he claimed, for what he had suffered.
Heracles had come to his house and to his hearth
as an old friend. But Eurytus thundered greatly against him
like the sea and spoke with great malice in his heart:
"Even if Heracles has inescapable arrows,"   265
he said, "in a contest of archery my sons
leave Heracles far behind." He added too
that Heracles was a free man's slave,
a broken thing!° Then he got him drunk at the banquet
and threw him out of the house. It was this that galled;
and when one day Iphitus came to the hill of Tiryns,   270
searching for the tracks of horses that had strayed,
the moment his eyes looked one way, his mind on something
    else,
Heracles hurled him from the top of that broad fortress.
But the king was angry at this act of his,
he who is the father of all, Zeus Olympian,   275
and had him sold and sent out of the country and did not
    relent,
since this was the only man he had ever killed
by guile. If he had taken vengeance openly,
Zeus surely would have pardoned his rightful victory:
for the gods like insolence no better than do men.   280
So they who were so arrogant with their vicious tongues,
themselves are all inhabitants of Hades,
while their city is enslaved. The women you see
come to you, finding, in place of prosperity,
an unenviable existence. These were your husband's wishes   285
which he commanded and I, faithful to him, fulfill.
You may be sure that he himself will come as soon
as he has made the holy sacrifice to Zeus,
god of his fathers, for his conquest. Of much news
happily reported, this must be the sweetest to hear.   290

CHORUS LEADER
  O Queen, now your delight is clear, both for what
  has come about already, and what you have heard promised.

DEIANIRA
  Yes, I should have every right to rejoice
  when I hear the news of my husband's great success.
  Surely my joy must keep pace with his good fortune.   295
  Still, if one gives it much thought, one knows a feeling
  of dread for the man who prospers so, lest he fall.
  For a terrible sense of pity came over me,
  my friends, when I saw these ill-fated women
  wandering homeless, fatherless, in a foreign land.   300
  Before they were, perhaps, the daughters of free men,
  but now they shall have to pass their lives as slaves.
  O Zeus, who turns the tide of battle, grant that I
  may never see you come like this against my children,
  and if you will come, at least not while I am alive.   305
  This is the fear I feel when I look at them.

                                              (To Iole.)

  O unfortunate girl, tell me who you are.
  Are you married? Are you a mother? To judge by your looks,
  you have never known treatment like this, but you
  are someone noble. Lichas, whose daughter is this girl?   310
  Who was her mother, and who was the father that begot her?
  Speak out, for on seeing her I pitied her most
  among these women, since only she understands.

LICHAS
  What do I know? Why do you question me? Perhaps
  in birth she is not among the humblest of that land.   315

DEIANIRA
  Of royal birth perhaps? Had Eurytus a daughter?

LICHAS
  I do not know. I made no long interrogation.

DEIANIRA

Did you not learn her name from one of her companions?

LICHAS

No, I did not. I performed my task in silence.

DEIANIRA

Then do tell us yourself, my poor child, for it   320
would be a great shame not to know who you are.

LICHAS

It will be quite unlike her manner up to now
if she begins to speak, I can assure you, since
she has not said a single thing, not one word yet.
She suffers constantly the weight of her misfortune   325
like pangs of labor, weeping and miserable, from the time
she left her windblown fatherland. Truly, her situation
is miserable indeed, and we must pardon her.

DEIANIRA

Then let her be, and let her go into the house
however she please. She should not have further grief   330
on my account to add to her present unhappiness.
What she has already is enough. Let us all
enter the house so you may hasten wherever you wish
to go and I may see to the preparations within.

> (Exit Lichas and the captive women into the house.
> The Messenger addresses Deianira.)

MESSENGER

Wait! Stay a moment here that you may learn,   335
without these others, who they are that you lead inside,
and, since you have heard nothing at all, you may discover
what you must. For of all this I have knowledge.

DEIANIRA

What do you want? Why have you stopped me from going in?

MESSENGER

Stay and hear me. The earlier message you had from me 340
was no waste of time, nor, I think, will this be.

DEIANIRA

Should we call the others back, or do you wish
to speak only to me and to my friends here?

MESSENGER

To you and your friends I may speak—leave the others.

DEIANIRA

They are gone now, so please give me an explanation. 345

MESSENGER

Nothing that man has just been telling you was spoken
in strict honesty. Either he is a liar now,
or he was no honest messenger before.

DEIANIRA

What are you saying? Tell me clearly everything
you know. I cannot understand what you have said. 350

MESSENGER

I myself heard this man say—and many men
were present who can bear me out—that for the sake
of this girl Heracles destroyed Eurytus
and his high-towered Oechalia; and, of the gods, it was
Love alone who bewitched him into this violence— 355
not his laborious service in Lydia for Omphale,
nor the fact that Iphitus was hurled to his death—
it was Love, whom he brushes aside in this new version.
But the truth is that when he could not persuade the father
to give the girl to him for his secret bed, 360
he fabricated a petty complaint, an excuse
to campaign against the girl's country, and sacked
the city.° And now, as you see, he is coming home 365
and has sent her here, not without a reason, lady,
and not to be a slave. You must not expect that!

It would not be likely if he is inflamed with desire.
    So I thought it best to reveal the whole affair
to you, my mistress, as I actually heard it from him,   370
and there were many others listening to this same story
in the public gathering of the men of Trachis who can
refute him as well as I. If what I say is unkind,
I am sorry, but still I have told the strict truth.

DEIANIRA

Oh! Oh! What has happened to me? I have   375
welcomed a secret enemy under my roof.
Oh, I am miserable, miserable! Is she truly nameless,
as the man who brought her here swore to me—
a girl so brilliant in her looks and in her birth?°

MESSENGER

She had Eurytus for her father and was called   380
Iole, but of course that man could tell you nothing
of her origin since he had never asked!

CHORUS LEADER

Damn all evildoers, but damn him most of all
who practices a secret, degrading evil.

DEIANIRA

What shall I do, ladies? I must ask you, for the story   385
that has now come out leaves me utterly stunned.

CHORUS LEADER

Go and talk to Lichas. Perhaps he would speak truth
if you insisted on knowing, whether he liked it or not.

DEIANIRA

I shall go. Your advice is not unreasonable.

MESSENGER

Shall I wait meanwhile? What do you wish me to do?   390

DEIANIRA

Stay, for I see the man has started from the house
of his own accord, without my summoning him.

(Lichas enters from the house.)

LICHAS

Lady, what should I say when I come to Heracles?
Give me instructions, for, as you see, I am on my way.

DEIANIRA

How quickly you are rushing off when you were   395
so long in coming, before we have even talked again.

LICHAS

If there is anything you wish to ask me, I am at your service.

DEIANIRA

Will I be able to trust in the truth of what you say?

LICHAS

Yes—great Zeus be my witness!—as far as my knowledge goes.

DEIANIRA

Tell me, then, who is the woman you brought with you?   400

LICHAS

A Euboean. But I do not know her parents.

MESSENGER

You there! Look here! To whom do you think you are talking?

LICHAS

And you—what do you mean asking such a question?

MESSENGER

You would be well advised to try to answer me.

LICHAS

I speak to her who commands, Deianira, daughter   405
of Oeneus and the consort of Heracles, if my eyes
do not deceive me—it is my mistress that I address.

MESSENGER

There it is, the very thing I wanted to hear.
You say she is your mistress?

LICHAS

It is the honest truth.

MESSENGER

Well, then, what do you think should be your punishment   410
if you are discovered to have been dishonest with her?

LICHAS

What do you mean "dishonest"? What are these tricky
riddles?

MESSENGER

No riddles at all! You are the one who is being tricky.

LICHAS

I am leaving. I have been a fool to listen so long.

MESSENGER

Not yet, not before you answer a brief question.   415

LICHAS

Say what you want. You'll not be at a loss for words.

MESSENGER

That captive girl whom you brought to the house, you know
whom I mean?

LICHAS

I do, but why do you ask about her?

MESSENGER

You look at her with no sign of recognition,
but did you not say she was Iole, the daughter of Eurytus?   420

LICHAS

Where on earth did I say so? Who is going to come
and testify that he was there and heard me talk?

MESSENGER

You spoke before many of the townspeople. A large crowd
in the public place of Trachis heard you say this.

LICHAS

Oh, yes—
They may have said they heard me. But to repeat an
    impression   425
is not the same as giving an accurate account.

MESSENGER

Impression, indeed! Did you not state under oath that you
were bringing this girl as a wife for Heracles?

LICHAS

I said that? A wife? By the gods, explain to me,
dear mistress—this stranger here, who on earth is he?   430

MESSENGER

A man who was there and heard you say her city was
completely crushed through desire for her; no woman
of Lydia destroyed it, but his manifest love for her.

LICHAS

Please have this fellow leave. No sensible person,
mistress, wastes his time exchanging words with a madman.   435

DEIANIRA

By Zeus who flashes lightning over the topmost glen
of Oeta, do not cheat me of the truth! Speak,
and you will find that I am not a spiteful woman
nor one who's ignorant about human nature—
that it doesn't always take pleasure in the same things.   440
How foolish one would be to climb into the ring
with Love and try to trade blows with him, like a boxer.
For he rules even the gods as he pleases, and
he rules me—why not another woman like me?
You see that I would be altogether mad   445
to blame my husband, because he suffers from this sickness,
or that woman. She has been guilty of nothing shameful,
and she has done no harm to me. No, it is
inconceivable. If you have learned to lie from him,

then you are not learning honest lessons. If you educate   450
yourself in this fashion, you succeed only
in seeming dishonest when you are trying to be decent.
Tell me the whole truth. To gain the reputation
of a liar is utter dishonor for a free man.
You cannot think that I won't find out. There are   455
many men to whom you have spoken, and they will tell me.

(Lichas remains silent.)

Are you afraid of hurting me? You are wrong.
The only thing that could hurt would be not to know.
Where is the danger in knowing? One man and many
   women—
Heracles has had other women before.   460
Never yet has one of them earned insults
from me, or spiteful talk, nor will this girl, even
if she is utterly absorbed in her passion,°
for I pitied her deeply when I saw her because
her own beauty has destroyed her life, and, against her will,   465
this unfortunate girl has sacked and enslaved the land
of her fathers. Now let all that flow away
on the wind. To you I have this to say: you may
be dishonest with others, but never lie to me.

CHORUS LEADER

   Obey her. What she says is good. You will have   470
   no cause to complain later, and you will gain our thanks.

LICHAS

   Well, dear mistress, I realize that you are not
   unreasonable. You see things as we mortals must.
   So I shall tell you the whole truth. I shall not hide it.
   It is just as this man said. A terrible longing   475
   came over Heracles—and it was for this girl.
   Because of her, Oechalia, the land of her fathers,
   was overthrown by his spear with great destruction.
   None of this did he tell me to hide, I must say

in fairness to him; none of this did he ever deny.   480
I myself, O my mistress, was fearful lest I
should cause pain in your breast by these words of mine.
It was I who did wrong, if you call this wrong.
But since, as it turns out, you know the whole story,
for your own sake as much as for his, be kind   485
to the woman and show that the words you spoke to her
before you knew were said in all sincerity.
Against all else he has won by sheer strength; but by
this love for her he has been completely defeated.

DEIANIRA

Those are my own thoughts too, and so too shall I act.   490
You may be sure I shall not choose to add to my
afflictions hopeless resistance to the gods. Now let us
go into the house. I have messages for you
to carry, and there are gifts to match the gifts you brought—
these too you must take. It would not be right to leave   495
empty-handed when you came so well provided.

(*Exit Deianira and Lichas into the house,*
and the Messenger to the side.)

CHORUS [*singing*]

STROPHE

Strong is the victory the Cyprian goddess always wins.
I pass by
the gods; I shall not tell how Zeus was tricked by her;   500
nor Hades, who lives in the night;
nor Poseidon, the shaker of the earth.
But for our lady's hand
who were the two valiant contenders in courtship?
Who were they who came out to struggle in bouts that were   505
all blows and all dust?

ANTISTROPHE

One was a strong river with the looks of a high-horned
four-footed bull,
Acheloüs from Oeniadae; the other   510

came from the Thebes of Bacchus,
shaking his back-sprung bow, his spears and club
—the son of Zeus. They met
together then in the middle, desiring
her bed. Alone, in the middle with them, their referee,   515
Cypris, goddess of love's bed.

EPODE

Then there was thudding of fists and clang of bows
and confusion of bull's horns;
and there was contorted grappling,   520
and there were deadly blows from butting heads
and groaning on both sides.
But the tender girl with the lovely
eyes sat far from them on a hillside,
waiting for the one who would be her husband.   525
So the struggle raged, as I have told it;°
but the bride over whom they fought
awaited the end pitiably.
And then she was gone from her mother,
like a calf that is lost.   530

(Enter Deianira from inside the house.)

DEIANIRA
  Dear friends, while our visitor is in the house
  talking to the captured girls before he leaves,
  I have come out to you, unobserved. I want
  to tell you the work my hands have done, but also to have
  your sympathy as I cry out for all I suffer.   535
  For here I have taken on a girl—no, I
  can think that no longer—an experienced woman, as
  a ship's master takes on cargo, goods that outrage my heart.
  So now the two of us lie under the one blanket
  waiting for his embrace. This is the gift my brave   540
  and faithful Heracles sends home to his dear wife
  to compensate for his long absence! And yet, when he

is sick as he so often is with this same sickness,
I am incapable of anger. But to live
in the same house with her, to share the same marriage,   545
that is something else. What woman could stand that?
For I see her youth is coming to full bloom
while mine is fading. The eyes of men love to pluck
fresh blossoms; from the faded flowers they turn away.
And this is why I am afraid that he may   550
be called my husband but be the younger woman's man.
But no sensible woman, as I've said before,
should let herself give way to rage. I shall tell you,
dear friends, the solution I have to bring myself relief.

I have kept hidden in a copper urn   555
for many years the gift of a Centaur, long ago.
While I was still a child, I took it from the wounds
of the hairy-chested Nessus as he was dying.
He used to ferry people, for a fee, across
the deep flood of the Evenus in his arms,   560
using no oars to help him nor ships' sails.
I too was carried on his shoulders when my father
sent me to follow Heracles for the first time
as his wife. When I was halfway across
his hands touched me lustfully. I cried out and at once   565
the son of Zeus turned around, raised his hands,
and shot a feathered arrow through his chest; into
his lungs it hissed. The beast spoke his last words to me
as he died: "Daughter of old Oeneus,
if you listen to me, you shall have great profit   570
from my ferrying, since you are the last I have brought across.
If you take in your hands this blood, clotted in
my wounds, wherever it is black with the bile
of the Hydra, the monstrous serpent of Lerna, in which
he dipped his arrows, you will have a charm over   575
the heart of Heracles, so he will never look
at another woman and love her more than you."

I have thought of this, my friends, for since his death
I have kept it in the house, tightly closed.
I followed all instructions he gave me while he still lived   580
and dipped this robe in the charm. Now it is all done.

I am not a woman who tries to be—and may
I never learn to be—bad and bold. I hate
women who are. But if somehow by these charms,
these spells I lay on Heracles, I can defeat   585
the girl—well, the move is made, unless you think
I am acting rashly. If so, I shall stop.

CHORUS LEADER

If there is reason for confidence in these measures,
you do not seem to us to have acted badly.

DEIANIRA

I have this much confidence only: there seem to be   590
good prospects, but I have never brought them to the test.

CHORUS LEADER

One can only tell from action. Whatever you think,
you have no way of judging before you try it out.

DEIANIRA

Well, we shall know soon. I see the messenger
coming out of doors, and he will be going shortly.   595
Only be discreet.
In darkness, even if one acts shamefully,
one will never fall into the shame of disgrace.

(Enter Lichas from the house.)

LICHAS

What am I to do? Command me, daughter of Oeneus.
I have already stayed too long, and now I am late.

DEIANIRA

Lichas, this is the very thing I have looked after   600
while you were talking to the foreign women inside.

Here is a gift made by my own hands for you
to take to my husband—this long, fine-woven robe.
When you give it to him, you must tell him that it
should touch the skin of nobody before it touches his,   605
nor should he let the light of the sun look upon it,
nor any holy enclosure, nor the gleam from a hearth,
until he himself stands, conspicuous before all,
and shows it to the gods on a day of bull-slaughtering.
For this was my vow: if I should ever see or hear   610
that he was coming safe to his home, in all piety
I would dress him in this robe to appear before
the gods to make new sacrifice in new clothing.
And you shall carry a token of this vow which he
will understand from the familiar encircled print   615
of my seal.
                Go now, and as a messenger
be sure to keep the rule not to exceed your orders.
In this way, with thanks both from my husband and
from me, you will earn our double gratitude.

LICHAS

If I, the messenger, practice this art of Hermes   620
soundly, I shall never fail in serving you.
I shall present this casket exactly as it is,
and in explanation I shall repeat your words.

DEIANIRA

Then you should be going now. You understand
completely how everything is here in this house.   625

LICHAS

I understand, and I shall report that all is well.

DEIANIRA

And, of course, since you saw it, you know the girl's
reception—you know I received her as a friend.

LICHAS

Yes, I do, and I am astonished and delighted.

DEIANIRA

What else is there to tell him? For I am afraid   630
you would be talking too soon of my longing for him
before I know if he feels longing for me.

(Exit Lichas to the side; exit Deianira into the house.)

CHORUS [*singing*]

STROPHE A

Safe harbors, hot springs among
the rocks, the high cliffs of Oeta—
all you who live by these and by the inmost reaches   635
of the sea in Malis,
the coast of the Maid who shoots the golden shaft,
and there at the Gates,
the famous gatherings of the Greeks—

ANTISTROPHE A

Soon again the lovely sounds   640
of the pipe will rise among you,
ringing out strongly in fitting clamor
along with the lyre, music
for the gods. The son of Zeus and Alcmene
hurries to his home   645
bearing the prizes of all valor.

STROPHE B

Gone from the city completely,
we missed him, waiting a long twelve months, while he
was on the sea, but we knew
nothing, and his loving wife,   650
all lamentation always, sadly, most
sadly, broke her heart.
But now Ares, god of war,
stung to madness, dispels the day of troubles.

ANTISTROPHE B

Oh let him come, let him come,   655
and his ship of many oars; let it

not stop before he ends his journey
at this city, leaving the island
hearth where, they say, he makes sacrifice.
Let him come from there   660
all desire when the beast's
inducements, all dipped in persuasion, have melted him.°

                           (Deianira enters from the house.)

DEIANIRA

   O my friends, I am afraid! Can it be
   I have gone too far in all I have just done?

CHORUS LEADER

   What is the matter, Deianira, child of Oeneus?   665

DEIANIRA

   I don't know. I have a foreboding that I'll be shown
   to have done great harm when I hoped to do good.

CHORUS LEADER

   Surely you do not mean your gift to Heracles?

DEIANIRA

   Yes, yes. Now I see that one should never
   plunge eagerly into anything obscure.   670

CHORUS LEADER

   Explain the cause of your fear, if it can be explained.

DEIANIRA

   Something has happened which, if I tell you, my friends,
   will seem a marvel such as you never thought to hear.
   Just now, when I anointed the robe I sent to be
   my husband's vestment, I used a tuft of fleecy white wool.   675
   This piece has disappeared, devoured by nothing in
   the house but destroyed by itself, eaten away
   and crumbled completely to dust. I want to tell you this
   in detail, so you may know the whole story.

I neglected none of the instructions that beast   680
the Centaur explained to me, lying in agony
with the sharp arrowhead in his side. I kept them
like an inscription on bronze that cannot be washed away.
And I only did what I was told to do—
I must keep this drug away from fire and always   685
deep in the house where no warm ray of light may touch it
until I should want to apply it freshly smeared.
And this is what I did. Now, when it had to do its work,
at home, inside the house, secretly I smeared it on
some wool, a tuft I pulled from one of the household sheep,   690
and then I folded my gift and put it in a casket
before the sun could shine on it, as you saw.

But when I went in again, I saw something
unspeakable, incomprehensible to human reason.
Somehow I had happened to throw the ball of wool,   695
which I had used to smear the robe, into the full heat
of the sun's rays, and, as it became warm,
it all ran together, a confused mass, and crumbled
to bits on the ground, looking most like the dust one sees
produced by someone sawing a piece of wood.   700
Like this it lies where it fell. But from the earth
on which it rests, clotted foam boils up
like the rich liquid of the blue-green fruit
from the vines of Dionysus, poured on the earth.
And now I do not know what to think. I see   705
myself as someone who has done a terrible thing.
From what possible motive, in return for what,
could the dying beast have shown me kindness, when he
was dying because of me? No, he beguiled me,
only to destroy the man who shot him. But I   710
have come to understand now when it is too late.
I alone, unless my fears are fanciful,
I, oh most unhappy, shall destroy him.
I know that arrow which struck Nessus injured even

Chiron, who is a god, and all animals,   715
whatever it touches, it kills. This same poison which seeped,
black and bloody, from the wounds of Nessus, how can
it fail to kill Heracles too? At least, this is
my fear. And yet I have made a decision: if he goes down,
under the same blow I will die with him.   720
I could not bear to live and hear myself called evil
when my only wish is to be truly good.

CHORUS LEADER

Terrible results are indeed to be feared, but one
should not expect the worst before anything has happened.

DEIANIRA

When the plans themselves are bad, there can be   725
no expectations that leave any place for courage.

CHORUS LEADER

But whenever people trip up unintentionally,
the anger felt is softer, and so it should be with you.

DEIANIRA

You may talk like this, since you have no share
in the wrong; you have no burden all your own.   730

CHORUS LEADER

Better to be silent now—say nothing more,
if you do not want to tell it to your son.
He is here, the one who went off to search for his father.

(Hyllus enters from the side.)

HYLLUS

Mother! I wish I could have found you not as you are
but no longer alive, or safe but someone else's   735
mother, or somehow changed and with a better heart
than now. Three ways—oh, for any one of them!

DEIANIRA

My son, what has happened that I should be so hateful?

HYLLUS

What has happened? Your husband, my father
—do you hear me?—you have killed him.   740

DEIANIRA

No, no, my child! What have you blurted out?

HYLLUS

Only what cannot fail to be. Once a thing
is seen, who can cause it never to have been?

DEIANIRA

How could you say this? Who on earth told you
that I did such an awful crime as you charge me with?   745

HYLLUS

I saw my father's ghastly fate with my own eyes
myself; I did not hear of it from anyone.

DEIANIRA

Where did you come upon him? Were you at his side?

HYLLUS

If you must hear, then I must speak out and tell you all.
After he sacked the famous city of Eurytus,   750
he marched away with the trophies and the first fruits of
    victory.
On a wave-beaten shore of Euboea there is
a point called Cenaeum, where he marked out altars
and a whole precinct for Zeus, god of all fathers.
    There I first saw him, glad since I had been missing him.   755
He was about to make great slaughter for sacrifice
when his own herald Lichas arrived from our home,
bringing with him that gift of yours, the deadly robe.
He clothed himself in it just as you had instructed
and killed first his bulls, twelve perfect victims,   760
the pick of the plunder; then he brought the number to
one hundred, driving a mixed herd to the altar.
And at first the poor wretch, his mind at ease,

rejoicing in his handsome dress, prayed to the gods.
But as the flame from the juicy pinewood fire   765
blazed high and bloody from the solemn rites,
the sweat broke out on his skin; the robe enfolded him
around his limbs, joined tightly to his sides
like the work of a sculptor. Spasms of pain
bit into his bones. Then like a vicious, murderous   770
viper's poison, it began to consume him.

Now he shouted for that unfortunate Lichas, who was
in no way guilty of your crime, demanding
to know the plot behind his bringing him this robe.
Unlucky man, he knew nothing and said it was   775
a gift from you alone, just as you had sent it.
And at that moment, as Heracles listened to his answer,
a piercing, tearing pain clutched at his lungs; he caught
Lichas by the foot where the ankle turns
and threw him against a wave-beaten rock that juts from
    the sea.   780
It pressed the pale brains out through his hair,
and, split full on, skull and blood mixed and spread.
All the people there cried out in horror for
the one man in his suffering, the other dead.
No one had the courage to come to Heracles.   785
He was being wrenched now to the ground, now in the air,
crying, shrieking. All around the rocks echoed,
the mountain headlands of Locris, the high cliffs of Euboea.
When he gave up at last, after throwing himself
miserably again and again to the earth, crying   790
and groaning again and again, damning his deadly match
with you, wretched woman, the whole marriage that he
had won from Oeneus, only to befoul his life,
he raised his eyes, distorted, from the dark smoke
that hung around him and saw me in the great crowd,   795
tears pouring down my face, and, looking at me, called:
"My son, come to me! Do not run from me

in my pain, even if you must die with me.
Take me away! Above all else I ask you to put me
in a place where no man can look at me.   800
If you have pity, at least carry me out of this land
as soon as you can, that I may not die here."
These were his orders; we placed him in the middle of
a boat and with difficulty landed him here,
howling in spasms of pain. You will be seeing him   805
at once, still alive or dead only now.

Mother, this is what you have planned and done to my father,
and you are caught. For this, may Justice the punisher
and the avenging Fury requite you. If it is right
and proper, I curse you; and it is right, since you   810
have given me the right by killing the best of all men
on earth, such as you shall never see again.

(Exit Deianira into the house.)

CHORUS LEADER   *(To Deianira.)*

Why do you go off in silence? Surely you see
that by silence you join your accuser and accuse yourself?

HYLLUS

Let her go, and I hope a fair wind blows   815
to carry her far out of my sight. For why should she
maintain the pointless dignity of the name
of mother when she acts in no way like a mother?
No, let her go—good-bye to her. And the delight
she gave my father, may she find the same herself.   820

(Exit Hyllus, also into the house.)

CHORUS [*singing*]

STROPHE A

See, maidens, how, suddenly, it has closed
with us, the prophetic word spoken
with foreknowledge long ago, that said
when the year of the twelfth plowing came to an end,

then it would bring an end for the trueborn son of Zeus   825
to his relay of labors. And now, surely,
at the right time, it all comes home.
How can he who no longer sees
still have, still, laborious
servitude, when he is dead?   830

If there clings to him in a murderous cloud
the Centaur's treacherous constraint
and his sides are soaked with venom
that Death begat and the shimmering serpent bred,
how shall he see another sun after today's   835
when the Hydra, horrible and monstrous, has
soaked in? From the black-maned beast's
treacherous words there comes to torture him
a murderous confusion,
sharp points brought to burning heat.   840

She, poor woman, knew nothing of this
but, seeing great injury for her home
from a new marriage swiftly approaching,
herself applied a remedy;   845
but what came from another's will, through a fatal meeting,
truly, now ruined, she laments,
truly, she weeps a pale,
foaming flood of tears. Doom
as it advances makes clear before
it comes a great disaster from treachery.   850

A fountain of tears burst open.
Such sickness, alas, has poured upon him, pain
that earns pity such as never before came upon this hero
at his enemies' hands.   855
Woe for the dark tip of the front-fighting spear
that won in battle this

fatal bride from steep
Oechalia. But that silent
handmaiden, Cyprian Aphrodite, 860
is revealed; it is her work.

(Wailing is heard inside the house.)

CHORUS LEADER°
Can I be mistaken? Do I hear something,
a cry of grief surging now through the house?
What can I say? 865
The sound is all too clear. They are shrieking for
misfortune inside. The house suffers a new blow.

(Enter the Nurse from the house.)

And see
this old woman who is coming toward us, to tell us
something, see how sad she is and how she frowns. 870

NURSE
Children, that gift she sent to Heracles,
truly it was the beginning of great sorrow for us.

CHORUS LEADER
What new calamity have you to tell us, old woman?

NURSE
Deianira has moved away upon the very last
of all her journeys, without taking a step. 875

CHORUS LEADER
No, you cannot mean she has died?

NURSE
                                You know all.

CHORUS LEADER
Then she is dead, the poor woman?

NURSE
                                I tell you again, she is.

CHORUS LEADER
Gone, poor thing! Can you tell us how she died?

NURSE
Horrible, the way it happened!

CHORUS LEADER
Tell us, woman,
the fate she met   880

NURSE
She killed herself
with a sword's point.°

CHORUS [*singing*]
Was her mind in a passion or sick,
that she ended her life with the cruel weapon?
How could she think of
death on top of death   885
and end her life all alone?

NURSE° [*singing*]
The grim steel cut her.

CHORUS LEADER [*speaking*]
And helpless did you see her awful act?

NURSE [*speaking*]
Yes, I saw it. For I was standing near her there.

CHORUS [*singing*]
Oh, what was it? How? Tell us.   890

NURSE [*speaking*]
She herself by herself set her hand to it.

CHORUS [*singing*]
What are you saying?

NURSE [*singing*]
The clear truth.

CHORUS
That bride, newly come,°
bore, bore a mighty
Fury for this house.   895

NURSE [*speaking*]
Yes, and if you had been near and had seen
what Deianira did, still more would you pity.

CHORUS LEADER
How could any woman bring her hands to this?

NURSE
Yes, it was terrible. You will learn everything
and bear me witness. When she went into the house, alone,   900
and saw her son in the courtyard, arranging a cushioned bed
to take with him as he went back to meet his father,
she hid herself where no one might look at her and groaned,
falling against the altars, that now they would be
deserted; and whenever she touched some household thing   905
she used to use before, the poor woman would weep.
Here and there, from room to room, she kept turning,
and if she saw some servant of the household who was
dear to her, she would look at her sadly and weep,
and she would call out loud to her fate and to   910
her house that would have no children any more.°

Then she stops all this, and suddenly I see her
rushing into the bedchamber of Heracles,
and secretly, from the shadows, I keep watch
over her. I see the woman casting sheets   915
and spreading them upon the bed of Heracles.
Then, as soon as she had finished, she leapt up
and sat there in the middle of her marriage bed,
and, bursting into torrents of hot tears, she said:
"O my bed, O my bridal chamber, farewell   920
now forever, for never again will you take me
to lie as a wife between these sheets of yours."

She says nothing more, but with a violent sweep
of her arm unfastens her gown where a pin
of beaten gold lies above her breast. She had   925
uncovered her whole side and her left arm.
And I go running off with all the strength I have
and tell her son what his mother is planning to do.
But in the time I have been rushing there and back
we see that she has cut her side to the liver   930
and the seat of life with a double-bladed sword.
Her son shrieked, for he realized, poor boy,
too late that in his anger he had driven her to this act:
he had just learned from people in the house that she
had done unwittingly the will of that wild beast.   935

Then the miserable boy abandoned himself utterly
to sobs and mourning for his mother; he threw himself
upon her lips and there, pressing his side to hers,
he lay and groaned over and over that he
had struck her thoughtlessly with a cruel accusation,   940
weeping because at one moment he was doubly
orphaned for all his life, losing his father and her.

This is the way things are within. If anyone
counts upon one day ahead or even more,
he is a fool. For there can be no tomorrow   945
until we have safely passed the day that is with us still.

(*Exit the Nurse into the house.*)

CHORUS [*singing*]

STROPHE A

Which shall I lament first?
Which is the more final disaster?
In my distress I cannot tell.

ANTISTROPHE A

The one we can see in the house,   950
the other awaits us in our thoughts—
to have and to await are all the same.

Oh for a strong blast
of fair wind coming to my hearth
to carry me away from this place   955
that I may not die of fright
from merely looking directly
at Zeus's valiant son.
They say he is coming to the house
in unassuageable pain,   960
an unspeakable wonder to see.

(Men enter from the side, carrying Heracles in a litter,
accompanied by an Old Man; Hyllus enters from the house.)

ANTISTROPHE B

Near, then, not distant
is he for whom I cried, like the shrill
nightingale. Here comes a company of strangers.   965
How are they carrying him? As though
mourning for a friend,
their steps are slow, soundless.
Ah! He is carried without a word.
Am I to think that he
is dead or only asleep?   970

HYLLUS [chanting, along with the Old Man and then Heracles]
    O my father!
    O my sorrow! What is left
    for me? How can I help?

OLD MAN
    Be silent, child, do not excite
    the wild pain that makes him savage.   975
    He still lives, though fallen. You must bite your lips.

HYLLUS
    What? Alive?

OLD MAN

Do not wake him, held fast in sleep.
Do not excite, do not set stirring
that awful returning   980
sickness.

HYLLUS

                    But it drives me mad,
so helpless under this unbearable weight!

HERACLES

O Zeus,
what land have I come to? Among what men
do I lie worn out by these   985
unceasing pains? O my agony!
The filthy thing eats me again.

OLD MAN

Now do you see how much better it was
to hide your sorrow in silence, nor scatter
sleep from his head   990
and eyes?

HYLLUS

                    No, I cannot stand it
when I see him in this suffering.

HERACLES

O altar steps of Cenaeum, is this
all the thanks you win me for all
the sacrifice I made on you?   995
O Zeus! Torture, torture is all
you give me! I wish I had never seen you
with these poor eyes that must face now
this inexorable flowering of madness.
Is there any singer of spells,   1000
any craftsman surgeon who can
lull this horror to sleep, but Zeus?
Even to see him would be a wonder!

(The bearers set the litter down.)

[*now singing*]

STROPHE

. . . .

Oh! Let me be.° Let
me sleep in my misery,   1005
let me sleep my last sleep.

Where are you touching me? Where are you laying me?
You will kill me, kill me.
You have prodded awake what slumbered.

It has caught me. Oh! It comes on again.   1010
O most ungrateful of the Greeks, where are all you
for whom I wore myself out purging so many beasts
from all the seas and woods? Now when I am sick,
will no one turn the beneficial fire, the sword on me?

Oh! Why will no one   1015
come and cut away
my head from my abominable body.

OLD MAN [*singing*]

Come, you are the man's son. The task is more
than my strength can manage. You must help. Your strength
can easily do more for him than I.

HYLLUS [*singing*]

I touch him,   1020
but to make him unconscious of pain, that is beyond
my power or any man's. Such is the will of Zeus.

HERACLES

ANTISTROPHE

My son, my son! Where are you? Help me, here,
here, lift me up. Oh! Oh! Oh god!   1025

It lunges, lunges again, the vile thing
is destroying me—
savage, unapproachable sickness.   1030

O Pallas! It is torturing me again. O my son,
pity me your father, draw the sword—no one 1035
will blame you—strike me in the breast, heal the pain
with which your godless mother has made me rage. Oh
I wish I could see her fallen too,
caught in just the same death she has dealt me! 1040

Sweet Hades, kinsman, brother of Zeus, lull me to sleep,
to sleep; with quick death end my agony.

CHORUS LEADER
My friends, I hear and shudder at our lord's misfortunes—
so great a man, hounded by such suffering. 1045

HERACLES [*now speaking*]
Many have been the toils for these hands, this back,
that I endured, hot and painful even to tell of.
But neither the wife of Zeus nor hateful Eurystheus
has ever condemned me to such agony as this
that the false-faced daughter of Oeneus has fastened 1050
upon my shoulders, a woven, encircling net
of the Furies, by which I am utterly destroyed.
It clings to my sides, it has eaten away
my inmost flesh; it lives with me and empties the channels
of my lungs, and already it has drunk up 1055
my fresh blood, and my whole body is
completely killed, conquered by these unspeakable fetters.
Neither the spear of battle, nor the army of
the earth-born Giants, nor the violence of beasts,
nor Greece, nor any place of barbarous tongue, not all 1060
the lands I came to purify could ever do this.
A woman, a female, in no way like a man,
she alone without even a sword has brought me down.

O my son, now truly be my trueborn son
and do not pay more respect to the name of mother. 1065
Bring her from the house with your own hands and put
her in my hands, that woman who bore you, that I may know

clearly whether it pains you more to see my body
mutilated or hers when it is justly tortured.
Come, my child, dare to do this. Pity me,   1070
for I seem pitiful to many others, crying
and sobbing like a girl, and no one could ever say
that he had seen this man act like that before.
Always without a groan I followed my painful course;
and now from such a cause I'm discovered a woman.   1075

Come close to me now; stand by your father and
look well at my misfortune; see what I suffer.
I shall take off the coverings and show you. Look,
all of you, do you behold this poor body?
Can you see how miserable, how pitiful I am?   1080

[*singing*]
Oh, oh, the pain!

[*speaking again*]
That malignant tearing scorches me again,
it shoots through my sides, it must have me struggle,
it will not let me be—miserable, devouring sickness.

[*singing*]
O King Hades, receive me!   1085
O flash of Zeus, strike!

[*speaking again*]
Drive against me, O king, hurl down the bolt
of lightning, father. Now it feeds on me again,
it has sprung out, it blooms. O my hands, my hands,
O my back, my chest, O my poor arms, see   1090
what has become of you from what you once were.
The lion that prowled the land of Nemea, that scourge of
    herdsmen,
that unapproachable, intractable creature,
with your strength once you overpowered it,
and the serpent of Lerna and that galloping army   1095

of double-bodied, hostile Centaurs, violent, lawless,
supremely strong, and the boar of Erymanthus,
and under the earth the hell hound with three heads,
irresistible monster, the awful Echidna's nursling,
and guarding the golden apples the dragon at the end of the
    earth—   1100
and I have had my taste of ten thousand other toils,
but these hands let no one set his trophies over me.
Now look at me, torn to shreds, my limbs unhinged,
a miserable ruin sacked by invisible disaster, I
who am called son of the most noble mother,   1105
I who am hailed as the child of Zeus in the heavens.
But I tell you this, even if I am nothing,
nothing that can even crawl, even so—
only let her come who has done this to me—
these hands will teach her, and she can tell the world: alive   1110
I punished the evil, and I punish them in death.

CHORUS LEADER
    O unhappy Greece, I can see how great
    mourning you shall have if you lose this man.

HYLLUS
    Father, since you let me speak to you now,
    hear me in silence while I speak, though you are sick.   1115
    I ask only for what is right. Give me yourself
    without this grim anger which stings you to such fury.
    Otherwise you cannot know just how misguided
    is the satisfaction your fury craves, the pain it feels.

HERACLES
    Say what you want and be done with it. I am too sick—   1120
    I can make no sense at all of your riddles.

HYLLUS
    It is about my mother that I come to speak,
    about her present state and her unwilling error.

HERACLES

Damn you! How dare you speak of her again, the mother
who is a father's murderer—and in my hearing?   1125

HYLLUS

Her state is such that one should not keep silent.

HERACLES

For sure, no silence for the crime she has committed!

HYLLUS

Nor for what she has done today, you will admit.

HERACLES

Speak, but beware. Do not disgrace yourself.

HYLLUS

I shall speak. She is dead. She is just now newly killed.   1130

HERACLES

By whom? It sounds miraculous, this news you portend.

HYLLUS

She is dead by her own hand and by no other.

HERACLES

Ah! She's dead too soon. She should have died by mine.

HYLLUS

Even your fury would turn aside if you knew all.

HERACLES

A strange beginning, but go on—what do you mean?   1135

HYLLUS

In all that she did wrong she had intended good.

HERACLES

Good? Does she do good when she kills your father?

HYLLUS

It was a charm for love she wanted to put on you
that failed—when she saw that new bride in her house.

HERACLES

Who in Trachis knows such deadly drugs as this?   1140

HYLLUS

Nessus the Centaur long ago persuaded her
to excite your desire with this potent charm.

HERACLES

Ah, ah! Now I am truly done for.
Lost! I am lost! I see the light no longer.
Ah! Now I know the doom that is upon me.   1145
Come, my child. You no longer have a father.
Call together all my children, your brothers,
and call the unhappy Alcmene who was the bride of Zeus
to her cost. You shall learn from me with my
last words all the prophecies I know.   1150

HYLLUS

But your mother is not here. It happens that
she is living now at Tiryns on the sea,
and of your children she has taken some with her
to care for, and others, I must tell you, are living in Thebes.
But all of us who are here—if there is anything,   1155
father, we must do, we shall listen and serve you.

HERACLES

Then hear your task. You have come to that point
where you must show the sort of man you are that you
are called my son. Long ago my father revealed
to me that I should die by nothing that draws breath   1160
but by someone dead, an inhabitant of Hades.
This was that beast, the Centaur, who has in death killed me
alive, even as it had been divinely revealed.
Now I shall show you how more recent prophecies
agree with this exactly and give support to the old.   1165
I went to the grove of the mountain-dwelling Selli who sleep
upon the ground, and I copied down the words
from my father's oak that speaks with many tongues,
which told me that, at this present, living time,

release from all the toils imposed on me would be   1170
complete. And I thought that then I would be happy.
But it only meant that I would die then.
For the dead there are no more toils. My son,
since all this is coming true so clearly, you must
be ready to stand by my side in the fight, and you must not   1175
hesitate and wait for my words to grow sharp.
On your own, agree to act with me; discover
yourself the finest rule—obedience to your father.

HYLLUS

Father, I am alarmed to see where your words lead,
but I shall obey you in whatever you decide.   1180

HERACLES

You must give me your right hand first of all.

HYLLUS

Will you tell me why you must have this strong pledge?

HERACLES

Quickly, give me your hand. Do not disobey me.

HYLLUS

Here, I give my hand. I shall deny you nothing.

HERACLES

Swear now by the head of Zeus who fathered me.   1185

HYLLUS

Swear to do what? Will you tell me that?

HERACLES

Swear to fulfill completely the task I give to you.

HYLLUS

I do swear, and I take my oath on Zeus.

HERACLES

And pray for punishment if you break your oath.

HYLLUS

I pray, though I shall keep my oath and not be punished.   1190

HERACLES

You know that high crag of Zeus on Mount Oeta?

HYLLUS

Yes. I have often stood there to sacrifice.

HERACLES

Then you must take my body up there, with your
own hands and with the help of any friends you wish;
you must fell a great supply of deep-rooted oak,   1195
and many trees of the lusty wild olive
you must cut down as well, and put my body on them,
and then take the flaming brand of a pine torch
and burn. Let me see no tears, no mourning. Do
your job without lamentation, without tears,   1200
if you are your father's son, or even below
I shall wait for you, a crushing curse forever.

HYLLUS

Oh, father! What are you saying? What have you forced me
to do?

HERACLES

What must be done. If you do not do it, then be
another man's son—do not call yourself mine.   1205

HYLLUS

Father, father, how can you? You are asking me
to be your murderer, polluted with your blood.

HERACLES

No, I am not. I ask you to be my healer,
the only physician who can cure my suffering.

HYLLUS

How would I cure your body by setting it on fire?   1210

HERACLES

If that frightens you, do the rest at least.

HYLLUS

I shall carry you there—that I could not begrudge you.

HERACLES

And you will complete the pyre as I told you?

HYLLUS

So long as I do not touch it with my own hands.
Everything else I shall do. You can be sure of me.   1215

HERACLES

Even that much is enough. Now after your other
great kindness, do me this one small favor.

HYLLUS

No matter how great a favor it is, it shall be done.

HERACLES

You know, of course, the girl who is the daughter of Eurytus?

HYLLUS

It is Iole you mean, I suppose.   1220

HERACLES

I see you know her. This, then, is what I tell you to do,
my son. When I die, if you wish to be pious
and remember the oaths you have sworn to your father,
you must take this girl as your wife, and do not
disobey me. No other man but you must ever   1225
have her who has lain with me at my side. You,
my son, must engage yourself to her bed.
Obey. Although you listen to me in greater matters,
disobedience in lesser things wipes out the favor.

HYLLUS

Ah! It is wrong to argue with a sick man,   1230

yet how can one stand to see him with such thoughts as
    these?

HERACLES

You speak as if you would do none of the things I ask.

HYLLUS

How could anyone, when she alone shares
the blame for my mother's death and your condition?
How could anyone choose to do that, unless   1235
avenging fiends had made his mind sick? Better
for me, too, to die than live with my worst enemy.

HERACLES

I see the man will not give me my due, though I
am dying; but I tell you, if you disobey
my commands, the curse of the gods will be waiting for you.   1240

HYLLUS

Oh! Soon, I can see, you will show how sick you are.

HERACLES

Yes! You rouse my agony from its sleep.

HYLLUS

So wretched, so helpless am I, no matter where I turn.

HERACLES

Because you do not choose to listen to your father.

HYLLUS

But shall I listen, father, and learn impiety?   1245

HERACLES

It is no impiety if you give my heart pleasure.

HYLLUS

Do you command me and make it right for me to do this?

HERACLES

I do command you, and I call the gods to witness.

HYLLUS

> I shall do it then, and I shall not forswear,
> while showing to the gods that it is your will. No one   1250
> could think me wrong in obeying you, father.

HERACLES

> In the end you act well. Now make your mercy
> follow swift upon your words. Put me on the pyre
> before another tearing, biting attack
> can come upon me. Hurry. Lift me up. The true   1255
> respite from suffering is this—my final end.

HYLLUS

> Nothing can prevent its full accomplishment
> for you, since you command and compel me, father.

HERACLES [*chanting, with Hyllus, to the end of the play*]
> *Come then, O my tough soul,*
> *before this sickness is stirred again,*   1260
> *set a steel bit in my mouth,*
> *hold back the shriek, and make an end*
> *of this unwanted, welcome task.*

> *(The bearers raise the litter and begin their exit to*
> *the side, followed by Hyllus and the Chorus.)*

HYLLUS

> *Raise him, my helpers. From you let me have*
> *much compassion now for what I do.*   1265
> *You see how little compassion the gods*
> *have shown in all that's happened; they*
> *who are called our fathers, who begot us,*
> *can look upon such suffering.*
> *No one can foresee what is to come.°*   1270
> *What is here now is pitiful for us*
> *and shameful for them;*
> *but of all men it is hardest for him*
> *who is the victim of this disaster.*

(To the Chorus Leader.)

Maiden, come from the house with us.   1275
You have seen terrible deaths
and agonies, many and strange, and there is
nothing here which is not Zeus.

(Exit all.)

ELECTRA

Translated by DAVID GRENE

ELECTRA: INTRODUCTION

The Play: Date and Composition

The date of *Electra*'s first production is not known. Nor do we know which other plays Sophocles presented along with it in the annual competition. On the basis of the play's style and dramatic technique many scholars have come to regard it as one of Sophocles' latest tragedies, probably composed after Euripides' *Electra* (which deals with the same story), perhaps between 420 and 410 BCE. But this assessment is largely subjective, and some scholars prefer to date Sophocles' play earlier than Euripides', in the 430s or 420s BCE.

The Myth

The story of the royal dynasty of the Pelopids, legendary rulers of Argos (or Mycenae), provided plots for a large number of Greek tragedies. Many of these focused on the story of Agamemnon and his family. The broad outlines of this story were familiar to all. The brothers Agamemnon and Menelaus, sons of Atreus, led an expedition against the city of Troy to recover Menelaus' wife Helen, who had eloped with the Trojan prince Paris. While Agamemnon was away at Troy, his wife Clytemnestra took another lover, his cousin Aegisthus, and the two of them murdered Agamemnon upon his return home from Troy. Clytemnestra was motivated to kill her husband in part because he had sacrificed their eldest daughter, Iphigenia, to the goddess Artemis in order to procure favorable winds for the expedition to Troy. (As for Aegisthus, he was eager to avenge his father Thyestes, several of whose children had been hideously murdered by his brother

Atreus, who was Agamemnon's and Menelaus' father.) Aegisthus and Clytemnestra then took over the throne of Argos/Mycenae and ruled there for many years.

Agamemnon and Clytemnestra had three children (apart from Iphigenia): two daughters, Electra and Chrysothemis, and a son, Orestes, who was just a baby when his father was murdered. In most versions of the story, Aegisthus and Clytemnestra intended to kill Orestes as well, but he was rescued (largely through Electra's intervention) and was sent off to be raised by a family friend, King Strophius of Phocis, whose own young son Pylades became Orestes' closest friend. During the next several years Orestes was abroad in exile from his native land while Electra was living in misery at home, preserving the memory of her father, hating the usurping murderers, and hoping for her brother's return to exact vengeance. This is the point at which Sophocles' play begins.

The precise means and process by which Orestes and Electra (and Pylades) carry out the act of vengeance varies in important ways from one narrative version to another. In Homer's *Odyssey*, we are told repeatedly that Orestes killed Aegisthus, while the killing of Clytemnestra remains much more vague and Electra is not mentioned. In many subsequent lyric poems (of which only a few small fragments survive), in a wide range of visual representations, and above all in Aeschylus' tragic trilogy the *Oresteia* (458 BCE), which established itself immediately as the classic treatment of the whole saga, Orestes continues to be the main focus. In most versions he is instructed by Apollo's oracle at Delphi to avenge his father's murder by stealth; so he returns home in disguise, accompanied by Pylades, and reveals his identity to Electra only once he has ascertained that she is indeed faithful to their father's cause. Then the brother and sister together plan the killing of the two usurpers, with Orestes (assisted by Pylades) performing the act himself while Electra provides support and encouragement. In most versions the killing of mother by son is the climactic and most shocking moment in the whole drama, and it is usually followed immediately by an onslaught of avenging Furies who seek to punish Orestes for his deed.

Sophocles' *Electra*, Aeschylus' *Libation Bearers* (the second play of the *Oresteia*), and Euripides' *Electra* constitute the only case in which we possess three plays on exactly the same topic written by each of the great Athenian tragedians. The comparison is fascinating, even while we should remember that scores of other plays, now lost, were also doubtless composed on this same theme, with each new version introducing further innovations and modifications. In comparing Sophocles' tragedy to the two others, it is striking that—whereas Euripides' play seems to make a number of obvious references, some of them apparently quite polemical, to the *Oresteia*—Sophocles' version seems to make almost no such direct allusions or revisions and follows quite an independent path. Among Sophocles' innovations are his inclusion of an old tutor who has been Orestes' mentor since childhood and who guides him and Electra through to the final stages of the vengeance, and a third sibling, Chrysothemis, whose rather timid and conventional behavior serves as an effective foil to Electra's boldness in seeking to avenge her father and her unrelenting hatred of her mother and Aegisthus. Sophocles also includes a sensational messenger speech, in which Orestes' fictitious death in a chariot wreck is vividly described, while Electra and Clytemnestra respond to it in opposite ways. Significantly, Sophocles reverses the usual order of the killings, so that Clytemnestra dies first and the play ends with the death of Aegisthus. This makes the matricide seem somewhat less climactic and horrendous than it is in Aeschylus and Euripides. Indeed, the possibility that the Furies will pursue Orestes seems to be almost completely ignored in our play. But scholars debate the significance of these elements for the overall interpretation of the play; and some believe that the ending has suffered damage and truncation, so that we do not have quite all that Sophocles wrote. (See the textual note on lines 1505–10.)

Transmission and Reception

We do not know whether Sophocles' *Electra* won the prize upon its first production. But it seems to have been a popular play throughout antiquity, being performed and read quite widely (more so than Euripides' *Electra*). And of course the whole story of Electra, Orestes, and Pylades continued to be frequently depicted in literature and art. Sophocles' recognition scene between Orestes and Electra was particularly admired, and we are told of famous performances in which the actor playing Electra affected the audience deeply, as he spoke his (her) lines while holding the urn that supposedly contained her brother's ashes. The play was one of the seven Sophoclean plays selected in the first or second century CE for school use. It thus survived into the Byzantine era, and was one of the "triad" of plays most widely copied and distributed between the tenth and fifteenth centuries. We possess over one hundred manuscripts of the play, some of them with quite extensive marginal notes (scholia) that include useful ancient commentary.

The character Electra has remained iconic throughout Western literature and art, from antiquity to the present, as a symbol of a daughter's devotion to her father (and hatred of her mother and stepfather), single-minded loyalty to her brother, and long-suffering determination to punish political and/or familial crimes. In the eighteenth and nineteenth centuries, it was Sophocles' version of her character and her story that was the most influential and inspirational: this lonely but indomitable female figure, ceaselessly voicing her grief, loyalty, and indignation despite every attempt to suppress her, resonated strongly with playwrights, poets, and painters. Since the beginning of the twentieth century, however, playwrights have tended to blend elements from all three Greek tragedians in composing their new versions of her story—as for example Eugene O'Neill does in *Mourning Becomes Electra* (1931), T. S. Eliot in *The Family Reunion* (1939), and more recently Yael Farber in *MoLoRa* (South Africa, 2004). But Jean Giraudoux's brilliant *Electra* (1937) is an exception: Sophocles is his clear inspiration. Films made on this theme have only loosely, though sometimes quite distinctly, picked up on Sophocles' original: for example, the Hungarian film *Electra, My Love*, directed by Miklós Jancsó (1974), or the acerbic comedy *Ellie*, directed by Peter Wittman (1984). But Electra is a household name, almost to the degree that Oedipus is: Sigmund Freud and Carl Jung obviously are partly responsible for this, with the "Electra complex," but Sophocles' play still remains the best-known version of her story. Electra has even reached Marvel Comics, where the character Elektra Natchios has been featured in several episodes, along with her brother Orestez.

The rather free adaptation of Sophocles' play by Hugo von Hofmannsthal (1904) has been especially influential in Germany, and an adaptation of this text was used as a libretto by Richard Strauss for his opera *Elektra* (1909; often since performed all over the world). In earlier periods, there had been numerous operas that more or less freely adapted parts of Electra's story: the most deserving of mention are *Electra* by J. C. F. Haeffner (1787, with libretto by A. F. Ristell) and *Idomeneo* by W. A. Mozart (1781). More definitely based on Sophocles, though still heavily adapted, is the opera by Mikis Theodorakis (1995, with Modern Greek libretto).

Until recently, Sophocles' *Electra* was one of the most frequently performed of all Greek tragedies. Productions of the original play, or adaptations of it, have been numerous ever since the eighteenth century, both on college campuses and in professional theaters: actors and audiences have relished the heroine's role for its emotional range and power, while the scenes of ironic misrecognition around the messenger speech and the urn, and the actual recognition of brother by sister, are among the most intensely theatrical in all of Greek drama. Particularly notable productions include those directed by Jane Addams at Hull-House, Chicago (1880s and 1890s); Max Reinhardt (in Hofmannsthal's adaptation, Berlin 1903); Margaret Anglin in the Hearst Greek Theater, Berkeley, California, 1915, 1918); several by the National Theatre of Greece at Epidaurus, directed by Dimitris Rondiris (1936–78), and later by Lydia Koniordou (1996) and by Peter Stein (2007); Michel Saint-Denis at the Old Vic (1951); Andrei Serban (selected scenes, first produced at La MaMa, New York City, in 1974; available on video); Carolos Koun and the Theatro Technis (1984); Deborah Warner with the Royal Shakespeare Company (1988, 1991); and Suzuki Tadashi (various locations, 1994–2001).

ELECTRA

Scene: Before the royal palace in Mycenae.

(Enter Orestes, Pylades, and Tutor, from the side.)

TUTOR

Son of Agamemnon, commander once at Troy,
now you are here, now you can see it all,
all that your heart has always longed for.
This is old Argos of your yearning, the grove
of Inachus' gadfly-haunted daughter, Io.   5
And here, Orestes, is the Lycian marketplace
of the wolf-killing god. Here on the left
the famous temple of Hera. Where we have come now,
believe your eyes, see golden Mycenae,
and here the death-heavy house of the Pelopids.   10

Once on a time, from amidst your father's murder,
I took you from this house, received you from the hand
of your sister, the one who shares your blood.
I saved you then. I have raised you from that day
to this moment of your manhood to be the avenger
of that father done to death. Orestes, now,   15
and you, Pylades, dearest friend, take counsel
quickly on what to do. Already the sunlight,
brightening, stirs dawning birdsong into clearness,
and the black, kindly night of stars is gone.
Before any man leaves the house, you two   20
must join together in discussion. We are where
we must not shrink. It is high time for action.

ORESTES

Dearest of servants:
very plain are the signs you show of your nobility
toward me. It is so with a well-bred horse: 25
even in old age, hard conditions
do not break his spirit. His ears are still erect.
So it is with you. You urge me, and yourself
follow among the first. Therefore, I will make plain
all that I have decided. Give keen ear   30
to what I say, and if I miss the mark
of what I should, correct me.

When I came to Pytho's place of prophecy
to learn how to win revenge
for my father's murder on those that killed him,
Phoebus spoke to me what I tell you now: 35
to take not help of shields nor host; instead,
by myself perform the slaughter, stealthily,
with just but crafty hand.
Now since this was the oracle we heard,
go you into this house when occasion calls you.
Know all that is done there, and, knowing, report   40
clear news to us. You are old. It's a long time.

They won't recognize you. They will not suspect you
with this silver hair of yours. Here is your story.
You are a stranger coming from Phanoteus,   45
their Phocian friend, the greatest of their allies.
Tell them a sudden accident befell
Orestes, and he's dead. Swear it on oath.
Say in the Pythian games he was rolled
out of his chariot at high speed.
Let that be your story.   50

    But we shall go first to my father's grave
and crown it, as the god bade us, with libations
and with luxuriant cuttings from my hair.
And then we shall come back here again
and in our hands a carved bronze-sided urn,
the urn that you know I hid here in the bushes.   55
By these means we shall bring them the pleasant news
with our tale of lies, that my body is no longer,
but has been burned and reduced to ashes.
What harm does it do me if by dying in word
in deed I come through alive and win my glory?   60
To my thinking, no word is bad when spoken with profit.
Before now I have seen wise men often
dying empty deaths as far as words reported them,
and then, when they have come to their homes again,
they have been honored more, even to the skies.
So in my case I venture to predict
that I who die according to this rumor   65
shall, like a blazing star, glare on my foes again.

Land of my father, gods of my country,
welcome me, grant me success in my coming,
and you, too, house of my father;
as your purifier I have come,
in justice sent by the gods.   70
Do not send me dishonored out of this country,
but ancestrally rich, restorer of my house.

This is all that I have to say. Old man,
let it be yours to go and mind your task.
We two must go away. It is the moment,   75
and the moment is greatest master of every act.

ELECTRA [*chanting from inside the house*]
  Ah! Ah! What misery!

TUTOR

Inside the house I thought I heard someone,
one of the servants, crying.

ORESTES

                  Might it not be   80
poor suffering Electra? Would you like us
to stay here and to listen to her crying?

TUTOR

No. Nothing must come before our trying
to carry out what Loxias has bidden us.
From there we must make our beginning,
pouring the holy offerings for your father.
For that, I say, will bring us victory,   85
and mastery in our enterprise.

                    (*Orestes and the others withdraw to the side.
                          Enter Electra from the palace.*)

ELECTRA [*chanting*]
  O holy light
  and air, copartner with earth,
  how many songs of lament,
  how many plangent strokes
  beating till my breast was bloody,   90
  have you heard from me
  when the gloomy night has withdrawn?
  And again in the house of my misery
  my bed is witness to my all-night sorrowing
  dirges for my unhappy father.

In the land of the foreigner   95
no murderous god of battles entertained him;
but my mother and the man who shared her bed,
Aegisthus, split his head with a murderous axe,
like woodsmen with an oak tree.
For all this no pity was given you   100
by any but me, no pity for your death,
father, so pitiful, so cruel.
But, for my part, I
will never cease my dirges and sorrowful laments,
as long as I have eyes to see
the ever-shining light of the stars and this daylight.   105
So long, like a nightingale who has lost her young,°
here before the doors of what was my father's house
I shall cry out my sorrow for all the world to hear.

House of Hades, house of Persephone,   110
Hermes of the underworld, mighty Curse,
and Furies, the Dread Ones, children of gods,
who look upon those who die unjustly,
who look upon the marriage bed secretly betrayed,
come all and help take vengeance for my father,   115
for my father's murder!
And send me my brother to my aid.
For alone I am no longer strong enough
to bear the burden of the grief that weighs against me.   120

(Enter the Chorus of Mycenaean women from one side.)

CHORUS [singing]

STROPHE A

Electra, child of the wretchedest of mothers,
why with ceaseless lament do you waste away
sorrowing for one long dead,
Agamemnon, godlessly trapped
by deceits of your treacherous mother,   125
betrayed by her evil hand?

May evil be the end
of the one who contrived the deed,
if it is allowed for me to utter this!

ELECTRA [*also singing*]
Daughters of truehearted families,
you have come to console me in my troubles.   130
I know, I understand what you say,
nothing of it escapes me.
But, all the same, I will not
cease my mourning for my poor father.
You whose love responds to mine in all ways,
allow me thus wildly to grieve,   135
I entreat you.

CHORUS

ANTISTROPHE A
But from the all-receptive Lake
of Death you shall not raise him,
groan and pray as you will.
Past the bounds of sense you dwell in grief   140
that is cureless, with sorrow unending,
and you are destroying yourself,
in a matter where the evil knows no deliverance.
Why do you seek
such unbearable suffering?

ELECTRA
Foolish indeed is the one   145
that forgets parents pitifully dead.
Suited rather to my heart
is the bird of mourning
that always laments "Itys, Itys,"
the bird of frenzied sorrow, Zeus's messenger.
And Niobe, that suffered all, ah!   150
I count you as a goddess
as you weep perpetually
in your rocky tomb.

CHORUS

Not alone to you, my child,
this burden of grief has come: 155
yet you exceed in your feeling far
those of your kin and blood.
Consider Chrysothemis and her life,
and Iphianassa,
and that one who grows up to prosperity in secret,
sorrowing, a prince,   160
whom one day this famed land of Mycenae
shall welcome home as noble heir,
returning here with Zeus' blessing, Orestes.

ELECTRA

I await him always
sadly, unweariedly,
I who am past childbearing,
past marriage,   165
always to my own ruin.
Wet with tears, I endure
an unending doom of misfortune.
But he has forgotten
what he has suffered, what he has known.
What message ever comes from him to me
that does not turn out false?   170
Yes, he is always longing to come,
but he does not choose to come, for all his longing.

CHORUS

Take heart, take heart, my child.
Still great above is Zeus,
who oversees all things in sovereign power.   175
Confide to him your overbitter wrath;
do not overburden yourself with hate against
your enemies, nor yet forget them quite:

for Time is a kindly god.
For neither he that lives
by Crisa's cattle-grazing shore, 180
the son of Agamemnon, will be neglectful,
nor the god that rules by Acheron's waters.

ELECTRA

But for me already the most of my life 185
has gone by without hope,
and I have no strength anymore.
I am one wasted in childlessness,
with no loving husband for champion.
Like some dishonored foreigner,
I serve in my father's house in these ugly rags 190
and stand at empty tables.

CHORUS

STROPHE C

Pitiful was the cry at the homecoming,
and pitiful, when on your father on his couch
the sharp biting stroke of the brazen axe
was driven home. 195
Craft was the contriver, lust the killer,
dreadfully begetting between them a shape,
dreadful, whether divine or human,
the one that did this. 200

ELECTRA

That day of all days that have ever been
most deeply hateful to me!
O night, horrible burden
of that unspeakable banquet,
shameful death that my father saw 205
dealt him by the hands of the two,
hands that took my own life captive,
betrayed, destroyed me utterly.
For these deeds may god in his greatness,
the Olympian one, grant punishment to match them, 210

and may they have no profit of glory,
they who accomplished such actions.

CHORUS

ANTISTROPHE C

Take heed you do not speak too far.
Do you not see from what
causes you suffer as you do?
Self-inflicted is the ruin   215
that you've fallen into so wretchedly.
You have won for yourself
superfluity of misfortune,
breeding wars in your sullen soul
evermore. You cannot fight
such conflicts hand to hand, with those who hold power.°   220

ELECTRA

Dreadful things compelled me,
to dreadful things I was driven.
I know it, I know my own spirit.
With dread all around me, I will not hold back
from this wild course of ruin, so long as I live.   225
For who, dear friends, who that thinks right
could expect there to be suitable comforting
words for me?
Let me be, let me be—no more comforting!
These ills of mine shall be called cureless   230
and never shall I cease my sorrow;
the number of my laments will be countless.

CHORUS

EPODE

But only in good will to you I speak
like a loyal mother, entreating you
not to breed ruin from ruin.   235

ELECTRA

What is the natural measure of my sorrow?

Come, how when the dead are in question
can it be honorable to forget?
In what human being is this instinctive?
Never may I have honor among such people,
nor, if I encounter any good thing,   240
may I live at ease with it, by restraining
the wings of shrill lament to my father's dishonor!
For if he that is dead
is earth and nothing,   245
lying in misery,
and they shall never in their turn
pay death for murderous death,
then shall all shame be dead
and all men's piety.   250

CHORUS LEADER [*speaking*]

    My child, it was with both our interests at heart
    I came, both yours and mine. If what I say
    is wrong, have your own way. We will obey you.

ELECTRA [*now speaking*]

    Women, I am ashamed if I appear
    to you too much the mourner with constant dirges.   255
    What I do, I must do. Pardon me. I ask you
    how else would any well-bred girl behave
    that saw the sufferings of her father's house
    as I have seen these, day and night, increasing
    and never a check?   260
    First there's my mother, the one who bore me, now
    a thing of hate. Then in my own house I live
    with those who killed my father. I'm their subject,
    and it's their decision whether I get   265
    or go without.
                What sort of days do you imagine
    I spend, watching Aegisthus sitting
    on my father's throne, watching him wear
    my father's self-same robes, watching him

at the hearth where he killed him, pouring libations? 270
Watching the ultimate act of insult,
my father's murderer in my father's bed
with my wretched mother—if mother I should call her,
this woman that sleeps with him.
She is so daring that she cohabits with 275
this foul, polluted creature and fears no Fury.
No, as though laughing at what was done,
she has picked out the day on which she killed
my father in her treachery, and on that day
has set a dancing festival and sacrifices 280
sheep, in monthly ritual, "to the gods that saved her."
So within that house I see, to my wretchedness,
the accursed feast named in his honor.
I see it, moan, and waste away, lament—
but only to myself. I may not even cry 285
as much as my heart would have me.
For this woman, all nobility in words,
abuses me: "You godforsaken, hateful thing,
are you the only one whose father is dead?
Is there no one else of humankind in mourning? 290
My curse upon you! May the gods below
grant you from your present sorrows no release!"
Such are her insults, unless she hears from someone
that Orestes is coming. Then she grows quite wild
and stands beside me shrieking: 295
"Aren't you the one responsible for this?
Is not this your doing, you who stole
Orestes from these hands of mine, conveying him
away? But you may be sure you will pay for it
and pay enough." She howls so, and next to her
is her distinguished bridegroom, urging the same, 300
that utter coward, total piece of mischief,
who makes his wars only with women's help.
But I forever wait for Orestes' coming,
to end our troubles. I wait and wait and die.

For his eternal going-to-do-something 305
destroys my hopes, both real and absent.

In such a state, my friends, one cannot
be moderate and restrained, nor pious either.
Evil is all around me, evil
is what I am compelled to practice.

CHORUS LEADER
Tell me, as you talk like this, is Aegisthus here, 310
or is he gone from home?

ELECTRA
                              Certainly, he's gone.
Do not imagine, if he were near, that I
would wander outside. Now he is on his estate.

CHORUS LEADER
If so, I can talk with you with better confidence. 315

ELECTRA
For the present, he is away. What is your wish?

CHORUS LEADER
Tell me: what of your brother? Is he really coming
or hesitating? That is what I want to know.

ELECTRA
He says he is—but does nothing of what he says.

CHORUS LEADER
A man often hesitates when he does a big thing. 320

ELECTRA
I did not hesitate when I rescued him.

CHORUS LEADER
                              Be easy.
He's a noble man and will surely help his friends. 325

ELECTRA
I believe in him, or else had not lived so long.

CHORUS LEADER

    Say no more now. I see your sister,
    blood of your blood, of the same father and mother,
    Chrysothemis, carrying grave-gifts in her hands
    such as are usually offered to those below.

(Enter Chrysothemis from the palace.)

CHRYSOTHEMIS

    What have you come to say here out of doors,
    sister? Will you never learn, in all this time,   330
    not to give way to your empty anger?
    Yet this much I know, and know my own heart, too,
    that I am sick at what I see, so that
    if I had strength, I would let them know how I feel.
    But under threat of punishment, I think,   335
    I must make my voyage with lowered sails,
    that I may not seem to be doing something and then
    prove ineffectual. I wish you'd do the same.
    And yet justice points not where my words are tending,
    but where your judgment stands. However, if
    I am to live, and not as a prisoner, I must
    in all things listen to the ones in power.   340

ELECTRA

    It is strange indeed that you who were born
    of our father should forget him
    and think only of your mother. All these warnings
    of me you have learned from her. Nothing is your own.
    Now you must make your choice, one way or the other,   345
    either to be rash and irrational
    or to be sensible—but forget your friends.
    Here you are saying: "If I had the strength,
    I would show my hatred of them!" Yet, when I
    try everything to take vengeance for our father,
    you do nothing to help—and even discourage my doing.   350
    Doesn't this add cowardice to the list of all our troubles?
    Tell me, or let me tell you, what benefit

would I achieve by giving up my mourning?
Do I not live? Yes, I know, badly, but
for me enough. And I hurt them   355
and so give honor to the dead, if there is, there
in that other world, anything that brings pleasure.
But you who tell me you hate them, hate in words only,
while in fact you are living with our father's murderers.

I tell you: never, not though they brought me all those gifts
in which you now feel pride, would I yield to them.   360
Have your rich table and your abundant life;
all the food I need is the quiet of my conscience.
I do not want to win your honor.
Nor would you if you were sound of mind. Now, when you
    could
be called the daughter of the best of fathers,   365
be called instead your mother's. Thus you'll seem to most
a traitor, betraying your friends and your dead father.

CHORUS LEADER

No anger, I entreat you. In the words of both
there is value for both, if you, Electra, can   370
follow her advice and she take yours.

CHRYSOTHEMIS

Ladies, I am used to her and her words.
I never would have mentioned this, had not
I learned of the greatest of misfortunes coming
her way to put a stop to her long mourning.   375

ELECTRA

Tell me of your terror. If you can speak to me
of something worse than my present condition,
I'll not keep arguing back.

CHRYSOTHEMIS

                      Well, I shall tell you
everything I know. They plan, if you don't stop

your present mourning, to send you away, to where   380
never a gleam of sun shall visit you.
You shall live out your life in an underground cave
outside this country and there bewail your sorrows.
With this in mind, reflect. And do not blame me
later when you are suffering.
Now is a good time to take thought.

ELECTRA
So this is what they have decided to do with me?   385

CHRYSOTHEMIS
Yes, this exactly, when Aegisthus comes home.

ELECTRA
As far as this goes, let him come home soon.

CHRYSOTHEMIS
Why such a prayer for evil, my poor sister?

ELECTRA
That he may come—if he will do what you say.

CHRYSOTHEMIS
Hoping that *what* may happen to you? Are you crazy?   390

ELECTRA
That I may get away from you all, as far as I can.

CHRYSOTHEMIS
Have you no care of this, your present life?

ELECTRA
Mine is indeed a fine life, to be envied!

CHRYSOTHEMIS
It might be, if you could learn common sense.

ELECTRA
Do not teach me falseness to those I love.   395

CHRYSOTHEMIS
That is not what I teach, but to yield to power.

ELECTRA

Keep practicing that flattery. It is not my way.

CHRYSOTHEMIS

It is a good thing, though, not to fall through stupidity.

ELECTRA

I shall fall, if I must, revenging my father.

CHRYSOTHEMIS

Our father does not blame me for this, I know.   400

ELECTRA

These are the kind of words that cowards praise.

CHRYSOTHEMIS

You will not heed me then? You will not agree?

ELECTRA

No, certainly.
May I not yet be so empty-witted.

CHRYSOTHEMIS

Then I must go on the errand I was sent.

ELECTRA

Where are you going? To whom   405
bringing those offerings?

CHRYSOTHEMIS

My mother sent me with libations for father's grave.

ELECTRA

What are you saying? To her greatest enemy?

CHRYSOTHEMIS

"Whom she herself killed"—you would add.

ELECTRA

Which of her friends persuaded her? Who thought of this?

CHRYSOTHEMIS

I think it was night terrors drove her to it.   410

ELECTRA

Gods of my father, now come to help at last!

CHRYSOTHEMIS

Why do "night terrors" make you confident?

ELECTRA

I'll tell you that when you tell me the dream.

CHRYSOTHEMIS

I cannot tell you much, only a little.

ELECTRA

Tell me it, all the same. A little story   415
has often made or ruined men before now.

CHRYSOTHEMIS

The story goes that she saw my father,
the father that was yours and mine, again
come to life, once more to live with her.
He took and at the hearth planted the scepter   420
which once he bore and now Aegisthus bears,
and up from out this scepter grew a branch
luxuriant with leaves, and shaded all the land
of this Mycenae. This is what I heard
from someone present when she told the Sun
about her dream.   425
              I know no more beyond this
except that it's for her fear she sends me now.
So, by our family's gods, I pray you: listen
to me and do not fall out of stupidity.
For if you reject me, you'll be back again in distress.° 430

ELECTRA

My dear one, not one thing that you are holding
allow to touch that grave, no, nothing!
It would not be god's law nor pious that you
should offer to my father libations

and burial offerings from that enemy woman.
Throw them to the winds! Or hide them deep   435
in the dust, somewhere where no particle of them
may ever reach my father where he lies.
But let them be stored up for her as treasures
below, against the day when *she* shall die.
I tell you, if she were not the most brazen   440
of all of womankind, would she have dared
to pour these enemy libations
over the body of the man she killed?
Consider if you think that the dead man,
as he lies in his grave, will welcome kindly
these offerings from her by whom he was robbed
of life and honor and foully mutilated?   445
And to wash her hands clean she wiped the clots of blood
off onto his head? Can you believe
that these offerings will bring absolution for her murder?
No, no. You let them be. You cut a lock
out of your own hair, from the fringe, and mine,
mine, too, his wretched daughter's. Such a small offering,   450
yet all I have! Give it to him, this rough°
lock of hair, and here, my girdle, unadorned.
Kneel then and pray that from the earth below
he may come himself, a friendly spirit, to help us
against his enemies. Pray that the boy Orestes   455
may live to fight and win against his enemies,
to set his foot upon them. And if so
in days to come we shall be able to dress
this grave with richer hands than we can now.
I think, oh yes, I think that it was he
that thought to send this evil-boding dream   460
to her.
        Yet, sister, do yourself this service
and help me, too, and help the dearest of all,
father of us both, that lies dead in the underworld.

CHORUS LEADER

The girl speaks piously. And you, my dear,
if you are wise, will follow her advice.   465

CHRYSOTHEMIS

I will do it. It is not reasonable for us two
to squabble about what is just. I must haste to do it.
But, my friends, if I attempt this, I must have your silence.
If my mother hears of this, I'm sure I shall regret   470
indeed the attempt that I'm about to make.

(Exit Chrysothemis to the side.)

CHORUS [*singing*]

STROPHE

If I am not a distracted prophet
and lacking in skill of judgment,
Justice foreshadowing the event   475
shall come, in her hands a just victory.
Yes, she will come, my child, in vengeance
and soon:
of that I am confident
since I lately heard   480
of this dream that blows sweet.
Your father, the king of the Greeks,
has never forgotten,
nor the axe of old,
bronze-cast, double-edged,   485
which did him to death
in shame and degradation.

ANTISTROPHE

There shall come many-footed, many-handed,
hidden in dreadful ambush,   490
the bronze-shod Fury.
Wicked indeed were they who were seized
with a passion for a forbidden bed,

for a marriage accursed, stained with murder.
In the light of this, I am very sure   495
that never, never shall we see
such a portent draw near without hurt
to doers and partners in crime.
There are indeed no prophecies for mortals
in dreadful dreams and soothsayings
if this night vision come not   500
well and truly to fulfilment.

EPODE

Horsemanship of Pelops long ago,
loaded with disaster,   505
how deadly you have proved
to this land!
For since the day that Myrtilus
sank to his rest in the sea,
wrecked utterly with the unhappy
wreck of his golden chariot,   510
for never a moment since
has destruction and ruin
ever left this house.   515

(Clytemnestra enters from the palace, with attendants.)

CLYTEMNESTRA

It seems you are loose again, wandering about.
Aegisthus isn't here, who always restrained you
from going abroad and disgracing your family.
But now that he is away you pay no heed
to me, although you have told a lot of people   520
at length how brutally and how unjustly
I lord it over you, insulting
you and yours.

             There is no insolence in myself,
but being abused by you so constantly
I give abuse in return.

Your father, yes,   525

always your father. Nothing else is your pretext—
that he was killed by me. By me. I know it,
well. There is no denial in me. Justice,
justice it was that took him, not I alone.
And you too would have served the cause of justice
if you had been right-minded.

     For this father of yours whom you always mourn,   530
alone of all the Greeks, had the brutality
to sacrifice your sister to the gods,
although he had not toiled for her as I did,
the mother that bore her, he the begetter only.
Tell me, now, why he sacrificed her. Was it   535
for the sake of the Greeks?
But they had no share in my daughter to let them kill her.
Was it for Menelaus' sake, his brother,
that he killed my child? And should he not then pay for it?
Had not this Menelaus two children who
ought to have died rather than mine? It was their parents   540
for whose sake all the Greeks set sail for Troy.
Or had the god of death some longing to feast
on my children rather than hers? Or had
that accursed father lost his love for my children
while feeling it still for those of Menelaus?   545
Was not this the act of a father thoughtless
or with bad thoughts? That is how I see it
even if you differ with me. The dead girl,
if she could speak, would bear me out.
I am not dismayed by all that has happened.
If you think me wicked, keep your righteous judgment   550
and blame your neighbors.

ELECTRA

This is one time you will not be able to say
that the abuse I receive from you was provoked
by something painful on my side.

                                        But if
you will allow me I will speak truthfully
on behalf of the dead man and my dead sister.   555

CLYTEMNESTRA

Of course, I allow you. If you always began
our conversations so, you would not be
so painful to listen to.

ELECTRA

                          I will tell you, then.
You say you killed my father. What claim more shameful
than that, whether with justice or without it?   560
But I'll maintain that it was not with justice
you killed him, but the seduction of that evil man,
with whom you now are living, drew you to it.
Ask Artemis the huntress what made her hold
the many winds in check at Aulis. Or
I'll tell you this, since we may not learn from her.   565
My father, as I hear, when at his sport,
started from his feet a horned dappled stag
within the goddess' sanctuary. He
let fly and hit the deer and uttered some boast
about his killing of it. The daughter of Leto   570
was angry at this and so detained the Greeks
in order that my father, to compensate
for the beast killed, would sacrifice his daughter.

Thus was her sacrifice—no other deliverance
for the army either homeward or toward Ilium.
He struggled and fought against it. Finally,   575
constrained, he killed her—not for Menelaus.
But if—I will plead in your own words—he had done so
for his brother's sake, is that any reason
why he should die at your hands? By what law?
If this is the law you lay down for men, take heed   580
you do not lay down for yourself pain and repentance.

If we shall kill one in another's requital,
you would be the first to die, if you met with justice.
No. Think if the whole is not a mere excuse.
Please tell me for what cause you now commit   585
the ugliest of acts—in sleeping with him,
the murderer with whom you first conspired
to kill my father, and breed children to him, and
drive out your former children, honorable ones   590
born of honorable wedlock. What grounds
for praise shall I find in this? Or will you say
that this, too, is retribution for your daughter?
If you say it, still your saying it is scandalous.
It isn't decent to marry with your enemies
even for a daughter's sake.

                        But I may not
even rebuke you! What you always say   595
is that it is my mother I am reviling.
Mother! I do not count you mother of mine,
but slave owner and mistress. My life is wretched
because I live with multitudes of sufferings,
inflicted by yourself and your bedfellow.   600
But the other, he is away, he has escaped
your hand, though barely: poor Orestes now
wears out his life in misery and exile.
Many a time you have accused me
of rearing him to be your executioner.
I would have done it if I could. Know that.   605
As far as that goes, you may publicly
proclaim me what you like—traitor, reviler,
a creature full of shamelessness. If I am
naturally skilled at such things, I do no shame
to your nature.

CHORUS LEADER

    I see she is angry, but whether it is in justice,   610
    I no longer see if there's concern for that.

CLYTEMNESTRA

What need have I of concern in her regard
who so insults her mother, though old enough
to know better? Don't you think that she will go
to any lengths, so shameless as she is?   615

ELECTRA

You may be sure I am ashamed of this,
even if you do not think so. I know that
I act improperly, so unlike myself.
But the hate you show for me, and all your actions,
compel me against my will to act this way.   620
For ugly deeds are taught by ugly deeds.

CLYTEMNESTRA

O shameless creature, I and my words and deeds
give you too much to talk of.

ELECTRA

It is you who talk, not I. It is your deeds,
and it's deeds invent the words.   625

CLYTEMNESTRA

Now by the Lady Artemis you shall not escape
the results of your behavior, when Aegisthus comes.

ELECTRA

You see? You let me say what I please, and then
you are outraged. You do not know how to listen.

CLYTEMNESTRA

Hold your peace at least. Allow me to sacrifice,   630
since I have permitted you to say all you will.

ELECTRA

I allow you, yes, I bid you, sacrifice.
Do not blame my tongue; for I will say no more.

CLYTEMNESTRA   *(To an attendant.)*

Come, do you lift them up, the offerings
of all the fruits of earth, that to this king here   635

I may offer prayers for freedom from my fears.
Phoebus Protector, hear me, as I am,
although the word I speak is muted. Not among friends
is it spoken, nor may I unfold the whole
to the light while this girl stands beside me,
lest with her chattering and malicious tongue   640
she sow in all the city bad reports.
Yet hear me thus, since this is how I will speak.
The dreams of double meaning I have seen
within this night, from them, Lycian king,   645
grant what is good for me prosperous outcome
but what is ill, turn it back upon
those that do us evil.
And if there are some that from my present wealth
plot to expel me with their stratagems,
do not permit them. Let me live out my life,   650
just as my life is now, to the end uninjured,
controlling the house of Atreus and the throne,
living with those I love as I do now,
enjoying prosperity, and with such children
as do not hate me nor cause bitter pain.
These are my prayers, Lycian Apollo; hear them   655
graciously. Grant to all of us what we ask.
For all the rest, although I keep silent,
I know you are a god and know it all.
It is natural that the children of Zeus see all.

(Enter Tutor, from the side.)

TUTOR

Excuse me, ladies, how may I know for certain,   660
is this the palace of the King Aegisthus?

CHORUS LEADER

This is it, sir. Your own guess is correct.

TUTOR

Would I then be right in thinking that this lady
is his wife? She has indeed a royal look.

CHORUS LEADER

Quite right. And here she is for you, herself.

TUTOR

Greetings, Your Majesty. I come with news
from a friend, good news for you and for Aegisthus.

CLYTEMNESTRA

I welcome what you have said. But I would like first
to know who sent you here.

TUTOR

                                                    It was Phanoteus
the Phocian, charging me with an important matter.   670

CLYTEMNESTRA

What is it, sir? Please tell me. I know well
you come from a friend and will speak friendly words.

TUTOR

Orestes is dead. There it is, in one short word.

ELECTRA

O no, O no! This is the day I die.

CLYTEMNESTRA

What's this you say, sir, what? Don't listen to her.   675

TUTOR

What I said and say again is "Orestes is dead."

ELECTRA

I am ruined, hopeless—I cannot go on living!

CLYTEMNESTRA   *(To Electra.)*
Mind your own business!

                                                    (To the Tutor.)

                                    Sir, tell me the truth:
in what way did he meet his death?

This
I was sent to tell, and I will tell you it all.   680
He went to the glorious gathering that Greece holds
in honor of the Delphic Games, and when
he heard the herald's loud proclamation
for the first contest—it was a running race—
he entered, looking brilliant, all eyes upon him.   685
His running was as good as his appearance:
he won the race and came out covered with honor.
There is much I could tell you, but I must tell it briefly.
I have never known a man of such achievement
or prowess. Know this one thing. In all the contests   690
the marshals announced, he won the prize, was cheered,°
proclaimed the victor as "Argive by birth,
by name Orestes, son of Agamemnon,
who once gathered and led the glorious Greek host."   695
So far, so good. But when a god sends ruin,
not even the strong man may escape.
                                Orestes,
when, the next day, at sunrise, there was a race
for chariot teams, entered with many contestants.   700
There was one Achaean, one from Sparta, two
Libyans, masters in driving racing teams.
Orestes was the fifth among them; he
had as his team Thessalian mares. The sixth
was an Aetolian with young sorrel horses.   705
The seventh was a Magnesian, and the eighth
an Aenian, by race, with a white team.
The ninth competitor came from god-built Athens,
and then a Boeotian, ten chariots in all.
They stood in their allotted stations where   710
the appointed judges placed them. At the signal,
a brazen trumpet, they were off. The drivers called
to their horses, and their hands vibrated the reins,
The course was filled with clamor of rattling chariots.

The dust rose up. The drivers, massed together,   715
applied the goad unsparingly, each one struggling
to advance the nave of his wheel or the snorting mouths
of his horses past his rival, wheels and backs
all slobbered by the breath of the teams behind them.°   720
So far they all stood upright in their chariots.
But the Aenian's hard-mouthed colts got out of hand
and bolted as they finished the sixth lap   725
and turned into the seventh; there they crashed
head-on with the Barcaean chariot. After that,
from this one accident, team crashed team
and overturned each other. All the plain
of Crisa was full of wrecks. But the man from Athens,   730
a clever driver, saw what was happening, pulled
his horses out of the way, and held them in check,
avoiding the disordered mass of teams in the middle.

      Orestes had been driving last and holding
his horses back, putting his trust in the finish.   735
But when he saw the Athenian left alone,
he sent a shrill cry through his swift horses' ears
and set to catch him. The two drove level,
the poles were even. First one, now the other,
would push his horses' heads in front.   740
Orestes always drove tight at the corners
barely grazing the edge of the post with his wheel,
loosening the reins of the trace horse on his right
while he checked the near horse.° In his other laps
the young man and his horses had come through safe.
But this time as he slackened the left rein
while the horse was still turning, unaware, he struck
the edge of the pillar and broke the axle box.   745
He was himself thrown from the rails of the chariot
and tangled in the reins. As he fell, the horses
bolted wildly to the middle of the course.
When the crowd saw him fallen from his chariot,
they cried out with pity for the young man, who'd done   750

such deeds and now was meeting such misfortune,
thrown earthward first, then with legs pointing
to the sky—until at last the charioteers
with difficulty stopped the runaway team
and freed him, but so covered with blood that no one   755
of his friends could have recognized the wretched corpse.
They burned him there on a pyre. Men of Phocis
chosen for the task are bringing in a small urn
of bronze the miserable ashes—all that's left
of this great frame, that he may have his grave   760
here in his father's country.
That is my story,
bitter as stories go, but for us who saw it,
greatest of all misfortunes that I've seen.

CHORUS LEADER

Ah, ah! The ancient family
of our lords has perished, it seems, root and branch.   765

CLYTEMNESTRA

Zeus, what shall I say? Shall I call it good luck?
Or terrible, yet for the best? Indeed,
my state is painful if I must save
my life by means of my own misfortunes.

TUTOR

My lady, why does this story make you dejected?

CLYTEMNESTRA

Mother and child! It is a strange relation.   770
A mother cannot hate the child she bore
even when injured by it.

TUTOR

Our coming here, it seems, then is to no purpose.

CLYTEMNESTRA

Not to no purpose. How can you say "no purpose"—
if you have come with certain proofs of death

of one who from my soul was sprung,   775
but severed himself from my breast, from my nurture, who
became an exile and a foreigner;
who after he quitted this land, never saw me again;
who charged me with his father's murder, threatened
terrors against me. Neither night nor day   780
could I find solace in sleep: each oncoming moment
kept nagging me like one about to die.
But now, with this one day I am freed from fear
of her and him. She was the greater evil;
she lived with me, constantly draining   785
the very blood of life—now perhaps I'll have peace
from her threats. The light of day will come again.

ELECTRA

Oh no, no! Now must I mourn indeed
your death, Orestes, when your mother here
pours insults on you, dead. Can this be right?   790

CLYTEMNESTRA

Not right for you. But he is right as he is.

ELECTRA

Hear, Nemesis, of the man that lately died!

CLYTEMNESTRA

Nemesis has heard what she should, and done things well.

ELECTRA

Insult us now. For now the luck is yours.

CLYTEMNESTRA

Will you not stop this, you and Orestes both?   795

ELECTRA

We are stopped indeed. We cannot make you stop.

CLYTEMNESTRA   *(To the Tutor.)*

Your coming will be worth much, sir, if you
have stopped my daughter's everlasting clamor.

TUTOR

Well, I will go now, if all this is settled.

CLYTEMNESTRA

O no! I should do wrong to myself and to   800
the friend who sent you if I let you go.
Please go inside. Leave her out here to wail
the misfortunes of herself and those she loves.

(Exit Clytemnestra and the Tutor into the house.)

ELECTRA

There's an unhappy mother for you! See
how agonized, how bitter, were the tears,   805
how terribly she sorrowed for her son
that met the death you heard of! No, I tell you,
she parted from us laughing. O what misery!
Orestes dearest, your death is my death.
By your passing you have torn away from my heart
whatever solitary hope still lingered   810
that you would live and come some day to avenge
your father and my miserable self.
But now where should I turn? I am alone,
having lost both you and my father. Back again
to be a slave among those I hate most   815
of all the world, my father's murderers!
Is this what is right for me?
                              No, this I will not:
live with them any more. Here, at this gate
I will abandon myself to waste away
this life of mine, unloved. If they're displeased,
let someone kill me, someone that lives within.   820
Death is a favor to me, life an agony.
I have no wish for life.

CHORUS [*singing, with Electra singing in response*]

STROPHE A

Where are Zeus's thunderbolts,
where is the blazing sun,

if they see all this and yet keep it hidden,
holding their peace?   825

ELECTRA
  Oh, oh!

CHORUS
  Why do you cry, child?

ELECTRA
  Ah!

CHORUS
  Speak no great word.   830

ELECTRA
  You will destroy me.

CHORUS
  How?

ELECTRA
  If you suggest a hope
  when all is plain, when they are gone
  to the house of Death, and when I waste   835
  my life away, then you are treading me further down.

CHORUS

                    ANTISTROPHE A
            King Amphiaraus, as I know,
            was caught by a woman's golden necklace,
            and now beneath the earth
            reigns over all the spirits there.   840

ELECTRA
  Oh, woe!

CHORUS
  Woe indeed, for the murderess . . .

ELECTRA
                            . . . she died!°

CHORUS

Yes.

ELECTRA

I know, I know. For him in sorrow
there came a deliverer.
None such for me. For one there was,
but he is gone, snatched away by death.

CHORUS

STROPHE B

Unhappy girl, unhappiness is yours!

ELECTRA

I bear you witness with full knowledge,
knowledge too full, bred of a life, 850
the crowded months surging with horrors
many and dreadful!

CHORUS

We know what you are saying.

ELECTRA

So do not then, I pray you, divert my thoughts to where ... 855

CHORUS

What do you mean?

ELECTRA

... there is no hope, no brother born
of the same noble lineage to help.

CHORUS

ANTISTROPHE B

Death comes to all mortal men. 860

ELECTRA

Yes, but to meet it so,
as he did, poor man,
tangled in the leather reins,
among the wild flurry of hoofs!

CHORUS
　　An unwatchable horror!　　　　　　　　　　　　

ELECTRA
　　True indeed, for he's now a stranger
　　that was hidden in earth, by no hand of mine,
　　knew no grave I gave him,
　　knew no weeping from me.　　　　　　　　　　

　　　　　　　　　　　　　　　(Enter Chrysothemis.)

CHRYSOTHEMIS
　　My dearest sister,
　　I am so glad, I have run here in haste,
　　regardless of propriety. I bring you
　　happiness and a relief from all
　　the troubles you have had and sorrowed for.

ELECTRA [*now speaking*]
　　Where could you find relief—and who are you　　875
　　to find it—for my troubles which know no cure?

CHRYSOTHEMIS
　　We have Orestes here among us—that is
　　my news for you—as plain as you see myself.

ELECTRA
　　Are you mad, poor girl, or can it be you laugh
　　at what are your own troubles as well as mine?　　880

CHRYSOTHEMIS
　　I swear by our father's hearth. It is not in mockery
　　I speak. He is here in person with us.

ELECTRA
　　　　　　　　　　Ah!
　　Poor girl! Who told you this that you believed him,
　　all too credulous?

CHRYSOTHEMIS

        My own eyes were the evidence 885
for what I saw, and no one else.

ELECTRA

              Poor thing!
What proof was there to see? What did you look at
that has set your heart incurably afire?

CHRYSOTHEMIS

I pray you, hear me by the gods,
and then, having heard me, call me sane or foolish. 890

ELECTRA

Tell me, then, if the story gives you pleasure.

CHRYSOTHEMIS

Yes, I will tell you all I saw.
When I came to our father's ancient grave,
I saw that from the very top of the mound
newly poured streams of milk were flowing, and his tomb 895
was crowned with a wreath of all the flowers
that grow. I saw in wonder, looked about
in case there might be someone near. But when I saw
that all was quiet, I approached the grave. 900
On top of the pyre I saw a fresh-cut lock of hair;
as soon as I saw that, something jumped within me
at the familiar sight. I knew I saw
the token of my dearest, loved Orestes.
I took it in my hands, never saying a word 905
for fear of saying what would be ill-omened,
but in pure joy my eyes were filled with tears.
Both then and now I know with certainty
this offering could come from him alone.
Whom else could this concern, save you and me?
I did not do it, I know, and neither did you. 910
How could you? For you cannot leave this house,

even to worship, but they will punish you for it.
Nor can it be our mother. She is not inclined
to do such things, and if she did, we'd notice it.
These offerings at the grave must be Orestes'. 915
Dear sister, take heart. It is not always the same
fortune that follows anyone. Till now
our fortune was hateful to us. But now perhaps
this day will seal the promise of much good.

ELECTRA
Oh, how I pity you, long since, for your foolishness!

CHRYSOTHEMIS
What is this? Are you not pleased by what I say? 920

ELECTRA
You don't know where you are, nor what you're thinking.

CHRYSOTHEMIS
Why, don't I have knowledge of what I saw quite plainly?

ELECTRA
He is dead, my poor dear. And your rescue at his hands
is dead along with him. Look to him no more. 925

CHRYSOTHEMIS
Alas! From whom on earth did you hear this?

ELECTRA
From one that was near to him, when he was dying.

CHRYSOTHEMIS
Where is that man then? I am lost in wonder.

ELECTRA
He's in the house, as our mother's welcome guest.

CHRYSOTHEMIS
Alas again! But who then would have placed 930
these many offerings on our father's tomb?

ELECTRA

I think perhaps that someone put them there
as a remembrance of the dead Orestes.

CHRYSOTHEMIS

Unlucky I! I was so happy coming,
hurrying to bring my news to you, not knowing   935
what misery we were plunged in. Now when I've come,
I find both our old sorrow and the new.

ELECTRA

That is how things are, yes. But now listen to me,
and you can relieve the suffering that weighs on us.

CHRYSOTHEMIS

So can I bring the dead to life again?   940

ELECTRA

This is not what I mean. I am no such fool.

CHRYSOTHEMIS

What do you bid me do, of which I am capable?

ELECTRA

To have the courage to follow my counsel.

CHRYSOTHEMIS

If I can help at all, I will not refuse.

ELECTRA

Look: there is no success without hardship.   945

CHRYSOTHEMIS

I know. As far as my strength goes, I will help.

ELECTRA

Hear me tell you, then, the plans that I have laid.
Friends to help—you know that we have none:
death has taken them and robbed us. We alone,
the two of us, are left.   950
While I still heard my brother lived and flourished,

I had my hopes that he would come again,
some day, to avenge the murder of our father.
But now that he's no more, I look to you,
that you should not draw back from helping me,
your trueborn sister, kill our father's murderer,   955
Aegisthus.
          There is nothing I should now conceal from you.
What are you waiting for, that you are hesitant?
What hope do you look to, that is still standing?
Now you must sorrow that you have been deprived
of our father's wealth; and you must grieve also   960
that you are growing older, to this point,
without a marriage and a husband. And
don't hope to get them now, for Aegisthus
is not such a fool as to allow children of yours   965
or mine to grow up, obviously to harm him.
But if you follow my plans,
first, you will win from that dead father, gone
to the underworld, and from our brother with him,
the recognition of your piety.
And, secondly, as you were born to freedom,   970
so in the days to come you will be called free
and find a marriage worthy of you: everyone
loves to look to the noble.
Do you not see how great a reputation
you will win for yourself and me by doing this?
For who of citizens and foreigners   975
that sees us will not welcome us with praise:
"These are two sisters. Look, friends, on them well.
They saved their father's house when their enemies
were riding high, and took their stand against murder,
sparing not to risk their lives upon the venture.   980
Therefore, we all should love them, all revere them,
and all at feasts and public ceremonies
honor these two girls for their bravery."
This is what everyone will say of us,

in life and death, to our undying fame.   985
My dear one, hear me. Labor to help your father
and help your brother; give me deliverance
from what I suffer, and deliver yourself, knowing this:
living shamefully, for the nobly born, is shameful.

CHORUS LEADER

In matters like this, forethought is an ally   990
to the one that gives advice and the one that gets it.

CHRYSOTHEMIS

Ladies, before she spoke, if she had good sense,
she would have held to caution; but she has not.

(To Electra.)

Where are you looking, that you arm yourself like this   995
with such audacity and call on me to help?
Can you not see? You are a woman—no man—
and your physical strength is less than is your enemies'!
Their fortune, day by day, grows luckier
while ours declines and comes to nothingness.   1000
Who then, plotting to kill such a man as this,
will escape unharmed and free of all disaster?
We two are now in trouble. Look to it that
we do not get ourselves trouble still worse
if someone hears what you have said.
There is no gain for us, not the slightest help,   1005
to win a noble reputation if
the way to it lies by dishonorable death.
For death is not the worst but when one wants
to die and cannot even have that death.
I beg of you, before you utterly
destroy us and exterminate our family,   1010
check your temper. All that you have said to me
I'll keep, for my part, unspoken and unfulfilled.
Be sensible, you, and, at long last, being weaker,
learn to give in to those that have the strength.

CHORUS LEADER

Follow her advice. There's no greater gain for humans   1015
than prudence and a reasonable mind!

ELECTRA

You have said nothing unexpected. Well
I knew you would reject what I proposed.
The deed must then be done by my own hand
alone. For I won't leave it unattempted.   1020

CHRYSOTHEMIS

Ah!
I would you had felt so when our father died:
you would have carried all before you.

ELECTRA

I was the same in nature then, weaker in judgment.

CHRYSOTHEMIS

Practice to keep that judgment through your life.

ELECTRA

That is advice which means you will not help me.   1025

CHRYSOTHEMIS

Yes—for the attempt most likely brings disaster.

ELECTRA

I envy you your "judgment," but hate your cowardice.

CHRYSOTHEMIS

I will be equally patient when you praise me.

ELECTRA

That you will never experience from me.

CHRYSOTHEMIS

There's a long future to determine that.   1030

ELECTRA

Be gone; for there's no help in you for me.

CHRYSOTHEMIS

There is, but there's no power of learning in you.

ELECTRA

Go and tell all this story to your mother.

CHRYSOTHEMIS

I do not hate you with such a hatred as that.

ELECTRA

Understand, at least, how you dishonor me.   1035

CHRYSOTHEMIS

It is not dishonor, only forethought for you.

ELECTRA

Must I then follow your idea of justice?

CHRYSOTHEMIS

You'll be our leader, once you come to your senses.

ELECTRA

It is terrible to speak well and be wrong.

CHRYSOTHEMIS

A very proper description of yourself.   1040

ELECTRA

What! Don't you think that I say these things with justice?

CHRYSOTHEMIS

There are times when even justice can bring harm.

ELECTRA

These are rules by which I would not wish to live.

CHRYSOTHEMIS

If you make your attempt, you'll find that I am right.

ELECTRA

Yes, I will make it. You will not frighten me.   1045

CHRYSOTHEMIS

Are you sure now? You will not think again?

ELECTRA

No enemy is worse than bad advice.

CHRYSOTHEMIS

You cannot agree with any of what I say?

ELECTRA

I have made my mind up—long ago, in fact.

CHRYSOTHEMIS

I will go away then. You cannot bring yourself°   1050
to approve my words, nor I your disposition.

ELECTRA

Go then. I'll never follow you,
not though you long for it. It is pure folly
to try to pursue vain and empty things.

CHRYSOTHEMIS

Well, if you think that you are right, go on   1055
thinking so. When you are deep in trouble, then
you will agree with what I said.

(Exit Chrysothemis into the palace.)

CHORUS [*singing*]

STROPHE A

Why, when we see above our heads the birds,
true in their wisdom,
caring for the sustenance   1060
of those that gave them life and help,
why do we not pay our own debts of gratitude so?
But, by Zeus of the lightning bolt,
by Themis, dweller in heaven,
not for long do we go unpunished.   1065
O voice that goes to the dead below,
carry the piteous message
to the Atridae in the underworld,
and tell of wrongs untouched
by joy of the dance.

Tell them that now their house is sick,   1070
tell them that their two children
fight and struggle, that they cannot
any more live in harmony together.
Electra, betrayed, alone,
is down in the waves of sorrow,
constantly bewailing her father's fate,   1075
like the nightingale lamenting.
She takes no thought of death;
she is ready to leave the light
if only she can kill the two Furies.
Was there ever one so noble
born to a father's house?   1080

Nobody truly good will choose to live
shamefully, if so living
they cloud their renown and die nameless.
O my child, my child, even so you°   1085
have chosen to share the life of mourning,
have rejected dishonor,
to win at once two reputations
as wise and best of daughters.

ANTISTROPHE B

I pray that your life may be lifted high   1090
over your foes,
in wealth and power as much as now
you lie beneath their hand.
For I have found you in distress   1095
but winning the highest prize
by piety toward Zeus
for observance of nature's greatest laws.

(*Enter Orestes and Pylades from the side, disguised as Phocian*
countrymen and accompanied by attendants who carry an urn.)

ORESTES

    I wonder, ladies, if we were directed right
    and have come to the destination that we sought?

CHORUS LEADER

    What do you seek? And what do you want here?   1100

ORESTES

    I have asked all the way here where Aegisthus lives.

CHORUS LEADER

    You have arrived and need not blame your guides.

ORESTES

    Would some one of you be so kind to tell
    the household we have come, a welcome company?

CHORUS LEADER

    This lady, as nearest of kin, could bear the message.   1105

ORESTES

    Then, lady, will you please report within
    that certain men of Phocis seek Aegisthus.

ELECTRA

    O no! Then are you bringing the certain proofs
    of those rumors we received before you came?

ORESTES

    I do not know about rumor. Old Strophius sent me   1110
    here to bring news about Orestes.

ELECTRA

    What is it, sir? How fear steals over me!

ORESTES

    Within this little urn, as you can see,
    we are bringing home his small remains. He is dead.

ELECTRA

    Ah, ah! This is it indeed, all clear.   1115
    Here is my sorrow visible, before me.

ORESTES

If you are one that sorrows for Orestes
and his troubles, know this urn contains his body.

ELECTRA

Sir, give it to me, by the gods. If he
is hidden in this urn—give it into my hands,   1120
that I may weep and cry lament together
for myself and my whole family with these ashes.

ORESTES [*speaking to his attendants*]

Bring it and give it to her, whoever she is.
It is not in enmity she asks for it.
One of his friends, no doubt, or of his blood.   1125

(*The attendants do as directed.*)

ELECTRA [*speaking*]   (*To the urn.*)

Precious memorial of my dearest love,
my most loved in the world, all that remains
of live Orestes, oh, how differently
from the hopes I sent you with do I receive you home!
Now all I hold of you is nothingness;
but you shone brilliantly, child, when from this house
I sent you forth.   1130
Would that I had left life before I sent you
abroad to a foreign country, when I stole you
with these two hands, saved you from being murdered.
Then on that very day you would have died,
and lying there would have found your share,   1135
your common portion of your father's grave.
Now far from home, an exile, on alien soil
without your sister near, you died unhappily.
I did not, to my sorrow, wash you with
these hands that loved you, did not lift you up,
as was my right, a weight of misery,   1140
from the fierce blaze of the pyre. The hands of strangers
gave you your rites, and so you come again,
a tiny weight enclosed in a tiny vessel.

Alas for all my nursing of long ago,
so constant—all for nothing—which I gave you   1145
with such sweet trouble. For you never were
as much your mother's love as you were mine;
none was your nurse but I within that household,
and I was always the one called "sister." Now
in one day all that is gone—for you are dead:
all, all you have snatched with you in your going, like   1150
a hurricane. Our father is dead and gone.
I am dead in you; and you are dead yourself.
Our enemies laugh. Frantic with joy she grows,
mother, no mother, the one you promised me
in secret messages so often you   1155
would come to punish. Now our evil fortune,
yours and mine, has stolen all this away,
and sent you back to me like this—no longer
the form I used to love, only your dust
and idle shade.

[*singing*]
Ah, ah!!

                    O body pitiable! Ah!   1160
O saddest journey that you went, my love,
and so have destroyed me! Ah!
O brother, loved one, you have destroyed me!

[*now speaking again*]
Therefore, receive me to your habitation,   1165
nothing to nothing, that with you below
I may dwell from now on. When you were on earth,
I shared all with you equally. Now I claim
in death no less to share a grave with you.
The dead, I see, no longer suffer pain.   1170

CHORUS LEADER
    Think, Electra, your father was mortal, and mortal
    was Orestes also. Do not sorrow too much.
    This is a debt that all of us must pay.

ORESTES

Ah!

What shall I say? What words can I use? It's impossible;

I am no longer master of my tongue.   1175

ELECTRA

What ails you? What is the meaning of your words?

ORESTES

Is this the glorious form of Electra that I see?

ELECTRA

Yes. This is she; and truly miserable.

ORESTES

Alas for this most lamentable event!

ELECTRA

Is it for me, sir, you are sorrowing?   1180

ORESTES

That body, so cruelly and godlessly abused!

ELECTRA

None other than myself must be the subject

of your ill-omened words, sir.

ORESTES

                              O, alas

for your life without husband or happiness!

ELECTRA

Why do you look at me so, sir? Why lament?

ORESTES

How little then I knew of my own troubles!   1185

ELECTRA

From what that has been said did you learn this?

ORESTES

I see you and your sufferings, so conspicuous.

ELECTRA

It's little of my suffering that you see.

ORESTES

How can there be things worse to see than this?

ELECTRA

Because I live with those that murdered him.   1190

ORESTES

Murderers? Whose? Where is this evil you hint at?

ELECTRA

My father's murderers; and I'm forced to be their slave.

ORESTES

Who is it that forces you to such subjection?

ELECTRA

She is called my mother—but she's like a mother in nothing.

ORESTES

How does she compel you? Hardship or violence?   1195

ELECTRA

With violence and hardship and all ills.

ORESTES

You have no one to help you or prevent her?

ELECTRA

No. There was one. You have shown me his dust.

ORESTES

Poor girl! When I look at you, how I pity you!

ELECTRA

Then you are the only one that ever pitied me.   1200

ORESTES

Yes. I alone came here and felt your pain.

ELECTRA

You haven't perhaps come from somewhere as our kinsman?

ORESTES

I will tell you—if these women here are friends.

ELECTRA

Yes, friends indeed. You may speak quite freely.

ORESTES

Give up this urn then, and you shall know all.   1205

ELECTRA

Don't make me do that, stranger—by the gods!

ORESTES

Do what I bid you. You will not be wrong.

ELECTRA

By your beard! Do not rob me of what I love most!

ORESTES

I will not let you keep it.

ELECTRA

                    O Orestes!
Alas, if I may not even give you burial!   1210

ORESTES

No words of ill omen! You have no right to mourn.

ELECTRA

Have I no right to mourn for my dead brother?

ORESTES

You have no right to call him by that title.

ELECTRA

Am I then so dishonored in his sight?

ORESTES

No one dishonors you. But this is not for you.   1215

ELECTRA

It is—if it's Orestes' body that I hold here.

ORESTES

But it's not Orestes'—except in make-believe.

ELECTRA

Where is the poor boy buried then?

ORESTES

                    Nowhere.
There is no grave for living men.

ELECTRA

                    How, boy,
what do you mean?

ORESTES

            Nothing that is untrue.   1220

ELECTRA

Is he alive then?

ORESTES

            Yes, if I am living.

ELECTRA

And are you he?

ORESTES

            Look at this signet ring
that was our father's, and know if I speak true.

ELECTRA

O happiest light!

ORESTES

            Happiest I say, too.

ELECTRA

Voice, have you come?

ORESTES

            Hear it from no other source.   1225

ELECTRA

Do my arms hold you?

ORESTES

Never again to part.

ELECTRA

Dearest of women, fellow citizens,
here is Orestes that was dead by contrivance,
and now by contrivance is restored to life again!

CHORUS LEADER

We see, my child, and at your happy fortune   1230
tears of gladness trickle from our eyes.

ELECTRA [singing, while Orestes speaks]

STROPHE

Child of the body that I loved the best,
at last you have come,
you have come, you have found, you have seen those you
yearned for.

ORESTES

Yes, I have come. But bide your time in silence.   1235

ELECTRA

Why?

ORESTES

Silence is better, that none inside may hear.

ELECTRA

No, by Artemis, ever virgin,
this I will never stoop to fear—
the women who live inside,   1240
a vain burden on the earth.

ORESTES

Yes, but consider that in women too
there lives a warlike spirit. You have proof of it.

ELECTRA

Ah, indeed!   1245
You have awakened our sorrow
the nature of which no cloud can cover,
nothing can undo,
no forgetfulness overcome,
our sorrow in all its evil.   1250

ORESTES

I know that too. But when the right moment comes,
then will be the time to remember what was done.

ELECTRA

ANTISTROPHE

Every moment, every moment of all time
would justly suit my complaints.   1255
For hardly now are my lips free of restraint.

ORESTES

And I agree. Therefore, hold fast that freedom.

ELECTRA

By doing what?

ORESTES

Where there is no occasion,
do not choose to talk too much.

ELECTRA

Who could find a fit bargain   1260
of words for such silence,
now you have appeared?
Past hope, past calculation,
I see you now.

ORESTES

You see me when the gods moved me to come.°

. . . .

ELECTRA

> You tell me then of a grace surpassing
> what I knew before, if in very truth
> the gods have given you to this house.
> This I do count an action divine.   1270

ORESTES

> Indeed, I hesitate to check your joy;
> only I fear your pleasure may be too great.

ELECTRA

EPODE

> Orestes, you have come at last,
> have made the journey worth all the world to me,
> have come before me at last.
> Now that I see you
> after so much sorrow,
> do not, I beg you . . .   1275

ORESTES

> What should I not do?

ELECTRA

> . . . do not deprive me
> of the joy of seeing your face.

ORESTES

> I would be angry if I saw this in anyone else.

ELECTRA

> You agree?

ORESTES

> Of course I do.   1280

ELECTRA

> My dear one, I have heard your voice,
> the voice I never hoped to hear.
> Till now I have held my rage speechless;°

I did not cry out when I heard bad news.
But now I have you. You have come,   1285
your dearest face before me
that even in suffering I could never forget.

ORESTES
Spare me all superfluity of speech.
Tell me not how my mother is villainous,
nor how Aegisthus drains my father's wealth   1290
by luxury and waste. Words about this
will shorten time and opportunity.
But tell me what we need for the present moment,
how openly or hidden by our coming now
we can put a stop to our enemies' mockery.   1295
And take care that our mother does not realize
by your radiant face, when we two go inside.
Keep groaning over my destruction, as it was
emptily described in words. For when we have triumphed,
then you may freely show your joy, and laugh.   1300

ELECTRA [*now speaking*]
Brother, your pleasure shall be mine. These joys
I have from you; they are not mine to own.
I would not agree to hurt you in the slightest,
even if this would bring great profit for myself.   1305
If I did so, I would not properly
be serving the god who watches over us.

　　　You know the situation. You have heard
Aegisthus is not at home; our mother is.
And don't be afraid that she will see my face   1310
radiant with smiles: our hatred is too old,
I am too steeped in it. And since I have seen you,
my tears of joy will still run readily.
How can they cease when on the selfsame day
I have seen you dead and then again alive?   1315
For me your coming is a miracle,
so that if my father should come back to life

I would think it no wonder but believe
I saw him. Since your coming is such for me,
lead as you will. Had I been all alone,
I would not have failed to win one of two things,   1320
a noble deliverance or a noble death.

ORESTES

Hush, hush! I hear one of the people within
coming out.

ELECTRA

          Please enter our house, dear guests—
more so, since what you are carrying in is that
which no one would refuse—nor be delighted,
if he receives it.   1325

TUTOR   *(Entering from the palace.)*
          Fools and madmen! No
concern for your own lives at all? No sense
to realize that you are not merely near
the deadliest danger, but in its very midst?   1330
If I had not, this while past, stood guard here
at the door, your plans would now be in the house
before your bodies. I and only I
took the precautions. Have done once and for all
with your long speeches, your insatiable   1335
cries of delight, and in with you at once!
As we are now, delay is ruinous:
it is high time to have done with our task.

ORESTES

How's everything inside, as I go in?

TUTOR

Well. There is no chance of your recognition.   1340

ORESTES

You have announced my death, I understand.

TUTOR

You are down in Hades, as far as they're concerned.

ORESTES

Were they glad of it? Or what did they say?

TUTOR

I will tell you at the end. As things are now,
all on their side is well—even what is not so.   1345

ELECTRA

Brother, who is this man? I beg you, tell me.

ORESTES

Do you not know him?

ELECTRA

                      I cannot even guess.

ORESTES

Do you not know him to whose hands you gave me?

ELECTRA

What, this man?

ORESTES

                 By his hands and by your forethought
I was conveyed away to Phocian country.   1350

ELECTRA

Is this the man, alone among so many,
whom I found loyal when our father was murdered?

ORESTES

This is he. There is no need for further questions.

ELECTRA

O light of day most loved! O only rescuer
of Agamemnon's house, how did you come   1355
back here? Are you indeed that man who saved
both Orestes and me from so many dangers?

O most loved hands, service of feet most kind!
To think you were standing beside me for so long,
and I didn't know you, and you gave no sign!
You killed me with your words while in reality
you were bringing sweet joy. Bless you, my father—   1360
for I think I see a father in you. Blessings!
Within a single day, of all mankind
I have most hated and loved you most.

TUTOR

Enough, I think. As for the story
of the happenings in between, there'll be many days   1365
and nights, as time comes round, to tell you all
clearly, Electra.

(To Orestes and Pylades.)

But as you two stand here
I say to you: now is your chance to act.
Clytemnestra is alone. No man is within.
If you hold back now, you will have others to fight   1370
more clever and more numerous than these.

ORESTES

Pylades, our need now is not for lengthy speeches,
but to get inside as quick as ever we can,
only first saluting the ancestral gods
whose statues stand beside the forecourt here.   1375

(Orestes, Pylades, and the Tutor exit into the palace.)

ELECTRA

Apollo, Lord, give gracious ear to them
and to me, too, that often made you offerings,
out of such store as I had, with prayerful hand.
So now, Lycian Apollo, I kneel before you,
I pray and entreat you, with all the resources   1380
that I possess: please be kind to us,
help us in the fulfilment of our plans

and demonstrate to all mankind the punishment
the gods exact for wickedness.

(*Exit Electra into the palace.*)

CHORUS [*singing*]

STROPHE A

See how the war god approaches,
breathing bloody vengeance, invincible Ares.   1385
They have gone under the roof of the house now,
those pursuers of evil crimes,
hounds that none may escape;
so that the dream that hung hauntingly
in my mind shall not wait long for fulfilment.   1390

ANTISTROPHE A

Stealthy, stealthy-footed, into the house
he goes, the champion of dead men,
into his father's palace rich from of old,
holding the blade of blood,
new-whetted, in his hands. Hermes,
the child of Maia, hiding the crafty deed in darkness,   1395
conducts him to its end, and delays not.

(*Electra enters from the palace.*)

ELECTRA [*mostly speaking, while Orestes speaks in response*]

STROPHE B

Dear friends, now is the moment that the men
are finishing their work. Wait in silence.

CHORUS LEADER

What do you mean? What are they doing?

ELECTRA

                                       She is preparing   1400
the urn for burial, and they stand beside her.

CHORUS LEADER

Why have you hurried out here?

ELECTRA

        To watch
that Aegisthus does not come on them unawares.

CLYTEMNESTRA   *(Cries out from within the palace.)*
  House, O house
  deserted by friends, full of killers!   1405

ELECTRA
  Someone cries out, inside. Do you hear?

CHORUS [*singing*]
  What I hear is a terror to the ear.
  I shudder at it.

CLYTEMNESTRA   *(Cries out again from within.)*
  Oh! Oh! Aegisthus, where are you?

ELECTRA
  Again, that cry!

CLYTEMNESTRA
        My son, my son,   1410
  pity your mother!

ELECTRA
        You had none for him,
  nor for his father that begot him.

CHORUS [*singing*]
                City,
  and miserable family, now
  that day-to-day fate of yours is coming to an end.°

CLYTEMNESTRA
  Oh! I am struck!

ELECTRA
        If you have strength—again!

CLYTEMNESTRA
  Once more! Oh!   1415

ELECTRA
>   If only Aegisthus were with you!

CHORUS [*singing*]
> *The curses are being fulfilled;*
> *those under the earth are alive;*
> *men long dead draw from their killers*
> *blood to answer blood.*   1420

>   (*Enter Orestes and Pylades from the palace.*)

CHORUS LEADER° [*now speaking*]
>   ANTISTROPHE B
> And here they come. The bloody hand drips
> with Ares' sacrifice. I cannot blame them.

ELECTRA
> Orestes, how have you fared?

ORESTES
>   In the house, all
> is well, if Apollo prophesied well.   1425

ELECTRA
> Is the wretched woman dead?

ORESTES
>   You need fear no more
> that your mother's arrogance will dishonor you.°

CHORUS [*singing*]
> *Stop! I can see Aegisthus*
> *clearly coming this way.*

ELECTRA
> Boys, back to the house!   1430

ORESTES
>   Where do you see him?

ELECTRA

  He's in our power,

  walking toward us from the suburb, full of joy.

CHORUS [*singing*]

  Back to the vestibule, quick as you can.

  You have done one part well; now here is the other.

ORESTES

  Don't worry, we will do it.   1435

ELECTRA

                              Go

  where you will, then.

ORESTES

                    See, I am gone.

ELECTRA

  Leave what is here to me.

                              (*Exit Orestes into the palace with Pylades.*).

CHORUS [*singing*]

  A few words spoken softly in his ear

  would be good, that unawares

  he may rush into his contest against Justice.   1440

                              (*Enter Aegisthus from the side.*)

AEGISTHUS

  Which of you knows where the Phocian visitors are?

  I am told they are come here with news for me

  that Orestes met his end in a chariot wreck.

  You there, yes, I mean you, who formerly   1445

  were so bold and insolent; I should think

  it is you this news concerns the most, and therefore

  you will know best to tell it to me.

ELECTRA

  I know it, of course. Were it not so, I would be

  an outsider to what concerns my best beloved.

AEGISTHUS

Where are the strangers then? Tell me that.   1450

ELECTRA

Inside. They have found a very generous hostess.

AEGISTHUS

And do they genuinely report his death?

ELECTRA

Better than that. They have brought himself, not news.

AEGISTHUS

Can I then see the body in plain sight?

ELECTRA

You can indeed. It is an unenviable sight.   1455

AEGISTHUS

What you say delights me—an unusual thing!

ELECTRA

You may delight, if you find these things delightful.

AEGISTHUS   (To the servants.)

Open the doors, I command you, for all to see,°
all Mycenaeans and Argives, and if there's anyone
who formerly had raised up empty hopes   1460
for Orestes, now he may look on the dead
and so accept my bridle, and thus avoid
a more forcible encounter with myself
and punishment to make him grow some sense.

ELECTRA

I have done everything on my side. At long last
I have learned some sense, agreement with the stronger.   1465

> (The doors of the palace are opened, to reveal a covered body
> on a bier, with Orestes and Pylades standing in front of it.)

AEGISTHUS

O Zeus, I see a revelation that has happened
not without the gods' anger. Or if that is something
I should not say, because of Nemesis,
I take it back. Lift all the covers from
that face, so kinship at least may have due mourning.

ORESTES

Handle it yourself. This is not mine,   1470
it's yours—to see and greet with loving words.

AEGISTHUS

True. I accept that. And you, will you call
Clytemnestra, if she is at home?

ORESTES

                                She is near you.
You need not look elsewhere.

AEGISTHUS   (Lifting the covering.)
                                What do I see?   1475

ORESTES

Something you fear? Do you not know the face?

AEGISTHUS

Who are these men that have driven me into their net
to my destruction?

ORESTES

                        Did you take so long
to find that your names are all astray
and those you call the dead are living?

AEGISTHUS

                                Ah!
I understand. And you who speak to me   1480
can only be Orestes.

ORESTES

Were you, so good a prophet, so long misled?

AEGISTHUS

This is my end then. But let me say one thing,
one short word.

ELECTRA

I beg you, brother; don't let him draw out the talking.
When men are in the middle of trouble, when one°   1485
is on the point of death, how can time matter?
Kill him as quickly as you can; and when you've killed him,
throw him out to find such burial as suits him,
out of our sights. This is the only thing for me
that can bring release from sufferings long endured.   1490

ORESTES   (To Aegisthus.)

In with you, then. It is not words that now
are the issue, but your life.

AEGISTHUS

Why into the house?
Why do you need the dark if what you do
is fair? Why is your hand not ready to kill me?

ORESTES

You are not to give orders. Go in, where you killed   1495
my father, so you may die in the same place!

AEGISTHUS

Is it completely necessary that this house
see the evils of the Pelopidae, now and to come?

ORESTES

Yours, at least. Of that I am an excellent prophet.

AEGISTHUS

Your father did not have the skill you boast of.   1500

ORESTES

   Too many words! You are slow to take your road.
   Go now.

AEGISTHUS

      You lead the way.

ORESTES

         No, you go first.

AEGISTHUS

   Afraid that I'll escape you?

ORESTES

            No, but you shall not
   die as you choose. I must take care that death
   is bitter for you. Justice shall be taken°   1505
   directly on all who act above the law—
   justice by killing. So we would have less crime.

                    (Exit Aegisthus into the palace, followed by
                         Orestes, Pylades, and Electra.)

CHORUS [*chanting*]
   O family of Atreus, how many sufferings
   were yours before you came at last so hardly
   to freedom, by this day's deed perfected.   1510

PHILOCTETES

Translated by DAVID GRENE

PHILOCTETES: INTRODUCTION

The Play: Date and Composition

Philoctetes was one of the last plays that Sophocles wrote. It was produced in 409 BCE, when he was eighty-five years old, and he won first prize in the annual competition that year. We do not know which other three plays Sophocles produced along with this one.

The Myth

The story of Philoctetes, who with his marvelous bow and arrows helped capture Troy, was an integral element in the saga of the Trojan War. His story is briefly mentioned in the *Iliad* and the *Odyssey* and was narrated in full in two post-Homeric epics, *The Cypria* and *The Little Iliad*, neither of which has survived except in a brief summary and few quotations. The story also figured in numerous other lyric poems and dramas (again, not preserved) before Sophocles came to compose this play. Sophocles himself had composed a previous tragedy, *Philoctetes at Troy*, about which nothing is known apart from its title.

Philoctetes' fame depended on a bow that had previously belonged to Heracles. Heracles bequeathed the bow to him just before he died, in gratitude for making the final preparations for Heracles' immolation and apotheosis on Mount Oeta (an event intimated at the end of Sophocles' *Women of Trachis*). Philoctetes had enjoyed the use of this special bow for several years, and when the Trojan War broke out he took it with him when he joined the Greek forces sailing to Troy from Aulis.

But Philoctetes did not reach Troy with the expedition and was not there during the ten long years of the war. In the course of his journey, when the Greek ships stopped off at the small island of Chryse, Philoctetes was bitten in the foot by a snake, after he unintentionally stepped into a sacred grove. His foot became diseased and caused him such agony that his screams, along with the foul smell of the wound, became intolerable to his fellow soldiers as they continued toward Troy. So Agamemnon, Odysseus, and the other Greek leaders decided to cast him ashore on the island of Lemnos, with only his bow for obtaining food and protection. In most versions of the story, Lemnos was inhabited (as indeed it was in the classical period); but in Sophocles' play it is a desert island and Philoctetes is living in a solitary cave.

In the tenth year of the war, an oracle delivered by the Trojan seer Helenus informed the Greeks that they could not capture Troy without the help of Philoctetes and his bow. (The precise details of the oracle are hard to determine in Sophocles' play, and the characters themselves seem confused at times about it: did it say that Philoctetes himself must be present, or only the bow?) A delegation of Greek leaders, headed by Odysseus, was dispatched to collect Philoctetes and bring him to Troy. This is the point at which our play begins. All three of the great tragedians wrote plays titled *Philoctetes* on this theme, and we possess a lively and illuminating essay by the first-century CE critic and orator Dio Chrysostom comparing the three different treatments (*Oration 62*). Both Aeschylus' and Euripides' plays certainly preceded Sophocles'. (We are informed that Euripides' *Philoctetes* was performed along with *Medea* in 431 BCE.)

In all the versions before our play, Odysseus and Diomedes are the two Greek chieftains assigned to get Philoctetes (by persuasion, deceit, or force) to rejoin the Greeks at Troy and assist at its capture. The wily Odysseus was always a resourceful engineer of effective strategies on behalf of Agamemnon and the rest of the Greek leadership, so this aspect of the story seems to have been unalterable. And while the means by which Odysseus succeeded vary from one version to another, all affirm that Philoctetes did go on to Troy and won himself great glory by his actions there.

In our play, however, Sophocles introduces two major innovations into the story. First, by making the island of Lemnos uninhabited, he consigns his hero to ten years of complete solitude, and also brings it about that the chorus, rather than being Lemnian inhabitants sympathetic to the hero's situation (as in Aeschylus and Euripides), are instead Greek sailors who have no previous acquaintance with him at all. Consequently Philoctetes' feeling of isolation is all the greater. Secondly, Sophocles makes Odysseus' companion not Diomedes, but Neoptolemus (otherwise known as Pyrrhus), the mighty but still adolescent and naive son of Achilles, who has recently joined the Greek forces at Troy. (In all other versions, Neoptolemus, coming to Troy following the death of his father, spends only a few days there before the city is captured; so he is not there when Philoctetes is first brought to Troy.) Neoptolemus and Philoctetes are not previously acquainted, a fact of which Odysseus takes full advantage in concocting his plans.

The original Athenian audience would have been well aware that each of these three characters is key to the eventual capture of Troy: Odysseus is the mastermind behind the wooden horse; Neoptolemus is the most violent and irresistible of the warriors who will emerge from the horse and carry out the massacre of the Trojans; and Philoctetes with his talismanic bow represents the blessing of Heracles and of the gods in general for this eventual Greek victory. Everyone watching the play thus knows that by the end Philoctetes must go to Troy, where his wound will be healed and he will win eternal fame. But they would not know how this outcome could be brought about, given Philoctetes' hatred of the Greek leadership (especially Odysseus), and they would have watched with fascination and puzzlement as Neoptolemus grows to respect and sympathize more and more with the embittered hero, to the point of agreeing to take him not to Troy but back home instead, contrary to Odysseus' instructions.

The interaction of these three characters, each radically different in personality, background, and motivation, provides Sophocles with rich opportunities for dramatic shifts of tone and suspense. In particular, as in so many of his plays, he builds a striking series of contrasts between the intransigent, proudly single-minded nature of his main hero, Philoctetes—who absolutely refuses to forgive his personal enemies for mistreating him, preferring to let his own pain persist rather than be healed and win glory at Troy if this will at all benefit them—and Odysseus—ever pragmatic, cold-blooded, and willing to resort to any kind of subterfuge if it will advance the collective Greek war effort. The youthful and idealistic Neoptolemus is caught between them, seeking to remain true to his father's principles of honesty and plain dealing, yet burning with eagerness to win the glory at Troy that seems to be within his reach, and increasingly ambivalent about his duty to the rest of the Greek leaders, including Odysseus. The intense discussions, contrasts of moral principles, and shifting patterns of allegiance among the three main characters recall some of the ideological conflicts and argumentative strategies of the Athenian democracy, as described by authors such as Thucydides and Plato: what does it take, and what tactics are justified, to bring about success in war and power politics? The complete absence of any female characters contributes even more to making this a particularly "political" play, by ancient Athenian standards. In the end, after several intricate twists of plot and moments of personal indecision, the appearance of a "god from the machine"—the deified Heracles—brings about the necessary yet paradoxical conclusion. The play has a "happy ending," even if it is one that may leave many members of the audience feeling uncomfortable.

Transmission and Reception

After the play's initial success, it seems to have continued to be quite widely known and read, though we cannot tell how often it was performed in the centuries that followed. The Roman tragedian Accius (second century BCE) composed a successful *Philoctetes*, which survives only in fragments, so we cannot tell how closely it was modeled on Sophocles' version. Later, perhaps during the second century CE, when seven Sophoclean tragedies were selected for school use (we do not know by whom), *Philoctetes* was included; and so a few copies survived through late antiquity into the Byzantine era. There are a dozen or so manuscripts from the period 1000 to 1400 that contain this play.

During the Renaissance, and especially in the Romantic era, Sophocles' portrayal of this lonely hero, living the life almost of a wild animal, in tune with his natural surroundings but also wounded and diseased, angry and disgusted by the callous machinations of exploitative political operators, resonated strongly with poets and—especially—with painters and sculptors. There exist innumerable neoclassical representations of a seminude, wounded Philoctetes stretched out in agony in front of a wild, craggy landscape. William Blake drew *Philoctetes and Neoptolemus at Lemnos* (1812); Franz Schubert composed a song (1817; text by J. B. Mayrhofer); and William Wordsworth composed one of his early sonnets on this theme (1827), beginning, "When Philoctetes in the Lemnian Isle . . ."

Small-scale productions of Sophocles' play were fairly common at colleges all over Europe, but it never achieved the popularity of other works by the playwright, such as *Ajax*, *Antigone*, and *Electra*. Later in the nineteenth century, André Gide wrote a play, *Philoctète* (written during 1892–98) that was not performed in public until 1937, in Paris: in Gide's version, Philoctetes ends up choosing to remain on the island, alone, after giving his bow to Neoptolemus to take to Troy. More of a public impact was made by Heiner Müller's bold adaptation (performed first in Munich, Germany, in 1968), in which Neoptolemus ends up killing Philoctetes and only his corpse is taken to Troy by Odysseus, along with the bow. Around the same time, the Modern Greek poet Yannis Ritsos published his long poem *Philoctetes* (1963–65), in which many Sophoclean themes are explored further. More recently, Seamus Heaney's rather faithful adaptation of Sophocles' play, titled *The Cure at Troy* (1991), has been performed in many locations around the world, reestablishing *Philoctetes* as one of the world's great tragic masterpieces. Less musical and less full of action than many Greek tragedies, *Philoctetes* nonetheless engages its audience deeply in problems of ethics, politics, loyalty, and male ideals of virtue and achievement, as well as in the possibility of redemption, forgiveness, and healing miraculously granted after years of unmerited suffering.

PHILOCTETES

Characters   ODYSSEUS
                 NEOPTOLEMUS, son of Achilles
                 CHORUS of Neoptolemus' sailors
                 PHILOCTETES
                 A SAILOR, disguised as a Merchant
                 HERACLES

Scene: A lonely spot on the island of Lemnos, with the two entrances to a cave.

             (Enter Odysseus and Neoptolemus with a sailor from the side.)

ODYSSEUS
   This is it; this is Lemnos and its beach
   down to the surrounding sea; desolate, untrodden
   by humans. Here I marooned him long ago,
   the son of Poias, the Malian, his foot   5
   diseased and eaten away with running ulcers.
      Son of our greatest hero,
   son of Achilles, Neoptolemus,
   I did what I was ordered by the kings, our commanders.
   We had no peace with him: at the holy festivals,
   we dared not touch the wine and meat; he screamed
   and groaned so, and those terrible cries of his
   brought ill luck on our celebrations; all
   the camp was haunted by him.   10
   Now is no time to talk to you of this,
   now is no time for long speeches.

I am afraid that he may hear of my coming
and ruin all my plans to take him.
It is you who must help me with the rest. Look about   15
and see where there might be a cave with two mouths.
There are two niches to rest in, one in the sun
when it is cold, the other a tunneled passage
through which the breezes blow sleep in summertime.
To the left, a little, you may see a spring—   20
if it is still unchoked—go this way quietly,
see if he's there or somewhere else and signal.
Then I can tell you the rest. Listen:
I shall tell you. We will both do this thing.   25

NEOPTOLEMUS
What you speak of is near at hand, Odysseus.
I think I see such a cave.

ODYSSEUS
Above or below? I cannot see it myself.

NEOPTOLEMUS
Above here, and no sound of any feet.

ODYSSEUS
Look, in case he is housed within, asleep.   30

NEOPTOLEMUS
I see an empty dwelling, with no one there.

ODYSSEUS
And nothing to keep house with?

NEOPTOLEMUS
A pallet bed, stuffed with leaves, for someone's sleep.

ODYSSEUS
And nothing else? Nothing inside the house?

NEOPTOLEMUS
A cup, made of a single block, a poor   35
workman's contrivance. And some kindling, too.

ODYSSEUS

It is his treasure house that you describe.

NEOPTOLEMUS

And look, some rags are drying in the sun
full of the oozing matter from a sore.

ODYSSEUS

Yes, certainly he lives here, even now   40
he's somewhere not far off. He cannot go far,
sick as he is, lame cripple for so long.
It's likely he has gone to search for food
or somewhere that he knows there is an herb
to ease his pain. Send your man here to watch,   45
that he may not come upon me without warning.
For he would rather take me than all the other Greeks.

NEOPTOLEMUS

Very well, then, the path will be watched.

(Exit Sailor to the side.)

Go on with your story; tell me what you want.

ODYSSEUS

Son of Achilles,   50
our coming here has a purpose; to it be loyal
with more than just your body. If you should hear
some strange new thing, unlike what you have heard
before, still serve us; it was to serve you came here.

NEOPTOLEMUS

What would you have me do?

ODYSSEUS

                              Ensnare
the soul of Philoctetes with your words.   55
When he asks who you are and whence you came,
say you are Achilles' son; you need not lie.
Say you are sailing home, leaving the Greeks

and all their fleet, in bitter hatred. Say
that they had prayed you, urged you from your home,   60
and swore that only with your help
could Troy be taken. Yet when you came and asked,
as by your right, to have your father's arms,
Achilles' arms, they did not think you worthy
but gave them to Odysseus. Say what you will
against me; do not spare me anything.   65
Nothing of this will hurt me; if you will not
do this, you will bring sorrow on all the Greeks.
If this man's bow shall not be taken by us,
you cannot ever sack the land of Troy.

Perhaps you wonder why you can safely meet him,   70
why he would trust you and not me. Let me explain.
You have come here unforced, unpledged by oaths,
made no part of our earlier expedition.
The opposite is true in my own case;
at no point can I deny his charge.
If, when he sees me, Philoctetes   75
still has his bow, there is an end of me;
and you too, for your presence with me, would die.
For this you must sharpen your wits, to become a thief
of the arms no man has conquered.

I know, young man, it is not your natural bent
to say such things nor to contrive such mischief.   80
But the prize of victory is pleasant to win.
Bear up: another time we shall prove honest.
For one brief shameless portion of a day
give me yourself, and then for all the rest
you may be called most scrupulous of men.   85

NEOPTOLEMUS
    Son of Laertes, what I dislike to hear
    I hate to put in execution.
    I have a natural antipathy
    to get my ends by tricks and stratagems.

So, too, they say, my father was. I am quite ready
to fight and capture this man, bring him by force,   90
but not by treachery. Surely a one-legged man
cannot prevail against so many of us!
I recognize that I was sent with you
to follow your instructions. I am loath
to have you call me traitor. Still, my lord,
I would prefer even to fail with honor   95
than win by cheating.

ODYSSEUS
You are a good man's son.
I was young, too, once, and then I had a tongue
very inactive and a doing hand.
Now when I go out to face the test, I see
that everywhere among the race of mortals
it is the tongue that wins and not the deed.

NEOPTOLEMUS
What do you tell me to do, except tell lies?   100

ODYSSEUS
I'm telling you to use a trick to take Philoctetes.

NEOPTOLEMUS
And why must I use a trick, rather than persuasion?

ODYSSEUS
He will not be persuaded, and force will fail.

NEOPTOLEMUS
Has he such strength to give him confidence?

ODYSSEUS
The arrows none may avoid that carry death.   105

NEOPTOLEMUS
Then even to encounter him is not safe?

ODYSSEUS
Not if you do not take him by a trick, as I say.

NEOPTOLEMUS

Do you not find it shameful to tell lies?

ODYSSEUS

Not if the lying brings our rescue with it.

NEOPTOLEMUS

How can a man not blush to say such things?   110

ODYSSEUS

When one does something for gain, one need not blush.

NEOPTOLEMUS

What gain for me that he should come to Troy?

ODYSSEUS

Only his weapons are destined to take Troy.

NEOPTOLEMUS

Then *I* shall not be, as was said, its conqueror?

ODYSSEUS

Not you without them, nor they without you.   115

NEOPTOLEMUS

They must be my quarry then, if this is so.

ODYSSEUS

You will win a double prize if you do this.

NEOPTOLEMUS

What? If I know, I will do what you say.

ODYSSEUS

You'd be called both a wise man and a good one.

NEOPTOLEMUS

Well, then I will do it, casting aside all shame.   120

ODYSSEUS

You clearly recollect all I have told you?

NEOPTOLEMUS

Yes, now that I have consented to it.

ODYSSEUS

                         Stay
and wait his coming here; I will go
so he may not spy my presence.
I will dispatch the scout back to the ship;   125
and if you are too slow, I will send him back here again,
disguised as a sea captain; so Philoctetes
will never know him.
Whatever clever story he presents, then   130
go along with it and use it as you need.
Now I will go to the ship and leave you in charge.
May Hermes, god of tricks, the escort, for us
be guide indeed, and Victory and Athena,
city protector, who preserves me always.

          (*Exit Odysseus to the side. The Chorus enters from the other side.*)

CHORUS [*singing*]

                    STROPHE A
We are strangers, my lord, and this land is strange;   135
what shall we say and what conceal from this suspicious man?
Tell us.
For one man's artful skill outdoes another's,
and his judgment too, if there resides
in his sovereign keeping Zeus's holy scepter.   140
To you, young lord, all this has come,
all the power of your forefathers. So tell us now
what we must do to serve you.

NEOPTOLEMUS [*chanting*]
Now—if you wish to see where he rests   145
on his crag at the edge—look, be not afraid.
But when the terrible wanderer returns,
the one who lives in this place, then watch
my signals and take your cues from me.
Help when you can.

CHORUS [*singing*]
ANTISTROPHE A

This we have always done, my lord,   150
have kept a watchful eye over your safety.
But now
tell us what places he inhabits
and where he stays. It is important   155
for us to know this,
lest he attack us unawares.
Where does he live? Where does he rest?
What footpath does he follow? Is he at home or away?

NEOPTOLEMUS [*chanting*]
This, that you see, is his two-doored home,
where he sleeps on the rock.   160

CHORUS [*chanting*]
Where is he gone, unhappy creature?

NEOPTOLEMUS [*chanting*]
I am sure
he has gone to find food somewhere near here;
stumbling, lame, dragging along the path,
he is trying to shoot birds to prolong his miserable life.
This indeed, they say, is how he lives.   165
And no one comes near to cure him.

CHORUS [*singing*]
STROPHE B

Yes, for my part I pity him:
how unhappy, how utterly alone, always   170
he suffers the savagery of his illness
alone, with no one to care for him,
with no friendly face near him,
but bewildered and distraught at each need as it comes.   175
How does the poor man hold out?
Oh powers divine,° oh unhappy generations of mortals
whose lives suffer extremes!

This man is as well born perhaps as any,   180
second to no son of an ancient house.
Yet now his life lacks everything,
and he makes his bed all alone,
with spotted and shaggy beasts for neighbors—
piteous in his pain and hunger,   185
suffering with incurable wretchedness;
there is only a blabbering echo,
that comes from the distance in response
to his bitter crying.   190

NEOPTOLEMUS [*chanting*]
I am not surprised at any of this:
this is a god's doing, if I have any understanding.
These afflictions that have come upon him
are the work of Chryse, bitter of heart.
As for his present loneliness and suffering,   195
this, too, no doubt is part of some god's plan
that he may not bend against Troy
the divine invincible bow
until the time has come, at which, so it's said,
Troy must indeed be conquered by it.   200

CHORUS
Hush.

NEOPTOLEMUS
What is it?

CHORUS [*singing*]

STROPHE C
Hush! I hear a sound,
the sound of a man in pain.
Is it here? Is it there?°
I hear a voice, now I can hear it clearly,   205
the voice of a man, moving along the path,
hard put to it to walk. It's far away,

but I can hear it; I can hear the sound well,
the voice of a man wounded; it is quite clear now.
Come now, my son.   210

NEOPTOLEMUS
Tell me, what?

CHORUS

ANTISTROPHE C
Time for new plans. He is here, almost with us.
His is no cheerful marching to the pipe
like a shepherd with his flock.
No, a bitter cry.
He must have stumbled far down on the path,   215
and his moaning carried all the way here.
Or perhaps he saw the ship in the unfriendly harbor,°
for it was a bitter cry.

(Enter Philoctetes, from the side.)

PHILOCTETES
Strangers, who are you that have put in, rowing   220
to a shore without houses or anchorage?
What countrymen may I call you? Who are your people?
Greeks you seem in clothing—dear to me.
May I hear your voice? Do not be afraid   225
or shrink from such as I am, grown a savage.
I have been alone and very wretched,
without friend or comrade, suffering a great deal.
Take pity on me; speak to me, if indeed
you come as friends.
Please—answer me.   230
It is not right for me not to get this from you,
or you from me.

NEOPTOLEMUS
Stranger, for your questions, since you wish to know,
know we are Greeks.

PHILOCTETES

                  Friendliest of tongues!
That I should hear it spoken once again   235
by such a man after long years! My boy,
who are you? Why have you come here? What has brought
    you?
What impulse? What friendliest of winds?
Tell me all this, that I may know who you are.

NEOPTOLEMUS

By birth, I'm from Scyrus that the sea surrounds;
I am sailing home. My name is Neoptolemus,   240
Achilles' son. Now you know everything.

PHILOCTETES

Son of a father that I loved so dearly
and of a land I loved, you that were reared
by that old man Lycomedes, what kind of venture
can have brought you to port here? Where did you sail from?

NEOPTOLEMUS

At present I am bound from Troy.   245

PHILOCTETES

                  From Troy?
But you did not sail with us to Troy at first.

NEOPTOLEMUS

You, then, are one that also had a share
in all that trouble?

PHILOCTETES

             Is it possible
you do not know me, boy, me whom you see here?

NEOPTOLEMUS

I never saw you before. How could I know you?   250

PHILOCTETES

You never heard my name then? Never a rumor
of all my terrible sufferings, even to death?

NEOPTOLEMUS
    I never knew a word of what you ask me.

PHILOCTETES
    Surely I must be wretched, and hated by gods   255
    that never a word of me, of how I live here,
    should have reached home or anywhere in Greece.
    Yet those who cast me away so impiously
    keep quiet about it and laugh, while my disease
    always increases and grows worse. My boy,
    you are Achilles' son. I that stand here   260
    am one you may have heard of, as the master
    of Heracles' arms. I am Philoctetes
    the son of Poias. Those two generals
    and Odysseus king of the Cephallenians   265
    cast me ashore here to their shame, alone,
    wasting with my sickness caused by the murderous bite
    of a viper mortally dangerous.
    Alone with this disease they left me here
    when our fleet put in on its way from the isle of Chryse.   270
    They were happy when they saw that I had fallen asleep
    on the shore in a rocky cave, after a rough passage.
    They went away and left me with some rags—
    as if for a beggar—and a handful of food.   275
    May the gods give them the like!
    Think, boy, of that awakening when I awoke
    and found them gone; think of the useless tears
    and groans for my condition, when I saw the ships—
    which I had once commanded—gone, and not
    a single man left there on the island,   280
    no one to help me or to lend a hand
    when I was seized with my sickness. I looked around:
    in all I saw before me nothing but pain;
    but of that a great abundance, boy.

    Time came and went for me. In my tiny shelter   285
    I must alone do everything for myself.

To meet my belly's needs, this bow of mine
shot pigeons as they flew by; then I must drag
my cursed foot, to where the feathered bolt
sped by the bow's thong had struck down a bird.   290
If I must drink, and it was wintertime—
the water was frozen—I must break up firewood.
Again I crawled and miserably contrived
to do the work. Whenever I had no fire,   295
rubbing stone on stone I would at last produce
the spark that kept me still in life.
A roof for shelter, provided I have fire,
gives me everything but release from pain.

Boy, let me tell you of this island.   300
No sailor by his choice comes near it.
There is no anchorage, nor anywhere
that one can land, sell goods, be entertained.
Sensible men make no voyages here.
Yet now and then someone arrives—not on purpose,   305
but time as long as this allows much to happen.
When they have come here, boy, they pity me—
at least they say they do—and in their pity
they have given me scraps of food and cast-off clothes;
but that other thing, when I dare mention it,   310
none of them will—to bring me home again.

It is nine years now that I have spent dying,
with hunger and pain feeding my insatiable
disease. That, boy, is what they have done to me,
the two Atridae, and mighty Odysseus.
May the gods that live on Olympus grant   315
that they pay for this, agony for my agony.

CHORUS LEADER
    In this, I too resemble your other visitors.
    I pity you, son of Poias.

NEOPTOLEMUS
                    I am a witness,
I also, of the truth of what you say.   320
I know it is true. I have dealt with those villains,
the two Atridae and the lord Odysseus.

PHILOCTETES
Have you, as well as I, then suffered wrong
from the cursed Atridae, so as to be angry at them?

NEOPTOLEMUS
Give me the chance to gratify my anger
with my hand some day!
Then will Mycenae and Sparta come to know   325
that Scyrus too is mother to valiant men.

PHILOCTETES
                    Well said, boy!
You come to me with a great hate against them.
Because of what?

NEOPTOLEMUS
                    I will tell you, Philoctetes—
for all that it hurts to tell it—
of how I came to Troy and what dishonor   330
they put upon me.
            When fatefully Achilles came to die . . .

PHILOCTETES
O stop! tell me no more. Let me understand
this first. Is he dead, the son of Peleus, dead?

NEOPTOLEMUS
Yes, he is dead; no man his conqueror
but shot by a god, they say, Phoebus the archer.   335

PHILOCTETES
Noble was he that killed and he that died.
Boy, I am at a loss which to do first,
ask for your story or to mourn for him.

NEOPTOLEMUS

    I would think that your own sufferings were quite enough,
    poor man, without mourning for those of others.   340

PHILOCTETES

    Yes, that is true. So again, tell me your story
    of how they have insulted you.

NEOPTOLEMUS

                    They came
    for me, did great Odysseus and the man
    that was my father's tutor, with a ship
    wonderfully decked with ribbons. They had a story—
    be it truth or lie—that it was divine decree   345
    that no one else, since he, my father, was dead,
    but I and I alone should take the towers of Troy.
        This was their story. And sir, it didn't take long
    for me quickly to embark with them.
    Chiefly, you know, I was prompted by my yearning   350
    for the dead man. I had hope of seeing him
    while still unburied. Alive I never had.
    And in addition, it was a splendid notion
    that I could go and capture the city of Troy.
    We had a favoring wind; on the second day   355
    we touched Sigeum. As I disembarked,
    all of the soldiers swarmed around me, blessed me,
    swore that they saw Achilles alive again,
    now gone from them forever. But he still lay
    unburied. I, his ill-fated son, wept for him;   360
    then, in a while, I came to the two Atridae,
    my friends,° as it seemed right to do, and asked them
    for my father's weapons and the other things of his.
    They needed brazen faces for their answer:
    "Son of Achilles, all that your father had,   365
    all else, is yours to take, but not his weapons.
    Another man now owns them, Laertes' son."
    I burst into tears, jumped up, enraged,

cried out in my pain, "You scoundrels, did you dare
to give those arms that were mine to someone else   370
before I knew of it?" Then Odysseus
spoke—he was standing near me—"Yes, and rightly,"
he said, "they gave them, boy. For it was I
who rescued them and him, their former owner."
My anger got the better of me; I cursed him outright
with every insult that I knew, sparing nothing,   375
if he should take my arms away from me.
And he, a man not usually given to quarreling,
was stung by what I said. He answered me:
"You were not where we were. You were at home,
out of the reach of duty. And since, besides,
you have so bold a tongue in your head, never   380
will you possess these arms to bring back home to Scyrus."
There it was. Abused, insulted, I lost
what should be mine and so sailed home. Odysseus,
that filthy son of filthy parents, robbed me.
Yet I do not blame him so much as the commanders.°   385
All of a city is in the hands of its leaders,
and likewise an army; those men who lack discipline
become bad through the instruction of their superiors.
This is the whole tale. May he that hates the Atridae
be as dear in the gods' sight as he is in mine.   390

CHORUS [singing]

STROPHE

Earth, Mountain Mother, sustainer of all,
mother of Zeus himself,
you who dwell by the great golden Pactolus,
then too, I called on you, revered Mother,   395
when all the insolence of the Atridae assaulted our lord,
O blessed one,
who rides the bull-killing lions,
when they gave his father's weapons, that wonder of the world,   400
to the son of Laertes.

PHILOCTETES [*speaking*]
You have sailed here, as it seems, with a clear tally;
your half of pain matches that of myself.
What you tell me rings in harmony. I recognize   405
the doings of the Atridae and Odysseus.
I know Odysseus would employ his tongue
on every ill tale, every rascality,
that could be brought to issue in injustice.
This is not at all my wonder, but that great Ajax   410
should stand by, see and allow it to happen.

NEOPTOLEMUS
He is no longer living, sir; never, indeed,
if he were, would they have robbed me of the weapons.

PHILOCTETES
What! Is he, too, dead and gone?

NEOPTOLEMUS
Yes, dead and gone. As such now think of him.   415

PHILOCTETES
But not the son of Tydeus nor Odysseus
whom Sisyphus once sold to Laertes!
They will not die; for they should not be living.

NEOPTOLEMUS
Of course, they are not dead; you may be sure
that they are in their glory among the Greeks.   420

PHILOCTETES
What of an old and honest man, my friend,
Nestor of Pylos? Is he alive? He might
have checked their mischief by his wise advice.

NEOPTOLEMUS
Things have gone badly for him. He has lost
his son Antilochus, who once stood by him.   425

PHILOCTETES

Ah!
You have told me the two deaths that most could hurt.
Alas, what should I look for
when Ajax and Antilochus are dead,
and still Odysseus lives, that in their place
ought to be counted among the dead?   430

NEOPTOLEMUS

He's a cunning wrestler; still, Philoctetes,
even the cunning are sometimes tripped up.

PHILOCTETES

Tell me, by the gods, where was Patroclus,
who was your father's dearest friend?

NEOPTOLEMUS

                              Dead, too.
In one short sentence I can tell you this.   435
War never takes a bad man except by chance,
it's always the good men.

PHILOCTETES

                    You have said the truth.
So I will ask you of one quite unworthy
but dexterous and clever with his tongue.   440

NEOPTOLEMUS

Whom can you mean except Odysseus?

PHILOCTETES

It is not he: there was a man, Thersites,
who never was content to speak just once,
though no one was for letting him speak at all.
Do you know if he is still alive?

NEOPTOLEMUS

                    I did not see him,
but I have heard that he is still alive.   445

PHILOCTETES

He would be; nothing evil ever perishes.
The gods somehow give them most excellent care.
They find their pleasure in turning back from Hades
the villains and tricksters, but the just and good
they are always sending out of the world.   450
How can I reckon the score, how can I praise,
when in praising gods' actions° I find these gods are bad?

NEOPTOLEMUS

For my own part, Philoctetes of Oeta,
from now on I shall take precautions.
I shall look at Troy and the Atridae both   455
from very far off. I shall never abide
the company of those where the worse man
has more power than the better, where the good
are always depleted and instead cowards rule.
For the future, rocky Scyrus will content me
to take my pleasure at home.   460
Now I will be going to my ship. Philoctetes,
good-bye, and best wishes. May the gods
relieve you of your sickness, as you would have it!
Let us go, men, that when god grants us sailing
we may be ready to sail.   465

PHILOCTETES

                    Boy, are you going,
already?

NEOPTOLEMUS

                    Yes, we must not miss our chance
to sail; we must be ready, not far afield.

PHILOCTETES

My son—I beg you in your father's name,
and in your mother's, in the name of all
that you have loved at home, do not leave me here   470
alone, living in sufferings you have seen

and others you have heard about from me.
I am not your main concern; but give me some passing
   thought.
I know that there is horrible discomfort
in having me on board. But put up with it.
To noble people, as you know, all meanness
is detested, while generosity brings glory. 475
If you leave me here, it is an ugly reproach;
but if you take me, much glory will be your reward,
if I shall live to see the land of Oeta.
Come! One day, hardly one whole day's space 480
that I shall trouble you. Endure this much.
Take me and put me where you will,
in the bilges, in the prow or stern, anywhere
where I shall least offend those that I sail with.
By Zeus himself, god of suppliants,
I beg you, boy, say "Yes," say you will do it! 485
Here I am on my knees to you, helpless,
a poor, lame man. Do not cast me away
so utterly alone, where no one ever walks by.
Either take me and set me safe in your own home,
or take me to Chalcodon's house in Euboea.
From there it will be no great journey for me 490
to Oeta and the ridge of Trachis and
the quick-flowing Spercheius,
so you can show me to my loving father.
For many a day I have feared that he is dead;
I sent messages with those who came to my island, 495
many of them, begging him to come
and bring me home himself. Either he's dead,
or, as I rather think, those messengers
made little of what I asked them, and just hurried home.
Now in you I have found both escort and messenger; 500
bring me safe home. Take pity on me.
Look how men live, always precariously
balanced between good and bad fortune.

If you are out of trouble, watch for danger.
And when you live well, then be most on guard   505
for your life, lest ruin take it unawares.

CHORUS [*singing*]

ANTISTROPHE

Have pity on him, my lord.
He has told us of a most desperate ordeal;
may such things never overtake friends of mine.
And, lord, if you hate the heartless Atridae,   510
I would set their ill treatment of him
to his gain and would carry him   515
in your quick, well-fitted ship
to his home and so avoid offense before the gods.

NEOPTOLEMUS

Take care that your assent is not too ready,
and that, when you have enough of his diseased company,   520
you're no longer consistent with what you've said just now.

CHORUS LEADER

No. You'll never be able to reproach me about this with
    justice.

NEOPTOLEMUS

I should be ashamed
to be less ready than you to render a stranger service.   525
Well, if you will then, let us sail. Let him
get ready quickly. My ship will carry him.
May the gods give us a safe clearance from this land
and a safe journey where we choose to go.

PHILOCTETES

God bless this day!   530
Man, dear to my very heart,
and you, dear sailors, how shall I prove to you
how you have bound me to your friendship!
Let us go, boy. But let us first kiss the earth,

reverently, in my homeless home of a cave.
I would have you know what I have lived from,   535
how tough the spirit that did not break. I think
the sight itself would have been too much for anyone
except myself. Necessity has taught me,
little by little, to suffer and be patient.

CHORUS LEADER

Wait! Let us see. Two men are coming.
One of them is of our crew, the other a foreigner.   540
Let us hear from them and then go in.

(Enter the Sailor from the side, disguised as a
Merchant, along with another sailor.)

MERCHANT

Son of Achilles, I told my companion here—
he with two others was guarding your ship—
to tell me where you were. I just happened on them;   545
I had no intentions this way. Just by accident
I came to anchor at this island.
I am sailing in command of a ship outward-bound
from Ilium, with no great company, for Peparethus—
a good country, that, for wine. When I heard
that all those sailors were the crew of your ship,   550
I thought I should not hold my tongue and sail on
until I spoke with you—and got my fair reward.
I guess you know nothing about your own affairs
and the Greeks' new plans for you—indeed, not just plans,   555
but actions in train already and not slowly.

NEOPTOLEMUS

Thank you for your consideration, sir.
I will remain obliged to your kindness
unless I prove unworthy. Please tell me
what you have spoken of. I would like to know
what are these new plans of the Greeks.   560

MERCHANT
　Old Phoenix and the two sons of Theseus are gone,
　pursuing you with a squadron.

NEOPTOLEMUS
　　　　　　　　　　Do they intend
　to bring me back with violence or persuade me?

MERCHANT
　I do not know. I tell you what I heard.

NEOPTOLEMUS
　Are Phoenix and his companions so eager　　　　　　　565
　to do this as a favor to the two Atridae?

MERCHANT
　It is being done.
　There is no delay about it. That you should know.

NEOPTOLEMUS
　How is it that Odysseus was not ready
　to sail as his own messenger on such
　an errand? It cannot be he was afraid?

MERCHANT
　When I weighed anchor, he and Tydeus' son　　　　　　570
　were setting off in pursuit of another man.

NEOPTOLEMUS
　Who was this other man that Odysseus himself should seek
　　him?

MERCHANT
　There was a man—perhaps you will tell me first
　who this is; and say softly what you say.

NEOPTOLEMUS
　This, sir, is the famous Philoctetes.　　　　　　　　　575

MERCHANT

                    Do not
ask me any further questions. Get yourself out,
as quickly as you can, out of this island.

PHILOCTETES

What does he say, boy? Why in dark whispers
does he bargain with you about me, this sailor?

NEOPTOLEMUS

I do not know yet what he says, but he must say it,   580
openly, whatever it is, to you and me and these.

MERCHANT

Son of Achilles, do not slander me
to the army for speaking about things I shouldn't.
There's many a thing I do for them and in return
get something from them, as a poor man may.

NEOPTOLEMUS

I am the enemy of the Atridae; and this man   585
is my greatest friend because he hates them too.
You have come to me as a friend, and so you must
hide from us nothing that you heard.

MERCHANT

Well, watch what you are doing, sir.

NEOPTOLEMUS

                    I have been careful
all along.

MERCHANT

        I shall put the whole responsibility
squarely upon you.   590

NEOPTOLEMUS

                    Do so; but speak.

MERCHANT

Well, then. The two I have spoken of,

the son of Tydeus and the mighty Odysseus,
are in pursuit of this man here.
They have sworn by the gods to bring him back with them
either by persuasion or by brute force.
And this all the Greeks heard clearly announced   595
by lord Odysseus; for he was much more confident
of success than was the other.

NEOPTOLEMUS

                What can have made
the Atridae care about him after so long—
one whom they, years and years since, cast away?   600
What yearning for him came over them? Was it the gods
who punish evil doings that now have driven them
to retribution for injustice?

MERCHANT

I will explain all that. Perhaps you haven't heard.
There was a prophet of very good family,
a son of Priam indeed, called Helenus.   605
He was captured one night in an expedition
undertaken single-handed by Odysseus,
of whom all base and shameful things are spoken,
captured by stratagem. Odysseus brought
his prisoner before the Greeks, a splendid prize.
Helenus prophesied everything to them   610
and, in particular, concerning the fortress of Troy,
that they could never take it till they persuaded
Philoctetes to come with them and leave his island.
As soon as Odysseus heard the prophet say this,   615
he promised at once to bring the man before them,
for all to see—he thought, as a willing prisoner,
but, if not that, against his will. And if he failed,
"any of them might have his head," he declared. My boy,
that is the whole story; that is why I urge you   620
and him and any that you care for to make haste.

PHILOCTETES

Ah!

Did he indeed swear that he would persuade me
to rejoin the Achaeans, did he so, that utter devil?
As soon shall I be persuaded, when I am dead,
to rise from Hades' house and come to the light again,   625
as his own father did.

MERCHANT

I do not know about that. Well, I will be going now
to my ship. May god prosper you both!

(Exit Merchant to the side with the other sailor.)

PHILOCTETES

Is it not shocking, boy, that the son of Laertes
should think that there are words soft enough to win me,
to let him put me in his boat, exhibit me
in front of all the Greeks?   630
No! I would rather listen to my worst enemy,
the snake that bit me, made me thus lame and useless.
But he will say anything; he will dare anything;
and now I know that he will come here.
Boy, let us go, that a great expanse of sea   635
may separate us from Odysseus' ship.
Let us go. For you know, swift action in due season
brings rest and peace when once the work is done.

NEOPTOLEMUS

When the wind at our prow falls, we can sail, no sooner.
Now it is dead against us.   640

PHILOCTETES

It is always fair sailing, when you're escaping evil.

NEOPTOLEMUS

Yes, but the wind is against them, too.

PHILOCTETES

                                        For pirates
when they can thieve and plunder, no wind is contrary.

NEOPTOLEMUS

If you will, then, let us go. Take from your cave   645
what you need most and love most.

PHILOCTETES

There are some things I need, but no great choice.

NEOPTOLEMUS

What is there that you will not find on board?

PHILOCTETES

An herb I have, the chief means to soothe my wound,
to lull the pain to sleep.   650

NEOPTOLEMUS

                    Bring it out then.
What else is there that you would have?

PHILOCTETES

                    Any arrow
I may have dropped and missed. For none of them
must I leave for anyone else to pick up.

NEOPTOLEMUS

Is this, in your hands, the famous bow?

PHILOCTETES

                    Yes, this,   655
this in my hands.

NEOPTOLEMUS

                    May I see it closer,
touch and kiss it like a god?

PHILOCTETES

                         For you, this will be granted,
and anything else of mine that is for your good.

NEOPTOLEMUS

I long for it, yet only with such longing   660
that if it is allowed, I may have it, else let it be.

PHILOCTETES

    Your words are holy, boy. It is allowed,
for you have given me the sunlight,
the sight of the sun shining above us here,
a hope to see my Oeta, my old father, my friends.   665
You have raised me up above my enemies,
when I was under their feet. You may be assured:
you may indeed touch my bow, then give it back
to me that gave it you—and proclaim that alone
of all the world you touched it, in return
for the good deed you did. It was for that,
for friendly help, I myself won it first.   670

NEOPTOLEMUS

I am glad to see you and take you as a friend.
For one who knows how to show and to accept kindness
will be a friend better than any possession.
Go in.

PHILOCTETES

    I will bring you with me. The sickness in me
needs to have you beside me.   675

(Neoptolemus and Philoctetes enter the cave together.)

CHORUS [*singing*]

STROPHE A

In story I have heard, but my eyes have not seen
him that once came near to Zeus's marriage bed:
I have heard how Zeus, son of Cronus, invincible,
caught him, bound him on a turning wheel.
But I know of no other,   680
whether by hearsay or by sight, of all mankind
who ever met with a destiny more hateful
than Philoctetes', who wronged no one, nor killed,
but lived, a just man among the just,
yet fell into misery quite undeservedly.   685
There is wonder, indeed, in my heart

how, how in his loneliness,
listening to the waves beating on the shore,
how he kept hold at all
on a life so full of tears.   690

He was lame, and no one came near him.
He suffered, and there were no neighbors for his sorrow
with whom his cries would find answer,
with whom he could lament the bloody plague
that ate him up.   695
No one who would gather
fallen leaves from the ground
to quiet the raging, bleeding sore,
running, in his maggot-rotten foot.   700
Here and there he crawled
writhing always—
suffering like a child
without the nurse he loves—
to whatever source of ease he could find   705
when the heart-devouring suffering relented.

No grain sown in holy earth was his, nor other food
of all enjoyed by us, men who live by labor,
save when with the feathered arrows shot by the quick bow   710
he got himself food for his belly.
Ah, poor soul,
that never in ten years' length
enjoyed a drink of wine   715
but looked always for standing pools of water
and tried to approach them.

But now he will end fortunate. He has fallen in
with the son of good men. He will be great, after it all.   720
Our prince in his seagoing craft will carry him
after the fullness of many months, to his father's home

in the country of the Malian nymphs,   725
by the banks of the Spercheius,
where the hero of the bronze shield ascended
to all the gods, ablaze in holy fire
above the ridges of Oeta.

(*Neoptolemus and Philoctetes reenter from the cave.*)

NEOPTOLEMUS

Come if you will, then. Why have you nothing to say?   730
Why do you stand like that, in silence transfixed?

PHILOCTETES

Oh! Oh!

NEOPTOLEMUS

What is it?

PHILOCTETES

Nothing to be afraid of. Come on, boy.

NEOPTOLEMUS

Is it the pain of your inveterate sickness?

PHILOCTETES

No, no, indeed not. Just now I think I feel better.   735
O gods!

NEOPTOLEMUS

Why do you call on the gods with cries of distress?

PHILOCTETES

That they may come as healers, come with gentleness.
Oh! Oh! Oh!

NEOPTOLEMUS

What ails you? Tell me; do not keep silence.   740
You are clearly in some pain.

PHILOCTETES

I am lost, boy.
I will not be able to hide it from you longer.

Oh! Oh!
It goes through me, right through me!
Miserable, miserable!
I am lost, boy. I am being eaten up. Ah!   745
By the gods, if you have a sword, ready to hand, use it!
Strike the end of my foot. Cut it off, I tell you, now.
Do not spare my life. Quick, boy, quick.   750

NEOPTOLEMUS
What is this thing that comes upon you suddenly,
that makes you cry and shriek so?

PHILOCTETES
                    You know, my son!

NEOPTOLEMUS
What is it?

PHILOCTETES
                    You know, boy, surely!

NEOPTOLEMUS
                    What do you mean?
I do not know.

PHILOCTETES
                    You surely know. Oh! Oh!

NEOPTOLEMUS
The terrible burden of your sickness.   755

PHILOCTETES
Terrible it is, beyond words' reach. But pity me.

NEOPTOLEMUS
What shall I do?

PHILOCTETES
                    Do not be afraid and leave me.
It always comes back after a while, I suppose when it's had
its fill of wandering in other places—my affliction.

NEOPTOLEMUS

You most unhappy man,
you that have endured all agonies, lived through them,   760
shall I take hold of you? Shall I touch you?

PHILOCTETES

No, not that, please! But take this bow,
as you asked to do just now, until the pain
of my sickness now upon me has grown less.   765
Keep the bow, guard it safely. Sleep comes upon me
when this affliction departs. There is no relief until then.
But you must let me sleep quietly;
and if they should come in the time when I'm asleep,
by the gods I beg you do not give up my bow   770
willingly or unwillingly to anyone;
and let no one trick you out of it, lest you prove
a murderer—your own and mine, who supplicate you.

NEOPTOLEMUS

I shall take care; be easy about that. It shall not pass
except to your hands and to mine. Give it to me now,
and may good luck go with it!   775

PHILOCTETES

                          Here,
take it, boy. Make a prayer to the gods' envy
that the bow may not be to you a sorrow,
as it was to me and to its former master.

NEOPTOLEMUS

You gods, grant us this; and grant us too
a journey speedy with a prosperous wind   780
to where god sends us and our voyage holds.

PHILOCTETES

Ah! Ah!
An empty prayer, I am afraid, boy:
the blood is trickling, dripping murderously

from its deep spring. I look for something new.
It is coming now, coming. 785
Ah!
You know my condition. Do not leave me now.
Ah!
O man of Cephallenia, if only it were you,
whose chest these pains transfix right through.
Ah! 790
        O Agamemnon and Menelaus, you two generals,
if only it were your two bodies that had fed 795
this sickness for as long as mine has. Ah!

Death, death, how is it that I can call on you,
always, day in, day out, and you cannot come to me?
Boy, my good boy, take up this body of mine
and burn it on what they call the Lemnian fire. 800
I had the resolution once to do this for another,
the son of Zeus, and so obtained the arms
that you now hold. What do you say?
What do you say? Nothing? Where are you, boy? 805

NEOPTOLEMUS
I have been in pain for you; I have long been
in sorrow for your pain.

PHILOCTETES
No, boy, keep up your heart. It is quick in coming
and quick to go. Only I entreat you, do not
leave me alone.

NEOPTOLEMUS
Do not be afraid. We shall stay. 810

PHILOCTETES
You will?

NEOPTOLEMUS
You may be sure of it.

PHILOCTETES
Your oath,
I do not think I need to put you to your oath.

NEOPTOLEMUS
No, it wouldn't be right for me go without you.

PHILOCTETES
Give me your hand upon it.

NEOPTOLEMUS
Here I give it you,
to remain.

PHILOCTETES
Now—take me away from here—

NEOPTOLEMUS
What do you mean?

PHILOCTETES
Up, up.

NEOPTOLEMUS
What madness is upon you? Why do you look   815
to the sky above us?

PHILOCTETES
Let me go, let me go.

NEOPTOLEMUS
Where?

PHILOCTETES
Oh, let me go.

NEOPTOLEMUS
Not I.

PHILOCTETES
You will kill me if you touch me.

NEOPTOLEMUS

Now I shall let you go, now you are calmer.

PHILOCTETES

Earth, take my body, dying as I am.
The pain no longer lets me stand.   820

NEOPTOLEMUS

In a little while, I think,
sleep will come on this man. His head is nodding.
The sweat is soaking all his body over,
and a black flux of blood and matter has broken
out of his foot. Let us leave him quiet, friends,   825
until he falls asleep.

CHORUS [singing]

STROPHE

Sleep that knows not pain nor suffering
kindly, lord, for us,
kindly, kindly come.
Spread your enveloping radiance,   830
as now, over his eyes.
Come, come, Lord Healer.
Boy, look to where you stand,
and where you are going; look to your plans
for the future. Do you see? He sleeps.
What is it we are waiting to do?   835
The critical moment that holds decision over all things
wins many a victory suddenly.

NEOPTOLEMUS [singing]

Yes, it is true he hears nothing, but I see we have hunted in vain,
vainly have captured our quarry the bow, if we sail without him.   840
His is the crown of victory, him the god said we must bring.
Shame shall be ours if we boast and our lies still leave victory
    unwon.

CHORUS

Boy, to all of this the god shall look.
Answer me gently;
low, low, whisper, whisper, boy.   845
The sleep of a sick man has keen eyes.
It is a sleep unsleeping.
But to the limits of what you can,
look to this, look to this secretly,   850
how you may do it.
You know of whom I speak.
If your mind holds the same purpose touching this man,
the wise can see trouble and no way to cure it.°

EPODE

It is a fair wind, boy, a fair wind: 855
the man is eyeless and helpless,
outstretched under night's blanket—
asleep in the sun is good—
neither of foot nor of hand nor of anything is he master,   860
but is even as one that lies in Death's house.
Look to it, look if what you say
fits the moment. As far as my mind,
boy, can grasp it, best is the trouble taken
that causes the least fear.

NEOPTOLEMUS [*speaking*]

Quiet, I tell you! Are you mad? He is stirring,   865
his eyes are opening; he is raising his head.

PHILOCTETES

Blessed the light that comes after my sleep,
blessed the watching of friends.
I never would have hoped this, my boy,
that you would have the pity of heart to support   870
my afflictions, that you should stand by me and help.
The Atridae, those brave generals, were not so,

they could not so easily put up with me.
You have a noble nature, Neoptolemus,
and noble were your parents. You have made light 875
of all of this—the offense of my cries and the stench.
And now, since it would seem my sickness
can forget me for a while and rest, raise me yourself,
raise me up, boy, and set me on my feet,
so that when my weariness releases me,
we can go to the ship and sail without delay. 880

NEOPTOLEMUS

I am glad to see you unexpectedly,
eyes open, free of pain, still with the breath of life.
In watching you suffer so, all the signs pointed
to your being no more. Now, lift yourself up. 885
If you would rather, these men will lift you. They
will spare no trouble, since you and I are agreed.

PHILOCTETES

Thanks, boy. Lift me yourself, as you thought of it.
Do not trouble them, let them not be disquieted 890
before they need by the foul smell of me; living
on board with me will try their patience enough.

NEOPTOLEMUS

Very well, then; stand up; take hold of me yourself.

PHILOCTETES

Do not be afraid; old habit will help me up.

NEOPTOLEMUS

Ah! What shall I do from now on? 895

PHILOCTETES

What is it, boy? Where are your words straying?

NEOPTOLEMUS

I do not know what to say. I am at a loss.

PHILOCTETES

Why are you at a loss? Do not say so, boy.

NEOPTOLEMUS

But this is where I've come to in this ordeal.

PHILOCTETES

Is it disgust at my sickness? Is it this   900
that makes you shrink from taking me?

NEOPTOLEMUS

All is disgust when someone leaves his own nature
and does things that are unlike him.

PHILOCTETES

But it is not unlike your father, either in word
or in act, to help a good man.   905

NEOPTOLEMUS

I shall be seen to be dishonorable:
that's what has been causing me pain.

PHILOCTETES

Not in your present actions. But your words make me
    hesitate.

NEOPTOLEMUS

Zeus, what must I do? Twice be proved rotten,
hiding what I shouldn't, saying what is most foul?

PHILOCTETES

Unless I am wrong, here is a man who will   910
betray me, leave me—so it seems—and sail away.

NEOPTOLEMUS

Not I; I will not leave you. But to your bitterness,
I might send you on a journey—and that's what I'm
    pained by.

PHILOCTETES

What are you saying, boy? I do not understand.

NEOPTOLEMUS

I will not hide anything. You must sail to Troy   915
to the Achaeans, join the army of the Atridae.

PHILOCTETES

What! What can you mean?

NEOPTOLEMUS

                        Do not cry yet
until you learn.

PHILOCTETES

Learn what? What would you do with me?

NEOPTOLEMUS

First save you from this torture, then with you
together go and lay waste the land of Troy.   920

PHILOCTETES

                        You would?
This is, in truth, what you intend?

NEOPTOLEMUS

                        Necessity,
a great necessity compels it. Do not be angry.

PHILOCTETES

Then I am lost. I am betrayed. Why, stranger,
have you done this to me? Give me back my bow.

NEOPTOLEMUS

That I cannot. Justice and interest   925
make me obedient to those in authority.

PHILOCTETES

You fire, you every horror, most hateful engine
of ruthless mischief, what have you done to me,
what treachery! Have you no shame to see me
that kneeled to you, entreated you, hard of heart?   930
You robbed me of my life, taking my bow.

Give it back, I beg you, give it back, I pray, my boy!
By your father's gods, do not take my life.

He does not say a word,
but turns away his eyes. He will not give it up.   935

Harbors and headlands, dens of wild creatures,
you jutting broken crags, to you I raise my cry—
there is no one else that I can speak to—
and you have always been there, have always heard me:
let me tell you what he has done to me, this boy,   940
Achilles' son. He swore to bring me home;
he brings me to Troy. He gave me his right hand,
then took and keeps my sacred bow,
the bow of Heracles, the son of Zeus,
and means to show me off to the Argives,
as though in me he had conquered a strong man
by force.   945
He does not know he is killing one that is dead,
a kind of vaporous shadow, a mere wraith.
Had I had my strength, he would not have conquered me,
for, even as I am, it was trickery that did it.
I have been deceived and am lost.
What can I do?
Give it back. Be your true self again. Will you not?   950
No word. Then I am nothing.

Two doors cut in the rock, to you again,
I come, but now unarmed, and all without
the means to feed myself! Here in this hovel
I shall shrivel to death alone. I shall kill no more
the winged bird nor wild thing of the hills   955
with that bow of mine. I shall myself in death
be a feast for those that fed me. Those that I hunted
shall be my hunters now.
Life for the life I took, I shall repay
at the hands of this man that seemed to know no harm.   960

My curse upon your life!—but not yet still
until I know if you will change again;
if you will not, may an evil death be yours!

CHORUS LEADER

What shall we do? Shall we sail? Shall we do as he asks?
Prince, it is you must decide.

NEOPTOLEMUS

A kind of compassion,   965
a terrible compassion, has come upon me
for him. I've been feeling it long since, more and more.

PHILOCTETES

Pity me, boy, by the gods; do not bring on yourself
men's blame for your crafty victory over me.

NEOPTOLEMUS

What shall I do? I wish I had never left
Scyrus, so hateful is what I face now.   970

PHILOCTETES

You are not bad yourself; by bad men's teaching
you came to practice your foul lesson. Now leave it to others
such as it suits, and sail away. Give me my weapons.

NEOPTOLEMUS

What shall we do, men?

(Enter Odysseus from the side.)

ODYSSEUS

You fool, what are you doing?
Hand that bow over to me, and back off!   975

PHILOCTETES

Who is this? Is that Odysseus' voice?

ODYSSEUS

It is.
Odysseus certainly; you can see me here.

PHILOCTETES

Then I've been sold out indeed; I am lost. It was he
who took me prisoner, robbed me of my weapons.

ODYSSEUS

Yes, I, I and no other. I admit that.   980

PHILOCTETES

Boy, give me back my bow, give it back to me.

ODYSSEUS

That he will never
be able to do now, even if he wishes it.
And you must come with the bow, or else these men
will take you by force.

PHILOCTETES

Me? Your wickedness and impudence are without limit.
Will these men really take me there by force?   985

ODYSSEUS

Yes, if you do not come of your own accord.

PHILOCTETES

O land of Lemnos and all-mastering brightness,
Hephaestus-fashioned, must I indeed bear this,
that he, Odysseus, drags me from you with violence?

ODYSSEUS

It is Zeus, I would have you know, Zeus this land's ruler,
who has determined. I am only his servant.   990

PHILOCTETES

Hateful creature,
what excuses you invent! You plead the gods
to screen your actions and make the gods out liars.

ODYSSEUS

They speak the truth. The road must be traveled.

PHILOCTETES

I say No.

ODYSSEUS

    I say Yes. You must listen.

PHILOCTETES

    Am I after all a slave, not free? Is that   995
    what my father sired me to be?

ODYSSEUS

                  No, but to be equal
    of the best, with whom it is destined you must take Troy,
    and demolish her stone by stone.

PHILOCTETES

    Never—I would rather suffer anything than this.
    There is still my steep and rugged precipice here.   1000

ODYSSEUS

    What do you mean to do?

PHILOCTETES

                  Throw myself down,
    shatter my head upon the rock below.

ODYSSEUS

    Hold him. Take this solution out of his power.

PHILOCTETES

    Hands of mine, prey of Odysseus' hunting,
    how you suffer now in your lack of the loved bowstring!   1005

    You who have never had a healthy thought
    nor a noble one, you Odysseus, how you have hunted me,
    how you have stolen upon me with this boy
    as your shield, because I did not know him, one
    that is no mate for you but worthy of me,
    who knew nothing but to do what he was bidden,   1010
    and now, you see, is suffering bitterly
    for his own faults and the evils brought on me.
    Your sneaky, dark-plotting soul taught him step by step

to be clever in mischief against his nature and will.   1015
Now it is my turn; now to my sorrow you intend
to tie me hand and foot and take me away,
away from this shore on which you cast me once
without friends or comrades or city, a dead man among the
   living.
Ah!
My curse on you! I have often cursed you before,
yet the gods give me nothing that is sweet to me;   1020
so you have joy in living, and I have sorrow
because my very life is linked to this pain,
laughed at by you and your two generals,
the sons of Atreus whom you serve in this.
And yet, when you sailed with them, it was by constraint   1025
and trickery, while I came of my own free will
with seven ships, to my undoing, I
who was then dishonored and cast away —
you say it was they that did it; but they say you.

     But now why are you taking me? For what?
I am nothing now. To you all I have long been dead.   1030
You god-hated wretch, how is it that no longer
am I lame and foul-smelling to you? How can you sacrifice
to the gods if I sail with you? Pour your libations?
This was your excuse for casting me away.
May death in ugly form come on you! It will so come,   1035
since you have wronged me, if the gods care for justice.
And I know that they do care for it, for otherwise
you never would have sailed here for my sake
and my future, had not the divine goad,
a need of me, compelled you.

     Land of my fathers, gods that look on men's deeds,   1040
take vengeance on these men, late but at last,
upon them all, if you have pity on me!
Wretchedly as I live, if I saw them
dead, I could think that I was free of my sickness.

CHORUS LEADER

He is a hard man, Odysseus, this stranger,   1045
and hard his words: no yielding to suffering in them.

ODYSSEUS

If I had the time, I have much I could say to him.
As it is, there is only one thing. As the occasion
demands, such a one am I.
When there is a competition of men just and good,   1050
you will find none more scrupulous than myself.
What I seek in everything is to win—
except in your regard: I willingly yield to you now.

Let him go, men. Do not lay a finger on him.
Let him stay here. We have these weapons of yours   1055
and do not need you, Philoctetes.
Teucer is with us who has the skill and I,
who, I think, am no inferior master of them
and have as straight an aim as you. Why do we need you?
Farewell: keep walking around Lemnos. Let us go.   1060
Perhaps your prize will bring me the honor you should
    have had.

PHILOCTETES

Oh! What shall I do? Will you appear
before the Argives in the glory of my weapons?

ODYSSEUS

Say nothing further to me. I am going.   1065

PHILOCTETES

Son of Achilles, your voice has no word for me?
Will you go away in silence?

ODYSSEUS

                    Come, Neoptolemus.
Do not look at him. Your generosity
may spoil our future.

PHILOCTETES

> You, too, men, will you go   1070
> and leave me alone? Do you, too, have no pity?

CHORUS LEADER

This young man is our captain. What he says to you
we say as well.

NEOPTOLEMUS   *(To the Chorus.)*

> Odysseus will tell me
> that I am too full of pity. Still
> remain, if this man will have it so, as long   1075
> as it takes the sailors to ready the ship
> and until we have made our prayer to the gods.
> Perhaps, in the meantime, he will have better thoughts
> about us. Let us go, Odysseus.
> You, when we call you, be quick to come.   1080

(Exit Odysseus and Neoptolemus to the side.)

PHILOCTETES [*singing, while the Chorus sings in reply*]

STROPHE A

Hollow cave in the rock, sun-warmed, ice-cold,
I was not destined, after all, ever to leave you.
Still with me, you shall be witness to my dying.   1085
Passageway, crowded with my cries of pain,
what shall be, now again, my daily life with you?
What hope shall I find of food to keep my wretched life alive?   1090
Come close now, birds that once were so timid,
come down the shrill winds; I no longer have strength to
> *catch you.*

CHORUS

It was you who doomed yourself,   1095
man of hard fortune. From no other,
from nothing stronger, came your mischance.
When you could have chosen wisdom,
with better opportunity before you,
you chose the worse.   1100

PHILOCTETES

Sorrow, sorrow is mine. Suffering has broken me,
who must live henceforth alone from all the world,
must live here and die here; 1105
no longer bringing home food nor winning
it with winged weapons and strong hands. 1110
Unnoticed, the crafty words of a treacherous mind
stole up on me. Would I might see him,
contriver of this trap,
for as long as I am, condemned to pain. 1115

CHORUS

It was the will of the gods
that has subdued you, no trickery
to which my hand was lent. 1120
Turn your hate, your ill-omened curses, elsewhere.
This indeed lies near my heart,
that you should not reject my friendship. 1125

PHILOCTETES

By the shore of the gray sea he sits and laughs at me.
He brandishes in his hand the weapon which kept me alive,
which no one else had handled. Bow that I loved,
forced from the hands that loved you, if you could feel,
you would see me with pity, successor to Heracles, 1130
that used you and shall handle you no more.
You have found a new master, a man of craft, 1135
and shall be bent by him.
You shall see crooked deceits and the face of my hateful foe,
and a thousand ill things such as he contrived against me.

CHORUS

A man should give careful heed to speak his own right;° 1140
and when he has said it, restrain his tongue from rancor and
    taunt.

Odysseus was one man, one out of many;
appointed by his commander he did this, a service to his friends.   1145

PHILOCTETES

ANTISTROPHE B

Birds my victims, and tribes of bright-eyed wild creatures,
tenants of these hills, no longer need you flee from me or my house.
No more do I have the strength of my hands, of my bow.   1150
Come! I'm lame, you have nothing to fear.°
It is a good time   1155
to glut yourselves freely on my discolored flesh.
For shortly I shall die here. How shall I find means of life?
Who can live on air without any of all that life-giving earth
    supplies?   1160

CHORUS

In the name of the gods, if there is anything that you hold in
    respect,
draw near to a friend that approaches you in all sincerity.
Know what you are doing, know it well.
It lies with you to avoid this doom.   1165
To feed it with your body is a pitiable destiny;
and he who dwells with it can never learn
how to endure the thousand agonies.

PHILOCTETES

EPODE

Again, again you have touched my old hurt,   1170
for all that you are the best of those that came here.
Why did you afflict me? What have you done to me?

CHORUS

What do you mean by this?

PHILOCTETES

You have hoped to bring me
to the hateful land of Troy.   1175

CHORUS

I judge that to be best.

PHILOCTETES

   Then leave me now at once.

CHORUS

   Glad news, glad news you give me.
   I am right willing to obey you.
   Let us go now to our places in the ship.   1180

PHILOCTETES

   No, by Zeus who listens to curses, do not go,
   I beseech you.

CHORUS

   Be calm!

PHILOCTETES

                Friends, stay!
   I beg you to stay.   1185

CHORUS

         Why do you call on us?

PHILOCTETES

   Ah, ah!
   It is the spirit that haunts me. I am destroyed.
   My foot, what shall I do with this foot of mine
   in the life I shall live hereafter?   1190
   Friends, come to me again.

CHORUS

   What to do? Your wishes now are different
   from your former bidding.

PHILOCTETES

   It is no occasion for anger
   when a man crazy with storms of pain
   speaks contrary to reason.   1195

CHORUS

   Unhappy man, come with us, as we say.

PHILOCTETES

Never, never! That is my fixed purpose.
Not though the lord of the lightning, bearing his fiery bolts,
come against me, burning me
with flame and glare.
Let Ilium go to hell and all those that under its walls   1200
had the heart to cast me away, crippled!
Friends, grant me one prayer only.

CHORUS

                              What is it you would seek?

PHILOCTETES

A sword, if you have got one,
or an axe or some weapon—give it me!   1205

CHORUS

What would you do with it?

PHILOCTETES

                              Head and foot,
head and foot, all of me, I would cut with my own hand.
My mind is set on death, on death, I tell you.

CHORUS

Why this?   1210

PHILOCTETES

    I would go seek my father.

CHORUS

Where?

PHILOCTETES

                  In the house of Hades.
He is no longer in the light.
City of my fathers, if only I could see you!
I, wretched man that I am, left your holy streams,   1215
to go help the Greeks, my enemies,
and now am nothing any more.

CHORUS LEADER [*speaking*]
    I should have been by now on my way to the ship,°
    if I did not see Odysseus coming here   1220
    and with him the son of Achilles.

> (*Enter Odysseus and Neoptolemus from the side.*
> *Philoctetes withdraws into the cave.*)

ODYSSEUS
    You have turned back; there is hurry in your step.
    Will you not tell me why?

NEOPTOLEMUS
    I am hurrying to undo the wrong that I have done.

ODYSSEUS
    A strange thing to say! What wrong was that?   1225

NEOPTOLEMUS
    I did wrong when I obeyed you and the Greeks.

ODYSSEUS
    What did you do that you think was unworthy?

NEOPTOLEMUS
    I caught a man with tricks and with treachery.

ODYSSEUS
    What man? Ah, do you have something rash in mind?

NEOPTOLEMUS
    Nothing rash. But to the son of Poias . . .   1230

ODYSSEUS
    What? I am afraid to hear what you will say.

NEOPTOLEMUS
    Back to the man I took it from, this bow . . .

ODYSSEUS
    You cannot mean you are going to give it back.

NEOPTOLEMUS

Just that. To my shame, unjustly I obtained it.

ODYSSEUS

By the gods, you speak in earnest?   1235

NEOPTOLEMUS

                                        Yes, unless
it is not in earnest to tell you the truth.

ODYSSEUS

What do you mean, son of Achilles, what are you saying?

NEOPTOLEMUS

Must I tell you the same story twice or thrice?

ODYSSEUS

I should prefer not to have heard it once.

NEOPTOLEMUS

You can rest easy. You have now heard everything.   1240

ODYSSEUS

Then there is someone who will prevent its execution.

NEOPTOLEMUS

Who will that be? Who will stop me?

ODYSSEUS

The whole assembly
of the Greeks and among them I myself.

NEOPTOLEMUS

You are a clever man, Odysseus, but
this is not a clever thing to say.

ODYSSEUS

                    In your own case
neither the words nor the acts are clever.   1245

NEOPTOLEMUS

                                        Still
if they are just, that's better than being clever.

ODYSSEUS

How can it be just to give up and surrender
what you won by my plans?

NEOPTOLEMUS

It was wrong,
a shameful wrong, which I shall try to redeem.

ODYSSEUS

Have you no fear of the Greeks if you do this?   1250

NEOPTOLEMUS

I have no fear of anything you can do,°
when I act with justice; nor shall I yield to force.

ODYSSEUS

Then we shall be fighting
not with the Trojans but with you.

NEOPTOLEMUS

Let that be as it will.

ODYSSEUS

Do you see my hand,
reaching for the sword?   1255

NEOPTOLEMUS

You shall see me do the same
and with no hesitation!

ODYSSEUS

I will let you alone;
I shall go and tell this to the assembled Greeks,
and they will punish you.

NEOPTOLEMUS

That is very prudent.
If you are always as prudent as this,
perhaps you will keep out of trouble.   1260

(Exit Odysseus to the side.)

Philoctetes, son of Poias, I call on you!
Come out from this rocky home of yours.

(*Philoctetes appears at the mouth of the cave.*)

PHILOCTETES

What cry is this at the door?
Why do you call me, strangers? What would you have?
Ah! This is a bad thing. Can there be some fresh mischief   1265
you come to do, to top what you have done already?

NEOPTOLEMUS

Be easy. I would only have you listen.

PHILOCTETES

I am afraid of that.
I heard you before, and they were good words, too.
But they destroyed me when I listened.

NEOPTOLEMUS

Is there no place, then, for repentance?   1270

PHILOCTETES

You were just such a one in words when you stole my bow,
inspiring confidence, but sly and treacherous.

NEOPTOLEMUS

I am not such now. But I would hear from you
whether you are entirely determined
to remain here, or will you go with us?   1275

PHILOCTETES

Oh, stop! You need not say another word.
All that you say will be wasted.

NEOPTOLEMUS

You are determined?

PHILOCTETES

More than words can declare.

NEOPTOLEMUS

    Well, I wish that I could have persuaded you.
    But if I cannot speak to some purpose, I have done.

PHILOCTETES

    Indeed, you will say it all   1280
    to no purpose, for you will never win my heart
    to friendship with you, who have stolen my life
    by treachery, and then came and lectured me,
    most hateful son of a noble father. Cursed be you all,
    first the two sons of Atreus, then Odysseus,   1285
    and then yourself!

NEOPTOLEMUS

                 Do not curse me any more.
    Take your bow. Here I give it to you.

PHILOCTETES

    What can you mean? Is this another trick?

NEOPTOLEMUS

    No. That I swear by the holy majesty
    of Zeus on high!

PHILOCTETES

    These are good words,   1290
    if only they are honest.

NEOPTOLEMUS

    The fact is plain.
    Stretch out your hand; take your own bow again.

(He hands the bow to Philoctetes. Odysseus
appears suddenly, from the side.)

ODYSSEUS

    I forbid it, as the gods are my witnesses,
    in the name of the Atridae and the Greeks.

PHILOCTETES

Whose voice is that, boy? Is it Odysseus? 1295

ODYSSEUS

You heard right—and near at hand!
And I shall bring you to the plains of Troy
by force, whether Achilles' son
will have it so or not.

PHILOCTETES (*Starting to aim at him.*)

You will be sorry for your words
if this arrow flies straight.

NEOPTOLEMUS

No, Philoctetes, no! 1300
Do not shoot.

PHILOCTETES

Let me go, let go my hand, dear boy.

NEOPTOLEMUS

I will not.

(*Exit Odysseus to the side.*)

PHILOCTETES

Why did you prevent me killing my enemy,
with my bow, a man that hates me?

NEOPTOLEMUS

This is not to our glory, neither yours nor mine.

PHILOCTETES

Well, know this much, that the princes of the army, 1305
the lying heralds of the Greeks, are cowards
when they face real combat, however keen in words.

NEOPTOLEMUS

Let that be. You have your bow. There is no further cause
for anger or reproach against me.

                    None.

You have shown your nature and true breeding,   1310
son of Achilles and not Sisyphus.
Your father, when he still was with the living,
was the most famous of them all, as now he is of the dead.

NEOPTOLEMUS
I am happy to hear you speak well of my father
and of myself. Now listen to my request.   1315
The fortunes that the gods give to us men
we must bear under necessity.
But men that cling willfully to their sufferings
as you do, no one may forgive nor pity.   1320
Your anger has made a savage of you. You will not
accept advice, although the friend advises
in pure goodheartedness. You loathe him, think
he is your enemy and hates you.
Yet I will speak. May Zeus, the god of oaths,
be my witness! Mark it, Philoctetes, write it in your mind.   1325
You are sick and the pain of the sickness is of divine origin
because you approached the guardian of Chryse,
the serpent that with secret watch protects
her roofless shrine to keep it from violation.
You will never know relief while the selfsame sun   1330
rises on this side and sets again on that,
until you come of your own will to Troy,
and meet among us the sons of Asclepius,
who will relieve your sickness; then with the bow
and by my side, you will become Troy's conqueror.   1335

I will tell you how I know that this is so.
There is a man of Troy who was taken prisoner,
Helenus, a good prophet. He told us clearly
how it should be and said, besides, that Troy   1340
must fall completely this summer. He even says,
"If I prove wrong, you may kill me."

Now since you know this, yield and be gracious.
It is a glorious increase of your gain,
for you, judged preeminent among the Greeks,
first, to come into hands that can heal you,   1345
and then to win the highest renown, by taking
Troy that has cost infinity of tears.

PHILOCTETES

Hateful life, why should I still be alive and seeing?
Why not be gone to Hades?
What shall I do? How can I distrust   1350
his words who in friendship has counseled me?
Shall I then yield? If I do so, how come
before the eyes of men, so miserable?
Who will say word of greeting to me?
Eyes of mine, that have seen all, can you endure   1355
to see me conversing with my murderers,
the sons of Atreus? With cursed Odysseus?
It is not the sting of wrongs past
but what I must look for in wrongs to come.
Men whose wit has been mother of villainy once   1360
have learned from it to be evil in all other things too.°
I must indeed wonder at yourself in this.
You should not yourself be going to Troy,
and you should be holding me back. They've done you wrong
and robbed you of your father's arms.° Will you go   1365
and help them fight, and compel me to do the same?
No, boy, no; take me home as you promised.
Remain in Scyrus yourself; let these bad men
die in their own bad fashion. We shall both thank you,   1370
I and my father. You will not then, by helping
the wicked, seem to be like them.

NEOPTOLEMUS

                    What you say
is reasonable; yet I wish that you'd trust the gods
and my word, and so set sail, with me as friend.   1375

PHILOCTETES

What, to the plains of Troy, to the cursed sons
of Atreus with this suffering foot of mine?

NEOPTOLEMUS

To those that shall give you redress,
that shall save you and your rotting foot from its disease.

PHILOCTETES

That's terrible advice: what do you mean by it?   1380

NEOPTOLEMUS

What I see fulfilled will be best for you and me.

PHILOCTETES

And saying it, don't you blush before the gods?

NEOPTOLEMUS

Why should one feel ashamed to do good to another?

PHILOCTETES

Is the good for the Atridae or for me?

NEOPTOLEMUS

I am your friend, and the word I speak is friendly.   1385

PHILOCTETES

How, then, do you wish to betray me to my enemies?

NEOPTOLEMUS

Sir, learn not to be defiant in misfortune.

PHILOCTETES

You will ruin me, I know it, by your words.

NEOPTOLEMUS

Not I. You do not understand, I think.

PHILOCTETES

Do I not know the Atridae cast me away?   1390

NEOPTOLEMUS

They cast you away; see if now they will restore you.

PHILOCTETES

  Never, if of my own will I must see Troy.

NEOPTOLEMUS

  What shall we do, since I cannot convince you
  of anything I say? It is easiest for me°   1395
  to leave my argument, and for you to live,
  as you are living, with no hope of cure.

PHILOCTETES

  Let me suffer what I must suffer.
  But what you promised to me and clasped my hand,
  that you'd bring me home, fulfill it for me, boy.
  Do not delay, do not speak again of Troy.   1400
  I have had enough of such talk.

NEOPTOLEMUS

  If you will then, let us go.

PHILOCTETES

                Noble is the word you spoke.

NEOPTOLEMUS

  Brace yourself, stand firm on your feet.

PHILOCTETES

                To the limit of my strength.

NEOPTOLEMUS

  How shall I avoid the blame of the Greeks?

PHILOCTETES

                Give it no thought.

NEOPTOLEMUS

  What if they come and harry my country?

PHILOCTETES

                I shall be there.   1405

NEOPTOLEMUS

  What help will you be able to give me?

PHILOCTETES

     With the bow of Heracles.

NEOPTOLEMUS

  Will you?

PHILOCTETES

     I shall drive them from your country.°

NEOPTOLEMUS

  If you will do what you say,
  come now; kiss this ground farewell, and come with me.

        (Heracles appears on high, above the cave of Philoctetes.)°

HERACLES [*chanting*]
  Not yet, not until you have heard
  my words, son of Poias.
  I am the voice of Heracles in your ears;   1410
  I am the shape of Heracles before you.
  It is for your sake I come and leave my home in the heavens.
  I come to tell you of the plans of Zeus,   1415
  to turn you back from the road you go upon.
  Hearken to my words.

  [*now speaking*]
  Let me reveal to you my own story first,
  let me tell you the labors and sufferings that were mine,
  and, at the last, the winning of deathless merit.   1420
  All this you can see in me now,
  all this must be your experience too:
  out of this suffering to win a glorious life,
     Go with this man to the city of Troy.
  First, you shall find there the cure of your cruel sickness,
  and then be adjudged best warrior among the Greeks.   1425
  Paris, the cause of all this evil, you shall kill
  with the bow that was mine. Troy you shall take.
  You shall win the prize of valor from the army
  and shall bring the spoils to your home,

to your father Poias, and the land of your fathers, Oeta. 1430
From the spoils of the campaign you must dedicate
some, on my pyre, in memory of my bow.

Son of Achilles, I have the same words for you.
You shall not have the strength to capture Troy
without this man, nor he without you, 1435
but, like twin lions hunting together,
he shall guard you, you him. I shall send Asclepius
to Ilium to heal his sickness. A second time
must Ilium fall to my bow. But remember this, 1440
when you come to sack that town, revere the gods.
All else our father Zeus thinks of less importance.
Holiness does not die with the men that die.
Whether they die or live, it cannot perish.

PHILOCTETES [*chanting, with Heracles and the Chorus chanting in*
response, to the end of the play]
   Voice that stirs my yearning when I hear, 1445
   my friend lost for so long,
   I shall not disobey.

NEOPTOLEMUS
   Nor I.

HERACLES
   Do not tarry then.
   The moment and the tide are hastening you on your way. 1450

PHILOCTETES
   Lemnos, I call upon you:
   Farewell, cave that shared my watches,
   nymphs of the meadow and the stream,
   the deep male growl of the sea-lashed headland 1455
   where often, in my niche within the rock,
   my head was wet with fine spray,
   where many a time in answer to my crying
   in the storm of my sorrow the mountain of Hermes sent its echo! 1460

Now springs and Lycian well, I am leaving you,
leaving you.
I had never hoped for this.
Farewell Lemnos, sea-encircled,
blame me not but send me on my way   1465
with a fair voyage to where a great destiny
awaits me, and the judgment of friends and the all-conquering
divinity who has brought this to pass.

CHORUS
Let us go all
when we have prayed to the nymphs of the sea   1470
to bring us safe to our homes.

                                        (Exit all.)

THE TRACKERS

Translated by MARK GRIFFITH

THE TRACKERS:
INTRODUCTION

The Play: Date and Composition

The Trackers (sometimes translated as *The Searchers*) is not a tragedy but a satyr-play. Satyr-plays were similar to tragedies in being based on heroic myth and employing many of the same stylistic features, but they were distinguished by having a chorus of half-human, half-horse followers of Dionysus—sileni or satyrs—and by always ending happily. Often the plot involved an exotic or romantic adventure or some marvelous new discovery or invention, with the naive satyrs reacting in wonder and fascination while the main characters go about their heroic business. The chorus was played by the same Athenian citizens as had played the tragic choruses in the three preceding plays, but costumed now in bald-headed masks, horse tails, and erect phalluses. The satyrs are generally characterized as being irrepressibly childish and/or slavish—impulsive, irresponsible, inept, and cowardly—but at the same time they are wonderfully energetic and divinely talented as musicians and dancers. The satyr chorus is always accompanied by their "father" Silenus, whose costume is a woolly body suit and who generally behaves in an even more shameless and opportunistic manner than his young "children." A vivid and informative picture of a satyr chorus preparing to perform, along with Silenus, heroic actors, and a pipe player, can be found on the famous Pronomos Vase, painted in Athens around the end of the fifth century BCE. (Images of this vase are widely available in books and on the web.)

Each playwright's dramatic tetralogy at the Great Dionysian Festival in Athens usually consisted of three tragedies followed by one satyr-play. Satyr-plays tend to be shorter and simpler than

tragedies, and to include frequent reference to wine, food, dancing, and sex, but without ever descending into the extreme cru-
dity and obscenity of comedy. They were also somewhat looser
formally and musically than tragedies, while playing up the
satyrs' own musical and choreographic skills. Usually satyr-plays
are set in the countryside or some exotic land, and in some re-
spects they seem to anticipate the later genres of pastoral poetry
and even the romantic novel.

One quarter of the 120 or so plays whose titles are listed in ancient sources as being the work of Sophocles were presumably
satyr-dramas, rather than tragedies. But on the basis of the titles
alone we often cannot tell which plays were tragedies and which
were satyr-plays, since the heroic characters and themes were
shared by both genres. The seven plays of Sophocles that were selected in antiquity to be read in schools, and that consequently
survived into the Byzantine period in manuscripts that can still
be read today, were all tragedies. None of his satyr-plays were
thus preserved. This is true also for Aeschylus, though papyrus
finds have contributed substantial passages from several of his
satyr-dramas. Only in the case of Euripides do we possess a whole
satyr-play, The Cyclops, preserved entire in a medieval manuscript.

Over 400 lines of The Trackers are preserved on an ancient papyrus that was discovered in 1907 in the course of excavations at
Oxyrhynchus, Egypt. Some of the lines are badly damaged, and
there are gaps at various places in the papyrus as well; nor do we
know how many lines are missing at the beginning and end. But
we probably possess about half of the entire play, and it is therefore possible to get a fairly good idea of its overall plot and dynamics.

The date of the play's production is not known; nor do we know
which other plays (tragedies) were performed with it.

The Myth

The plot of the play involves the theft of Apollo's cattle by his baby
brother, Hermes, and the invention of the lyre. Both these events

are narrated in the *Homeric Hymn to Hermes*, a hexameter poem probably composed in the sixth century BCE that describes in a semihumorous style the sensational antics that the newborn Hermes gets up to and their long-lasting cultural consequences. Our play follows the main outlines of that narrative, while also making some distinctive changes of its own.

Hermes, the god of thieves, trade, messages, and mischief, was one of the twelve Olympian gods. He was the son of Zeus and the goddess Maia, an otherwise unimportant divinity (daughter of Atlas); so he was a half brother of Apollo, Zeus' "number one" son (by Leto). Immediately after his birth, baby Hermes was given to the mountain nymph Cyllene to look after, in a remote mountainous region of Arcadia. He immediately began to demonstrate precocious powers, as well as a delicious sense of humor. Within a day of being born, he jumped from his crib, killed a tortoise, and made out of its shell the first lyre. (Greek lyres were regularly made with tortoiseshell sounding boards, and one of the standard terms for "lyre" in Greek actually means "tortoise.") Hermes is thus the inventor of the Greeks' most popular and culturally valued musical instrument.

According to the *Hymn to Hermes*, the young god thereupon begins to feel hungry (this is very odd for an immortal—gods do not usually eat food as humans do), so he sets off on a long journey to the north, where he finds the sacred cattle of his brother Apollo grazing and steals them. After driving the cattle all the way back with him to Arcadia, he then, in order to confuse Apollo and any other potential investigators, contrives to turn them around and drag them backward into a cave: thus no tracks are visible leading into the cave. He kills two cows and prepares their meat for a sacrificial feast. In due course, Apollo is informed by an old man that Hermes was the one who stole the cattle. Confronting him, he finds the little god (now just six days old) lying in his crib in swaddling clothes and protesting his innocence. After some argument and threats—and many bald-faced lies and false oaths from Hermes—father Zeus, highly amused, eventually persuades him to confess and reveal the whereabouts of the cattle. A friendly deal is finally negotiated between the brothers: Apollo gets back his cattle; Hermes gives him also the lyre in recompense for the theft and slain cows and shows him how to play it; and Hermes himself is given a herald's sacred staff and dominion over wild animals and flocks. Hermes also invents for himself the shepherd's pipes (syrinx) which will be his distinctive musical instrument for the future. The two brothers are henceforth firm friends and partners, and the etiology of their respective powers and prerogatives in Greek tradition has been established.

In *The Trackers*, the order of some of these events—and perhaps the motivation for them too—may have been somewhat different from that in the *Hymn*. (Most important is the fact that in our play Hermes does not create the lyre until after he has stolen the cattle.) Although we are missing the very beginning of the play, it is clear enough that the action begins with Apollo issuing a proclamation that he will provide a splendid reward of a golden crown for anyone who can help him find and recover his cattle. Silenus and the satyrs quickly show up to volunteer for this, and apparently are offered the prospect of "freedom from slavery" if they are successful. Unfortunately we lack a portion of the text in which it must have been made clear what exactly this means: to whom are the satyrs currently enslaved? Normally in satyr-drama the satyrs are understood to be cheerful "slaves of Dionysus," happy in that status because their servitude involves no actual work, only drinking, dancing, and sexual indulgence. So it seems unlikely that Apollo in our play is offering them emancipation from servitude to Dionysus, though some scholars have argued this. More likely, at the beginning of the play the satyrs are for some reason enslaved to someone else, perhaps to Apollo himself (just as in Euripides' *Cyclops* they have been unexpectedly enslaved to Polyphemus) and are eager to be freed so that they can resume their playful duties in Dionysus' entourage.

As the play proceeds, the satyrs become "trackers" of the lost cattle, sniffing their scent and following their tracks; and so they arrive at the cave where Hermes has hidden the cattle—at which point they hear the strange new sounds of a lyre, by which they are both frightened and entranced. As Cyllene emerges from the cave to talk to them, they learn more about this miraculous musical invention, in particular the fact that the person who made it has employed cowhide (as well as tortoiseshell). This new piece of evidence clinches their suspicion that the stolen cattle are inside the cave and that Hermes must be the thief; and it appears that the satyrs may also see some cattle nearby. But at this point the papyrus breaks off, so that we cannot tell exactly how the denouement of the play was brought about. It seems that Apollo reappeared at the end to talk to the satyrs and perhaps deliver their reward (a few words from him are decipherable among the tattered remains of the papyrus); presumably Hermes appeared as well. What kind of "freedom" were the satyrs granted? We do not know. But it is clear that the invention of music—or of a new kind of music—has transformed their lives, as it will transform that of all humankind to come.

Thanks to the recovery of those parts of *The Trackers* that survive almost intact, along with the other more fragmentary bits and pieces, we possess a rare and precious specimen of that distinctive blend of fantasy and adventure, pathos and absurdity, that lies at the heart of the dramatic genre of satyr-drama. Hermes himself, like Dionysus, was a god of playfulness, of disguise, and of music—and the world of satyr-drama is one that, in reassuring contrast to the tragic world, is populated by divinities whose interventions guarantee unexpected rescues and fortunate outcomes, an alternative reality in which humans and gods, heroes and bumpkins, will all find a happy ending. This is a world more akin to *A Midsummer Night's Dream* than to *Hamlet*. Every festival of dramatic competition at the City Dionysia ended by reaffirming that satyric mood, and *The Trackers* seems to have been typical of the genre in focusing attention specifically on the magical power of music, with simple animal and vegetable products being miraculously transformed by technology into a source of enchantment and joy.

The play does not seem to have been much read or performed in antiquity after its first production. On the whole, while new satyr-dramas continued to be written and performed throughout the Hellenistic period (and the Roman poet Horace in his *Art of Poetry* devotes considerable attention to the genre), there is little evidence of fifth-century satyr-plays being widely read or studied in schools. The papyrus containing *The Trackers* was apparently written in the second century CE. It was discovered in 1907, and first published in 1912. Before the discovery of this papyrus text, only a few very short quotations from the play by ancient scholars were known.

Modern performances or adaptations of the play have—not surprisingly, given its fragmentary state—been rare, though in recent years greater interest is being shown in satyr-drama as a genre overall and in this play in particular. The most notable adaptation is Tony Harrison's brilliant *The Trackers of Oxyrhynchus* (performed in 1988 at Delphi; a revised version staged at the National Theatre, London, in 1990): it interweaves passages from Sophocles' original play with dialogue between Bernard Grenfell and Arthur Hunt, the first excavators and publishers of the papyrus, while exploring issues of high versus low art and the status of the Greek classics in a postcolonial Egyptian context.

THE TRACKERS

Characters   APOLLO
                SILENUS, father of the satyrs
                CHORUS of satyrs
                CYLLENE, a mountain nymph (attendant of
                Hermes' mother, Maia)
                HERMES (a baby)

Scene: In front of a cave on Mount Cyllene in Arcadia.

[The opening lines of the play are lost.° At the point where
the papyrus begins to be somewhat legible, Apollo has arrived in Arcadia in search of his missing cattle and is calling
on anyone nearby to help him.]

APOLLO
. . . I came here quickly . . . and now I announce to all,
. . . both mortals and gods too, that if anyone
from near or far can help me now recover   5
the precious things I've lost . . .
I'll provide a fine reward. For I am suffering
great pain of heart: all of my milking cows   10
and all my baby calves as well are gone.
I'm tracking their hoofprints, far here from their stalls:
it's strange, and clever—I'd never have imagined
that anyone, whether god or mortal human,   15
would ever dare to attempt a deed like this.
      So since I've come here, distraught and hesitant,
I'm spying, searching, making proclamations

on all sides, to gods and humans too,
so that no one can be unaware of what has happened.   20
I'm out of my mind with fervor for the hunt,
and I've visited every nation, every corner of the land . . .°

. . . .

. . . to Thessaly, to the plains of Boeotia . . . ,   30
and now I've come to this Dorian peninsula
of Pelops seeking allies . . .   35
                    and to the region
around Mount Cyllene . . .°
If any shepherd, or farmer, or charcoal burner   40
is near at hand to hear my words, or else
any of those nymph-born rustic spirits,
the satyrs, I proclaim to one and all:
whoever finds the stolen property
of Apollo Paean, a great reward awaits!

                                    (*Enter Silenus from the side.*)

SILENUS

I heard a mighty voice, surely a god's,   45
calling out for help in loud proclamations:
so, with all the energy that an old person can muster,
I've rushed here, running hard, to your assistance,
Phoebus Apollo, eager to be your friend
and devoted benefactor, if I can succeed
in tracking down this missing treasure for you.   50
For that gold-wreathed prize that you've established
seems most appropriate for me to win.
And my sons, the satyrs, with many pairs of eyes to help,
I'll send them out searching too, if you will do
all you say, and provide a big reward.

APOLLO

Be assured, I'll provide it. Just carry out the task!   55

SILENUS

I'll bring you the cows. Just carry out your promise!

APOLLO

The finder, whoever he is, will get the reward.
It's ready and waiting . . .°

. . . .

SILENUS

. . . So what is it? Is there something more?

APOLLO

Freedom, for you and for your sons as well.°   63

(Exit Apollo to one side. Enter the Chorus of satyrs, from the other side.)

CHORUS [*singing*]

. . . . °

Come on now . . . move your feet!   65
Oh, oh! . . . Get after that thief . . . !
Listen to father's voice! . . .   72
How did that sneaky theft happen by foot . . . ?
If only I can be so lucky . . . !
Freedom for father . . .   75
May the god we love help us now to achieve
success in our labor, since he has shown us
brilliant samples of gold!

SILENUS

Goddess Fortune, divine guiding spirit,
grant me success in the venture that I've set out on   80
at such high energy, to track down the loot,
the prey, the spoils of Phoebus' stolen cattle!
If anyone has witnessed this, by sight or hearing,
he'll be my friend indeed by telling me,
and lord Apollo's perfect benefactor.   85

. . . . °

. . . Does anyone know, or nobody, what's going on?   90
. . . Come on, it seems we should all be getting to work,
following the scent closely, sniffing the air . . .   95
. . . that way we can track down our quarry,
and all will be well.

(*The Chorus splits into two groups.*)

CHORUS A [*singing*]
A *god, god, god, god! Ah, ah!* 100

[*now speaking*]
It looks as if we have them!

CHORUS B
Yes, here they are! These are the cattle's hoofprints!

CHORUS A
Quiet! A god is leading our colony!

CHORUS B
What are we to do, sir? Were we getting it right?
How does it look to those guys over there? 105

CHORUS A
It looks great to us! Everything looks clear now!

CHORUS B
Look, look! The exact imprint of their hooves again!

CHORUS A
Look closely here! This one measures just the same! 110

CHORUS B
Come here, run! . . . Take hold of this . . . !

CHORUS A
If any mooing from the cattle reaches your ear . . .

CHORUS B
I don't yet hear their voices at all clearly,
but here are the hoofprints for sure, and the trail 115
of the cattle, plain to see: you can't mistake them.

CHORUS A
But hey!
The footprints—they're back-to-front, by Zeus!
They're facing backward! Just look at them!

What's going on here? What kind of formation is it?   120
The front's been switched to the rear, and all the rest
are intertwined and facing in both directions.
That cattle driver was possessed by a weird confusion!

(Sounds begin to be heard from inside the cave.)

SILENUS

What about *you*? What's this strange technique
that you've invented? What is it? Bizarre!
Lying full-length on the ground, you're hunting and
    tracking?   125
What's your system? I don't get it. You're just like a hedgehog
lying in a bush, or like a monkey
bending over to blow off steam at someone.
What is all this? Where on earth did you learn it?
Tell me—I've no knowledge of this method.   130

CHORUS

Uh Uh Uh Uh!

SILENUS

What are you howling about? What's so frightening?
Who are you looking at? Why are you so panicked?
Why are you dancing so crazily? Are you digging down
because you're hoping to find millet seeds underground?
And why so quiet, when you're normally so talkative?   135

CHORUS

Shhh, be quiet!
. . . Listen!

SILENUS

How can I listen when I can't hear anybody's voice?

CHORUS

Do as I say!   140

SILENUS

You're not really helping me . . .

CHORUS

    Just listen for yourself now, father, for a little while,
    to the sound that has so overwhelmed us here
    a sound that no human being has ever heard before!

SILENUS

    Why are you so shocked and scared by a sound?   145
    You waxwork dummies!—cowardly, filthy creatures
    scared of the shadows, terrified by everything:
    as helpers you're all gutless, chaotic, slavish,
    just a bunch of bodies, tongues, and phalluses!   150
    If ever someone needs you, then you're loyal
    and trusty—in words, but you avoid any action.

        To think: with a father like yours, you wretched beasts,
    who in his youth set up many monuments,
    all finely wrought, of his prowess and valor
    at the homes of nymphs! I never turned to flight,   155
    I was never a coward, I never cringed
    at the sounds of cattle grazing on the hilltops!

                                (Gesturing toward his phallus.)

    No, my spear stood straight and strong, and I performed
    glorious deeds which now you are besmirching,
    in response to some unfamiliar sound of shepherds
    calling to charm their flocks.
                        Why are you so frightened,   160
    like children, before you've even seen anything?
    You're throwing away all that golden wealth
    that Phoebus told you about and guaranteed,
    and the freedom that he promised to bestow
    on you and me. You're just abandoning it,   165
    and going to sleep! If you don't get back on track
    and seek out those cattle and that cowherd,
    wherever they've gotten to, then you'll be sorry—
    and you'll be the ones making the bad noises,
    out of sheer cowardice.

CHORUS LEADER

    Father, join us and help us in our search;

    then you'll know for sure if there's any cowardice.   170

    If you're with us, you'll see for yourself

    you're talking nonsense.

SILENUS

    I'll come and join you, and rally you by my address,

    calling you all to action with a hound-rousing pipe tune.

    So come on, set your feet into position

    in three lines dancing a single path,

    while I stand close and direct your performance.   175

CHORUS [singing]

    U u u! ps ps! ah ah!

    Tell me, what is your trouble?

    Why did you moan, why did you mutter

    and look at me so weirdly?

        We've got him—who is this, in the first turn?

    You're caught! He's come, he's come!   180

    You're mine now, under arrest!

    Who's this at the second turn . . . ?°

    Dracis, Grapis, and you there

    Ourias, Ourias—you've gone off track!

    . . . .

    Look, here's a trail . . .

    Stratios, Stratios, follow this way! . . .

    There's a cow inside . . . !

    Come on, follow me,   190

    this way . . .

    . . . .

        (The sound of a lyre is heard from inside the cave.)

CHORUS LEADER

    Father, why so quiet? Isn't it true   203

    what we said? Can't you hear the sound, or are you deaf?

        (The lyre is heard again.)

SILENUS
Oh, oh!

CHORUS LEADER
What is it?

SILENUS
I'm not staying here!

CHORUS LEADER
Please do stay!   205

SILENUS
No way! You can all keep looking and tracking
and getting rich, by capturing them for yourselves
if you like, the cattle and the gold. But I
for my part have decided not to spend
another minute in this place.

CHORUS LEADER
I don't think we should give up . . .   210
. . . and leave, before we know
quite definitely who's making this strange sound!°

. . . .
. . . and he'll much enjoy all of this.
But I'll provide a pounding of my feet,
and with my leaps and kicks, thick and fast,
I'll compel him to listen, however deaf he may be.   220

(They dance.° Enter Cyllene from inside the cave.)

CYLLENE
Wild creatures, why have you mounted this assault
with so much shouting, on my woodland hill here,
green and home to animals? What new art,
what style is this of yours? What transformation
from those duties you formerly used to have
in pleasing Dionysus, your master—
always drunk, dressed in fawnskins,   225

holding a thyrsus lightly in your hands,
and calling out "euhoi!" as you followed behind the god,
with his cousins, the nymphs, and a crowd of goatherds.°
    But now, I do not recognize what's happened.
Where are these latest crazy twists and turns
whirling you off to? They're amazing! I heard   230
commands being shouted as well, like hunters calling
to dogs approaching the lair of their wild quarry.
But then I hear cries of "thief" and a "proclamation" . . .°   235

.   .   .   .

. . . giving this up, with kickings and leapings
your band of trackers came close . . .
So hearing you all so utterly out of your minds   240
I worry that you may be sick . . .
    . . . But you shouldn't be accosting one who's innocent!

CHORUS [*singing*]

STROPHE

Deep-girdled nymph, do not be so angry!
We are not here looking for quarrels
or fighting; our tongues mean no harm,   245
no breach of hospitality or friendship.
Don't be so quick to criticize us,
but freely tell, who or what was it
that amazed us so
from this place of yours underground
by emitting such a heavenly voice?   250

CYLLENE

These words are better than your former ones,
and you'll be much more successful in your hunting
using this method, rather than parades
of strength and rude attempts on a poor nymph!
It is not my style to engage in loud abuse.   255
    So tell me calmly, as clearly as you can,
just what is the matter? What is it you need?

CHORUS LEADER [*now speaking*]
Mighty Cyllene, ruler of this region,
I shall tell you in a moment why I came here:
but first, you tell us—what's this voice that sounds   260
and who of mortals torments us so with it?

CYLLENE
You must understand quite clearly: if you reveal
to anyone what I'm about to tell you,
you'll suffer the punishment yourselves.
The whole affair's a secret, guarded by the gods,   265
so that no knowledge of the story should get to Hera.
For Zeus secretly came here, to this home
of Maia, Atlas' daughter, and seduced her,
in deception of his wife, the deep-girdled goddess.   270
He begot a son, Maia's only child,
and I am nursing him here in my own arms
since his mother's strength is ravaged by sickness.
    So day and night I take care of his needs,
sitting beside the cradle as he lies   275
in his swaddling clothes, providing food and drink
and change of bedding. And he is growing, growing
each day in a way one never could imagine:
it's miraculous—I'm amazed and scared!
He came into the world not six days ago
and already he's outgrown a child's dimensions
and acquired the size and vigor of a teenager: 280
he keeps sprouting higher with no sign of stopping;
such is the child that our storehouse now contains.
Hermes is his name, by his father's choice.
And the voice you've heard, echoing loud all round,
he created this with a brand new instrument,
all in one day, the same day he was born.   285
He flipped [a creature] on its back . . .
. . . such a sweet source of pleasure the child produced
. . . full of loud cries.°

CHORUS [*singing*]

ANTISTROPHE

Unbelievable! . . .°   290
you mean a child . . .
an animal . . .
a voice . . .
. . . was able to produce such utterance?   297

CYLLENE
Don't disbelieve: this goddess' words invite your trust.

CHORUS LEADER
How can I believe a dead thing's voice makes such a sound?

CYLLENE
Believe me, it's true! The animal was silent   300
while living, yet found a voice when it was dead.

CHORUS LEADER
What did it look like? Long or round or short?

CYLLENE
Short, pot-shaped, wrinkled, with spotted skin.

CHORUS LEADER
It sounds a bit like a cat, or perhaps a panther?

CYLLENE
Completely unlike! Round, and with short legs.

CHORUS LEADER
You don't mean like a mongoose, or maybe a crab?   305

CYLLENE
Not like those either—try another direction!

CHORUS LEADER
Then was it like one of those horned beetles from Aetna?

CYLLENE
Now you're getting closer to what that creature resembles!

CHORUS LEADER

Which part of it makes the sound, the inside or the outside?

CYLLENE

It has a hard shell, like what oysters have.   310

CHORUS LEADER

So what do you call this animal? Can you tell me?°

CYLLENE

It's a "tortoise," and the part that makes the sound
is called by the boy a "lyre." ...
...and the skin ...
that's how it resounds ...   315
...there's no wood, but pegs are driven in tight,
all the way through to hold the instrument together.

...and this one thing is his cure and solace   325
for any pain or trouble. Quite beside himself
he takes joy in playing and singing melodies,
and the harmonious inflections of the lyre
raise his spirits and uplift him. So that's how
the child constructed a voice for a dead animal!

CHORUS [singing]

STROPHE

A lovely voice from the plucked strings
goes out over this place,
and brilliant images of sound are flowering now   330
throughout the region.
But step by step I must bring to a head
the matter that I've been pursuing:
you have to know, lady, that this god,
whoever he is that's invented all of this,
he's the one, and nobody else, who is
the thief—you have to know it for sure!   335
Don't get angry with me about this;
please, don't hold it against me!

CYLLENE

What do you mean? What's this complaint of theft?

CHORUS LEADER

I don't mean to distress you . . .

CYLLENE

. . . are you calling him a thief?   340

CHORUS LEADER

. . . along with the stolen property!

CYLLENE

. . . if you're telling the truth.

CHORUS LEADER

. . . I am telling the truth.

. . . cattle . . . he fitted . . . after cutting up . . .°   347

CYLLENE

             . . . finally I understand
that you are just jawing at me for being stupid.
The only reason you're doing so is for fun;
and as far as I'm concerned, you may keep on   355
insulting me, if it makes you happy or seems
to profit you: so, keep on playing your games!
But against this child, whose status as Zeus' son
is uncontested, do not try to bring
new charges against a newborn!
He was not born a thief from his father's side,   360
nor does stealing run in his mother's family.
Look elsewhere, if you want to find your thief.
This house and this family are noble; fix your crime°
on someone else more fitting, not on him!   365
      But you're always just a child: even full-grown
as a young man, with your little yellow beard,
you strut around like a goat, all full of yourself.
Stop rubbing that smooth-skinned bald-spot of yours in
     pleasure!

You really shouldn't say these stupid things
and joke around, since the gods will make you cry
later, so I can enjoy the last laugh.   370

CHORUS [*singing*]

ANTISTROPHE

Turn and twist, weave your clever words,
invent whatever you like,
your cleaned-up sayings! You won't convince me
of the main thing:
that this person here who fashioned
that instrument out of leather hide   375
obtained those skins from any other cattle
than Loxias Apollo's.
Don't try to divert my steps
from that path!°

. . . .

. . . utter rascal . . . the truth . . . the child's a thief . . . if it's
   true . . .°

CYLLENE
   . . . many cows are grazing.   397

CHORUS LEADER
   But there used to be more than there are now!

CYLLENE
   So who [do you think] has got them, you scoundrel?

CHORUS LEADER
   The child who's sitting inside there, locked up.   400

CYLLENE
   Stop accusing and insulting the son of Zeus!

CHORUS LEADER
   I'll stop, if someone will just bring out the cattle.

CYLLENE
   You and your talk of cattle are making me sick!

CHORUS LEADER

If they're making you sick, drive out the cattle right now!° 404

. . . .

CHORUS [*singing*]

...Come on now...

Oh, oh! 436

...Ah, ah!

That one you said... 444

. . . .

(*Enter Apollo, from the side.*)

CHORUS

Loxias!...You are here...

...see, here are your cattle... 450

. . . .

APOLLO

...your payment...

...freedom°... 457

[The rest of the play is lost. We do not know how much is missing. If we follow the *Homeric Hymn to Hermes*, we may surmise that Hermes eventually came out and engaged in a dialogue with Apollo, in which he confessed to stealing the cattle; the cattle were duly restored to their rightful owner; and in addition Hermes gave the lyre to Apollo. As for the satyrs, whether or not Apollo gave them the previously promised reward, presumably they ended up as Dionysus' attendants once again. See the Introduction.]

TEXTUAL NOTES

(Line numbers are in some cases only approximate.)

AJAX

SCENE: The staging of this opening scene is uncertain. Most scholars think Athena appears on high, probably on the roof of the stage building; but some have argued that she enters with Odysseus from the side.

168: More literally, "mighty vulture," but the Greeks did not distinguish clearly between these two kinds of birds.

262: Or possibly, "I think we are lucky."

269: This translation follows a modern emendation of the manuscripts' reading, "we are ill no longer . . ."

405-7: Text and interpretation very uncertain.

432: The name Ajax in Greek is written AIAS, and in the vocative it is AIAI, which looks and sounds exactly like the common expression for "alas!" or "agony!" So Ajax is suggesting that his name is etymologically derived from that word, *agony*.

476: Text uncertain.

554: This line, "ignorance is bliss," is almost a repetition of the previous line, and is missing in ancient quotations of this passage. Most modern editors delete it.

571: This line is deleted by many modern editors.

575: "Eurysaces" means "broad shield" in Greek.

601: Reading uncertain.

700-702: An ancient papyrus, as well as other ancient citations, gives "Mysian" here (referring to Phrygia and the cult of Cybele, mother of the gods). The medieval manuscripts read "Nysian" (meaning "of Dionysus"). Then two or three words seem to be missing at the end of 702.

714: The words "and ignites them again" are omitted by some ancient sources and modern editors, though they are contained in all the medieval manuscripts.

760: Some manuscripts read "useless."

802: The precise reading is uncertain, but the general sense is not in doubt.

815-65: The original staging of this scene is much debated by modern scholars (see Introduction, pp. 13-14). The setting is no longer Ajax's tent, but a lonely place on the shore. The text does not indicate where exactly Ajax plants the sword—whether in plain sight of the audience, or on a special wheeled mechanism (*ekkyklema*) that can later be rolled away, or behind some kind of temporary screen of bushes brought on by stagehands. See too the notes on lines 865 and 989 below.

839-42: Some ancient and modern scholars have considered these lines to be interpolated.

855-58: Many editors delete these lines as a probable interpolation.

865: Scholars disagree how this suicide was originally staged. The body of Ajax must remain somewhere on stage, visible to the other characters and to the audience for the rest of the play, but the actor playing Ajax will shortly need to be available to play Teucer. So some means of substitution must have been employed; see note on 815-65.

869: Text uncertain.

936: The word "priceless" is a modern restoration; several syllables are missing at this point in the Greek text.

989: It is not clear whether Tecmessa now exits through the main door (in which case we are to imagine that this is once again the entrance to Ajax's tent), or, more likely, she departs by a side entrance to make her way back to the Greek camp, imagined now as being at some distance away. See the note on lines 815-65.

1023: This is the probable meaning of the line, with a modern emendation.

1105-6: Many editors delete these two lines as an interpolation.

1416-17: Text uncertain.

77: Some editors emend the word for "place," to read "matter" or "crisis."

84: A line in the manuscripts before 85 has been deleted as an interpolation: it reads, "or we fall if your father has perished."

267–68: Text and meaning quite uncertain.

362–64: Two lines are deleted here by most modern editors as an interpolation: "He said that Eurytus was king of that country, and he killed the king her father."

379: Some of the manuscripts assign this line to the Messenger.

463: The text is ambiguous: another possible translation would be, "even if he is utterly absorbed in his passion."

526: Text uncertain.

661–62: Text uncertain.

862–898: The chorus's words during this scene should perhaps be distributed among different chorus members, rather than spoken and sung in unison.

881–82: Some words are missing in the manuscripts; the general sense is not in doubt.

887: Some editors give this line as well as 883–86 to the chorus.

894: An alternative reading gives "that bride unfeasted" (i.e., not officially married).

911: Text and interpretation of this line are doubtful.

1004: A line is missing before this.

1270–78: Some editors give all these lines to the chorus. Some give just lines 1275–78 to the chorus (as do some of the medieval manuscripts).

ELECTRA

106: Another possible translation would be, "like the nightingale who has killed her child."

220: The text here is uncertain.

428–30: Some editors reject these lines as an interpolation.

451: Text and interpretation are uncertain: the manuscripts' reading means literally "nonshining."

691: An unmetrical and ungrammatical line in the manuscripts here, "the double-track race and pentathlon, as are customary," is omitted by modern editors.

720: After this the medieval manuscripts have three lines that many (but by no means all) modern editors transpose to follow line 740 instead: see the note on lines 741-43.

741-43: These three lines have been transposed here from 720-22 by several modern editors.

841-43: Text very uncertain.

1050-54: Some editors delete these lines, regarding them as interpolated.

1085-87: Text uncertain: perhaps "you have chosen a glorious life."

1264: One line is missing after this.

1283: Two or three words are missing here in the manuscripts, but the general sense is not in doubt.

1413: Text and interpretation uncertain.

1422-23: Modern editors mostly assign these lines to the chorus; the manuscripts assign them to Electra. "Blame" is also a modern conjecture, accepted by almost all editors, for the manuscripts' "speak."

1428: Two lines may be missing here, alternated between Electra and Orestes.

1458: This emendation is accepted by almost all editors, for the manuscripts' "I bid you be silent, and to reveal the doors."

1485-86: One manuscript omits these two lines, and some editors delete them.

1505-10: Some editors think these final lines have suffered damage in transmission, and that several more lines have also dropped out, leaving the ending incomplete.

PHILOCTETES

177: The manuscripts read, "Oh hands of mortals," but both meter and sense seem to require this emendation.

204: The manuscripts assign this one line (improbably) to Neoptolemus.

217: Some editors interpret differently, "perhaps he saw no ship in the unfriendly harbor."

361: An alternative reading gives, "I came to the Atridae in a friendly manner."

385-88: Some modern editors regard these lines as an interpolation.

452: Some editors emend to read, "in surveying divine activities, I find the gods are bad."

852-54: The precise reading and interpretation of these lines are uncertain.

1140: Text uncertain. Some editors read, "A man should take heed to say what is just."

1153: The text translated here is an emendation of the manuscripts' reading, "The place is slackly guarded, and need not be feared."

1218-21: Some editors delete these lines as an interpolation.

1251-52: A line or two may have dropped out here.

1361: Precise text and interpretation uncertain.

1365: The manuscripts contain one extra line here, which all modern editors omit: "They judged wretched Ajax second to Odysseus in the award of your father's weapons."

1395: This is the reading of most of the manuscripts. Some editors adopt a simple emendation which gives, "It is time now to leave my argument . . ."

1407-8: The text of these two lines is uncertain; some words are missing in the manuscripts.

1408: Heracles' role is played by the same actor who played both Odysseus and the Sailor/Merchant. Some modern critics have suggested that the audience is meant to think that this is Odysseus, in disguise, but it seems unlikely that Sophocles would have provided no clue anywhere in the text to such a significant impersonation. Heracles' voice might nonetheless have sounded somewhat similar to Odysseus', and some spectators might well have wondered if this was really Heracles they were hearing.

THE OPENING LINES: It is not clear how many lines are missing before the first words that are legible on our papyrus; perhaps only a few. But some scholars have surmised that a more extensive passage must have preceded in which Apollo explained the circumstances of the loss of his cattle. Further on (at the point marked as line 100 in modern editions) the papyrus contains an indication in the margin which may indeed have been intended to signal that this was the hundredth line of the play, in which case almost nothing has been lost at the beginning.

23: The next six lines are entirely lost.

30-39: Only isolated words can be read in these lines.

58: The next four lines are lost.

63: Only the first half of the line is readable; the rest is a conjecture.

64: The first twelve lines of the chorus' entry song are largely lost; the few legible bits are translated.

86-90: These next five lines of interchange between Silenus and the chorus are completely lost.

182: The twenty lines after this are very fragmentary. From what is legible it appears that the chorus members are calling out to one another—and perhaps to their dogs as well—by name, as they focus their search on the entrance of the cave.

212: Text uncertain; and after this the next four lines are missing.

221: Presumably the satyrs now perform an especially vigorous dance (such as the one represented on the Pronomos Vase), accompanied by the pipe player.

228: Reading and interpretation uncertain: possibly "with your cousins the nymphs," and "with a crowd of followers" or "with a crowd of children."

235: These next few lines are largely lost.

285-87: Much is missing, but the lines seem to describe allusively baby Hermes' killing of the tortoise, turning it "upside down," and creating a "crying" lyre from its shell.

290-97: Most of these lines (sung, as the antistrophe to the strophe 243-50) are lost; the few decipherable bits are translated.

311-15: The general sense of 311-12 is fairly secure; but 313-15 are more badly damaged; 316–17 are transmitted separately by an ancient source as coming from this play. Then 318–25 are almost completely lost, but they must have included mention of the cowhide top with which Hermes covered the upturned tortoiseshell to create the lyre.

339–51: The beginnings of all these lines are missing, and the sense uncertain, but the references to "cutting up" and "cattle" are unmistakable. Lines 348–51 are lost almost completely.

363–64: Text very uncertain.

378: The next two lines (completing the antistrophe) are lost.

379–96: Of these seventeen lines, apparently spoken by the Chorus Leader and Cyllene in alternation, only tiny traces remain.

404: After this, about thirty lines are completely missing. The remainder of the papyrus (436–57) contains only short bits of lines, but enough to indicate that the chorus sings a song, greets the return of Apollo, and begins a dialogue with him.

457: Here the continuous papyrus ends. Further tiny scraps of what may be another column of writing contain too little for any sense to be recovered.

GLOSSARY

Achaeans: inhabitants of Achaea, a region in Greece on the northern coast of the Peloponnese; the name is sometimes used to refer to all the Greeks; they are also sometimes called Argives or Danaans.

Acheloüs: largest river in all of Greece, located in Aetolia, the region north of the Gulf of Corinth and west of Phocis.

Acheron: a river or lake in the underworld across which the dead are ferried.

Achilles: son of Peleus and Thetis; father of Neoptolemus; greatest warrior of the Greeks at Troy; after his death, his armor was given to Odysseus.

Aeacus: grandfather of Ajax; father of Telamon and Peleus; king of Aegina.

Aegean Sea: the body of water that separates eastern Greece from the mainland of Anatolia (modern-day Turkey).

Aegisthus: son of Thyestes; cousin of Agamemnon; first the lover and later the husband of Clytemnestra after they killed Agamemnon.

Aenian: the Aenians were a tribe in southern Thessaly.

Aetna: volcanic mountain in Sicily.

Aetolia, Aetolian: region in central Greece (and its inhabitants) north of the Gulf of Corinth, west of Phocis.

Agamemnon: son of Atreus; brother of Menelaus; husband of Clytemnestra; father of Iphigenia, Electra, Chrysothemis, and Orestes; king of Argos/Mycenae and leader of the Greek expedition against Troy.

Ajax: son of Telamon and Eriboea; husband of Tecmessa; father of Eurysaces; ruler of Salamis; the next-best warrior of the Greeks at Troy after Achilles. His name in Greek suggests "grief" or "woe."

Alcmene: wife of Amphitryon; mother of Heracles by Zeus.

Amphiaraus: seer and warrior from Argos; one of the Seven, who fought against Thebes. Though reluctant, he was persuaded by his wife, Eriphyle, who had been bribed by a golden necklace, to join that expedition, in which he died.

Antilochus: son of Nestor; killed by Memnon at Troy.

Apollo: son of Zeus and Leto; brother of Artemis. God of oracular prophecy, poetry, healing, and archery; worshipped especially at Delos and in his Pythian sanctuary at Delphi. Also known as Loxias, Paean, Phoebus, or Lycian.

Arcadia: mountainous region in the central Peloponnese (southern Greece); birthplace of Hermes (and in some versions, of Pan and the satyrs).

Ares: god of war; son of Zeus and Hera.

Argive: referring to Argos; in general, Greek.

Argos: a city and region in the eastern Peloponnese in southern Greece, not always distinguished clearly from Mycenae.

Artemis: daughter of Leto and Zeus; sister of Apollo; goddess of the hunt, childbirth, and virginity, who protected wild animals and boys and girls before they reached adolescence; according to some sources she was born on the island of Ortygia, which was either an old name for Delos or a separate island.

Asclepius: son of Apollo and Coronis; the most eminent Greek healing hero. The sons of Asclepius (Asclepiadae) were famous among the Greeks at Troy for their medical skill.

Athena: daughter of Zeus; goddess of wisdom and warfare; patron goddess of Athens.

Athens: main city in the plain of Attica in southeastern Greece.

Atlas: one of the Titans; son of Iapetus and brother of Prometheus; father of Maia. He was imagined as perennially supporting the heavens on his shoulders.

Atreus: father of Agamemnon and Menelaus; brother of Thyestes. In retaliation for Thyestes' seducing Atreus' wife, Atreus killed several of Thyestes' children and served them up for him to eat unwittingly in a cannibal feast.

Atridae: the sons of Atreus (Agamemnon and Menelaus).

Aulis: a harbor in eastern Greece in Boeotia, opposite Chalcis (Euboea), at which the Greek fleet assembled in preparation for sailing to Troy.

Bacchants: female followers of Dionysus.

Bacchus: Dionysus.

Barcaean: from Barce, a Greek city in Libya (North Africa).

Bear among the stars: the constellation of Ursa Major.

Boeotia: region in central Greece, containing Thebes and other cities.

Cadmus: founder of Thebes; Heracles is an adopted son of Thebes, and thus a "descendant of Cadmus."

Calchas: Greek seer who accompanied the army to Troy.

Cenaean Zeus: Zeus worshipped on Cape Cenaeum.

Cenaeum: cape located on the northwestern promontory of Euboea.

Centaurs: mythical savage beings, half human, half horse, against whom Heracles waged war.

Cephallenia (Cephallenian): cluster of islands in the Ionian Sea off the west coast of central Greece, including Ithaca.

Chalcodon: legendary leader of the Euboeans.

Chiron: son of Cronus and Philyra; a gentle Centaur; healer; educator of heroes (Heracles, Achilles, Jason, et al.); he was accidentally wounded by one of Heracles' poisoned arrows, ultimately giving up his immortality to end the pain.

Chryse: island in the Aegean Sea on which Philoctetes was bitten by the snake; also the name of the nymph to whom the island was sacred.

Chrysothemis: a third daughter of Agamemnon and Clytemnestra; sister of Iphigenia, Orestes, and Electra.

Clytemnestra: daughter of Tyndareus; sister of Helen; wife of Agamemnon; mother of Iphigenia, Electra, Chrysothemis, and Orestes. With her lover (later husband) Aegisthus, she killed Agamemnon, then was killed by Orestes. Also written Clytaemestra.

Cnosian: of Cnossos, a city on Crete.

coast of the Maid: coast near Thermopylae which was under the protection of Artemis, the virgin goddess (Maid).

Cretan deep: the Aegean Sea around Crete.

Crete (Cretan): large island to the south of mainland Greece.

Crisa: town in Phocis on the lower slopes of Mount Parnassus.

Cronus: one of the older generation of gods; father of Zeus, Poseidon, Hera, et al.; husband of Rhea.

Cyllene: mountain in Arcadia on which Hermes was born; also the name of a mountain nymph who lived there as an attendant of Maia and became the nurse of baby Hermes.

Cypris, Cyprian: Aphrodite, so named because she emerged from the sea on Cyprus, an island in the eastern Mediterranean south of Anatolia (Turkey); the island was famous for its sanctuaries dedicated to Aphrodite.

Death, god of death: Hades.

Deianira: daughter of Althaea and Oeneus; second wife of Heracles; mother of Hyllus.

Delos: Aegean island in the center of the Cyclades; birthplace of Apollo and Artemis.

Dionysus: son of Zeus and Semele; god of wine, music, and dance; usually attended by a retinue of nymphs and satyrs.

Dodona: city in Epirus in northwestern Greece, west of the Pindus Mountains; location of the most important oracle of Zeus, whose priestesses were known as "doves." The priests were the Selli.

Dorian: one of the major ethnic groups of the ancient Greeks, supposedly founded by Dorus, one of the sons of Hellen who was the mythic fore-father of all the Greeks. The Dorians were supposed to have originally come from the northeastern regions of Greece, ultimately settling in the Peloponnese.

Doves: the priestesses at Dodona.

Earth: wife of Ouranos (Heaven), but also sometimes identified with Cybele, the Anatolian mother of the gods.

Echidna: half woman, half snake; mother of many monsters, including Typho, Cerberus, the Lernaean Hydra, and the Chimera.

Electra: daughter of Agamemnon and Clytemnestra; sister of Orestes, Chrysothemis, and Iphigenia.

Enyalios: Ares.

Eriboea: wife of Telamon; mother of Ajax.

Erinyes: *see* Fury, Furies

Erymanthus: mountain in Arcadia; hunting and killing the Erymanthian boar was one of Heracles' labors.

Euboea: long island east of Boeotia (central Greece).

Eurysaces: son of Ajax and Tecmessa. His name means "broad shield," a characteristic weapon of Ajax.

Eurystheus: grandson of Perseus; he became king of Mycenae/Argos instead of Heracles through Hera's machinations and devised the twelve labors for Heracles to perform.

Eurytus: king of Oechalia, killed by Heracles; father of Iole and Iphitus.

Evenus: river in eastern Aetolia, east of the Acheloüs River.

Fury, Furies: female avenging spirit(s) concerned with bloodguilt; children of Night. In *The Women of Trachis*, the "encircling net" which kills Hera-cles is "of the Furies" because it is deadly.

Gates: Thermopylae ("hot gates"), a narrow pass on the Malian Gulf with natural hot springs.

Giants: children of Earth (not always distinguished from the Titans) who fought against the Olympian gods and were defeated by them, partly through Heracles' assistance.

Hades: brother of Zeus and Poseidon; god of the underworld. His name is sometimes used synonymously for the underworld itself.

Heaven: in Greek = Ouranos; husband of Gaia and father of the Titans.

Hector: son of Priam and Hecuba; husband of Andromache; leader of the Trojan army against the Greeks; killed by Achilles.

Helenus: son of Priam; Trojan seer.

Helios: god of the sun.

Hell: Hades.

Hellas: Greece.

Hephaestus: god of fire and metalwork.

Hera: Olympian goddess, wife and sister of Zeus.

Heracles: son of Zeus (or Amphitryon) and Alcmene; greatest of all Greek heroes; original possessor of Philoctetes' bow.

Heraclid: descendant of Heracles.

Hermes: son of Zeus and Maia; god of deception, trickery, communication, heralds, travel, trade, and music; he also escorted dead souls to the underworld.

Hydra: snake which inhabited the marshes of Lerna (hence "Lernaean Hydra"); slain by Heracles as his second labor. Its blood was poisonous.

Hyllus: son of Heracles and Deianira.

Ida: mountain located just to the southeast of Troy.

Ilium: another name for Troy.

Inachus: the main river of Argos; legendary king of Argos and father of Io, from whom the royal family of Argos was descended.

Io: daughter of Inachus; she bore Epaphus to Zeus; because of Hera's jealousy, Io was transformed into a heifer and tormented by a gadfly.

Iole: daughter of Eurytus; new bride or concubine of Heracles after he destroyed her home city of Oechalia; wife of Hyllus after Heracles' death.

Iphianassa: another sister of Orestes and Electra, briefly mentioned in Sophocles' *Electra* but otherwise ignored. In that play she appears to be a different person from Iphigenia.

Iphigenia: the eldest daughter of Agamemnon and Clytemnestra; sacrificed by her father at Aulis to Artemis, to procure favorable winds for the expedition to Troy.

Iphitus: son of Eurytus; killed by Heracles.

Itys: son of Procne; killed by his mother to avenge her husband Tereus' rape of her sister Philomela. Procne was turned into a nightingale, a bird associated with lament.

Laertes: father of Odysseus; husband of Anticleia.

Lake of Death: Acheron, in Hades.

Laomedon: father of Priam and Hesione (she was mother of Teucer); early king of Troy.

Lemnian fire: Moschylus, the volcano on Lemnos.

Lemnos: island in the northern Aegean Sea where the Greeks abandoned Philoctetes.

Lerna: marshy region south of Argos; home of the Hydra.

Leto: goddess, the mother of Apollo and Artemis.

Libya, Libyan: a region in North Africa on the coast of the Mediterranean, west of Egypt.

Lichas: slave and herald of Heracles.

Locris: region in central Greece opposite Euboea.

Lord Healer: Asclepius.

lord of the lightning: Zeus.

Love: Eros; god of sexual desire.

Loxias: Apollo.

Lycian: belonging to Apollo. The Greeks associated this name with the word for "wolf."

Lycian well: spring on Lemnos named after Lycian Apollo.

Lycomedes: king of Scyrus; father of Deidamia. He helped raise Neoptolemus while Achilles was at Troy.

Lydia: region in western Anatolia (modern-day Turkey); its chief city is Sardis.

Lydian woman: *see* Omphale

Magnesia: the northeastern region of Thessaly, in northern Greece.

Maia: daughter of Atlas; seduced by Zeus, she became the mother of Hermes.

Maid: Artemis, the virgin goddess.

Malis (Malian): a region in southern Thessaly; home of Poias.

Menelaus: son of Atreus; brother of Agamemnon; husband of Helen; king of Sparta.

Mountain Mother: Cybele, Anatolian goddess known as mother of the gods; sometimes identified with Rhea, Zeus' mother, or with Gaia (Earth).

Mycenae: city in the northeastern Peloponnesus; home of Agamemnon; not always clearly distinguished from nearby Argos.

Myrtilus: charioteer of Oenomaus; Pelops bribed Myrtilus to sabotage his master's chariot so that he was killed during their race. Pelops then killed Myrtilus.

Mysia: region in northwest Anatolia (modern-day Turkey).

Nemea: town and sanctuary of Zeus in the northeastern Peloponnesus. The killing of the Nemean lion was Heracles' first labor.

Nemesis: goddess of vengeance.

Neoptolemus: son of Achilles and Deidamia; also known as Pyrrhus; he arrived at Troy after the death of his father and participated ferociously in the sack of the city.

Nessus: Centaur who tried to rape Deianira and was killed by Heracles.

Nestor: the oldest, wisest Greek warrior at Troy; king of Pylos; father of Antilochus.

Niobe: a Greek heroine; when she boasted that she had many children, while Leto had only two, Apollo and Artemis, these latter were offended and killed all of her children with their arrows. In ceaseless grief, she was turned to stone, her tears becoming streams of water.

Odysseus: son of Laertes (or in some traditions, of Sisyphus); husband of
    Penelope; father of Telemachus; king of Ithaca; Greek warrior at Troy
    renowned for his intelligence and guile.
Oechalia: city of uncertain location in Euboea, ruled by Eurytus; home of
    Iole; destroyed by Heracles.
Oeneus: father of Deianira.
Oeniadae: town in southern Acarnania in western Greece located near the
    mouth of the Acheloüs River.
Oeta: mountain in central Greece located in southern Thessaly; location of
    Heracles' funeral pyre; this region was home of Philoctetes.
Olympus: mountain on which the gods make their home, located in Pieria
    in northern Greece.
Omphale: a Lydian queen whom Heracles served as slave for a year as pun-
    ishment for killing Iphitus.
Orestes: son of Agamemnon and Clytemnestra; brother of Electra and
    Chrysothemis, and of Iphigenia.
Ortygia: *see* Artemis
Pactolus: river, rich in gold dust, that rises from Mount Tmolus in Lydia and
    flows through Sardis.
Paean: a name for Apollo as healer and savior; or a kind of poem addressed
    to the god, expressing thanks or prayers for help.
Pallas: epithet of Athena, often used in place of her name.
Pan: woodland god of Arcadia; worshipped especially on Salamis. Accord-
    ing to one tradition Pan was the father of the satyrs.
Paris: son of Priam; abducted Helen from Menelaus' home and took her to
    Troy. Also known as Alexander.
Patroclus: best friend of Achilles; killed by Hector at Troy.
Peleus: father of Achilles; husband of Thetis; grandfather of Neoptolemus.
Pelopids, Pelopidae: descendants of Pelops; the royal family of Argos/
    Mycenae.
Pelops: son of Tantalus; father of Atreus and Thyestes; gave his name to the
    Peloponnesus ("Island of Pelops") in southern Greece.
Peparethus: small island located off the southern coast of Thessaly.
Phanoteus: a nobleman of Phocis; friend of Aegisthus.
Philoctetes: son of Poias; Greek hero who inherited Heracles' bow
    and assisted at the capture of Troy, after first spending several years
    marooned on the island of Lemnos.
Phocis, Phocian: a region (and its people) in central Greece on the northern
    shore of the Gulf of Corinth, near Delphi.
Phoebus: epithet of Apollo meaning "bright."
Phoenix: aged advisor of Achilles.

Phrygia (Phrygian): northwest-central region of Anatolia (modern-day Turkey); sometimes used to refer also to Troy.

Pleuron: town in Aetolia located between the Acheloüs and Evenus Rivers.

Poias: father of Philoctetes; ruled in Oeta (Thessaly).

Poseidon: god of the sea, horses, and earthquakes; brother of Zeus and Hades.

Priam: king of Troy; father of Hector, Paris, Helenus, and many other sons and daughters.

Pylades: son of Strophius of Phocis; the loyal comrade of Orestes.

Pylos: city on the southwestern coast of the Peloponnese; home of Nestor.

Pytho, Pythian: another name for Delphi; the name Pytho comes from the serpent Python that Apollo slew.

Salamis (Salaminian): small island in the Saronic Gulf about ten miles west of Athens.

Scamander: river in the plain of Troy.

Scyrus: island in the Aegean Sea, northeast of Euboea; home of Neoptolemus.

Selli: priests of the sanctuary of Zeus at Dodona.

Sigeum: promontory near Troy, in northwest Anatolia (modern-day Turkey).

Silenus: father of the satyrs; sometimes known as Papposilenus.

Sisyphus: legendary founder of Corinth; a trickster figure who famously deceived the gods on multiple occasions; in some accounts, the father of Odysseus.

Sparta: city in Laconia in the southeastern Peloponnese.

Spercheius: a river in central Greece which flows into the Malian Gulf.

Strophius: king of Phocis; father of Pylades; when Clytemnestra and Aegisthus killed Agamemnon, Orestes was rescued and brought to Strophius for safekeeping.

Sun, sun god: Helios.

Sunium: promontory on the southern tip of the Attica peninsula (ca. forty-five miles southeast of Athens), on which a temple to Poseidon was built.

Tecmessa: wife (slave concubine) of Ajax; mother of Eurysaces.

Telamon: father of Ajax and Teucer; king of Salamis.

Teleutas: father of Tecmessa; king of Phrygia.

Teucer: son of Telamon and Hesione; half brother of Ajax; an accomplished archer at Troy.

Thebes: the most important city in Boeotia.

Themis: primeval goddess of custom and established law.

Thersites: ugly and argumentative Greek soldier at Troy who came into conflict with Agamemnon and Achilles.

Theseus: son of Aegeus or Poseidon; father of Acamas and Demophon; king of Athens and the Athenians' most popular mythical hero.

Thessaly: large region in northeast-central Greece.

thyrsus: a wand carried by worshippers of Dionysus, made of a fennel stalk with ivy vines and leaves wound around it and topped by a pine cone.

Tiryns: city in the Argolid plain; located about nine miles southeast of Mycenae.

Trachis: main town in the region of Malis, east of Mount Oeta and south of the Spercheius River in Thessaly (east-central Greece).

Troy, Trojan: wealthy city (and its inhabitants) in northwest Anatolia (modern-day Turkey) besieged and sacked by Agamemnon and the Greeks; also called Ilium.

Tydeus: an Argive hero, father of Diomedes.

wolf-killing god: *see* Apollo; Lycian

Zeus: king of gods and men; father of Heracles and several other Greek heroes.